PRO LOGO

General Advisor to Palgrave:
Professor Christian Pinson, INSEAD

Translation: Joe LaCour

Pro Logo

Brands as a factor of progress

Michel Chevalier

and

Gérald Mazzalovo

First published 2003 in France by
Éditions d'Organisation
as *Pro Logo: Plaidoyer pour les marques*
This edition published 2004 by
PALGRAVE MACMILLAN
Houndmills, Basingstoke, Hampshire RG21 6XS and
175 Fifth Avenue, New York, N.Y. 10010
Companies and representatives throughout the world

PALGRAVE MACMILLAN is the global academic imprint of the Palgrave Macmillan division of St. Martin's Press, LLC and of Palgrave Macmillan Ltd. Macmillan® is a registered trademark in the United States, United Kingdom and other countries. Palgrave is a registered trademark in the European Union and other countries.

ISBN 1-4039-1825-2

This book is printed on paper suitable for recycling and made from fully managed and sustained forest sources.

A catalogue record for this book is available from the British Library.

A catalog record for this book is available from the Library of Congress.

Editing and origination by
Curran Publishing Services, Norwich

10 9 8 7 6 5 4 3 2 1
13 12 11 10 09 08 07 06 05 04

Printed and bound in Great Britain by
Creative Print & Design (Wales), Ebbw Vale

Contents

List of figures

List of plates

Provocation:

Profaning the sacred:

Commercializing values of solidarity:

A few good ads:

Managing a brand's esthetic:

Acknowledgments

This book, though conceived and written by the two authors, is also the result of much collaboration without which the project could not have taken shape in its final form.

We gratefully thank the owners of the trademarks who have given us permission to reproduce their logo and/or their publicity, and also the photographers and their models. Almost every organization we contacted gave us permission. In alphabetical order, they comprise these 38 brands:

- Bally
- Benetton
- Bulgari
- Chanel
- Coca-Cola
- Crédit du Nord
- Ducados
- Elle Espagne
- Eram
- Guess
- Kenneth Cole
- Lanvin
- Lycra
- Michelin
- Pirelli
- Shell
- Swatch
- The Body Shop
- Versace
- Banco Sabadell
- BMW
- Burberry
- Christian Dior
- Cooper
- Diesel
- Ducati
- Emanuel Ungaro
- Fortuna
- Jaguar
- Lancel
- Lightware
- Mecca-Cola
- Mondaine
- Salvatore Ferragamo
- Sisley
- Swiss Air Lines
- Tissot
- Volkswagen

All the trade marks cited in this book are the registered trade marks of their respective owners.

Other individuals such as the cartoonist Martin Morales, who works for the Spanish daily *abc*, and the agencfy Oriani & Orione-Photogroup allowed us to complete the illustration of this book with their documents.

Our thanks also go to the authors who gave us permission to use their copyright material in order to develop our thesis. In order of mention in the book, they are:

- David Aaker and Jean-Noel Kapferer, pioneers of the idea of brand identity.

- Martine Floch, widow of Jean-Marie, careful defender of the thoughts of the man who inspired the section of the book regarding semiotic analysis and brand identity.

- François Schwebel of Creative Business and Andrea Semprini, sparring partners and disciples of Jean-Marie Floch.

We are grateful to Hugues Leroy whose suggestions enabled us to significantly improve the form and content of the book.

Finally special acknowledgement goes to Carol, Sophie and our children without whom this project would have made little sense.

Michel Chevalier
Gérald Mazzalovo

Introduction

Some consumers will literally walk a mile for a Camel, or wait in line for hours to buy the new Swatch watch. Others have carried on real intimate relationships with a make of automobile or motorcycle; meanwhile all their children can talk about for months at a time is a certain clothing label that's all the rage at school.

But is this proof that these consumers are totally subjected to the diktats of the major brands? Are they the victims of manipulation by advertising, or symbols of a society that is fundamentally mercantile? Is absolute brand fetishism a threat to our civilization?

Our opinion is that if some people do show a marked preference for a given brand, it's simply because they feel that its products are the best. They feel that the manager of that brand has done his or her best to win their trust, and above all to keep it. We feel there are many positive factors inherent in such a system.

But recently, a certain intellectual trend is challenging that. This current, while it may have already existed, has crystallized in the wake of Naomi Klein's book.[1] Let us be clear: *No Logo* is a serious study which gives a well-documented journalistic panorama of anti-brand activism. We feel that the mobilization of consumers and users represents important progress towards fairer trade, and it would be very harmful to call it into question. Yet the foundations of *No Logo*'s analysis appear relatively weak to us, and we doubt that the book can really serve as the foundation for tomorrow's protests, though it does succeed at times in capturing a certain "spirit of the times."

---

1 Naomi Klein, *No Logo*, London: Flamingo, 2001 (and other editions worldwide). The book is referred to repeatedly in the text; for simplicity we have not repeated the bibliographical details each time.

That Zeitgeist is more what we are concerned with here. It is character-ized by a set of fairly vague perceptions that are more or less consistent with Naomi Klein's theses, which they sometimes cite as their inspiration, but are all very negative towards branded products. This "No global" trend seems to find an echo in a certain latent hostility among consumers, even when they are not mobilized in protest.

Brands get bad press. The omnipresent advertising bombardment, which seems to blend with news of the most alarming events happening in the world on our television screens, throws suspicion on them. In these times of collective anxiety in the face of globalization, they are the ideal scapegoat. Since they are highly visible, they must be guilty.

Here is an overview of these latent grievances that consumers hold:

First, brands are blamed for all the evils of globalization. Brand produc-ers relocate their production facilities, exploiting their workers under the pretext of bringing progress, causing poverty in the wealthy countries and exploitation of workers in the poor countries.

Their hegemony is visible at all levels, both in the major macroeconomic equilibriums and in our individual consciousness, which they attempt to manipulate. Even though the number of brands has decreased in the devel-oped countries over the past 20 years, consumers feel besieged on all sides by messages whose content and form either shock them or, often, leave them feeling bewildered. It's as if the notoriety of a brand were a license to promote anything and everything.

Finally, consumers today seem to complain of what appears to be a decrease in the quality of the products they use regularly. Nothing is "like it used to be." The introduction of innovative materials in the manufacture of products and the standardization of production one or two generations ago were positive factors in the perception of corporations and that of their clientele. Today they have become synonymous with a reprehensible homogenization and a deterioration of quality.

The confluence of the protest movement led by radical activists and the growing resentment among consumers has resulted in a melting pot of somewhat confused values, in which brands are held up as the sign of a future world where human beings will no longer be anything but machines, programmed to consume.

We feel that this vision of things is exaggerated and erroneous. What is more, it is also fed by fashion – because, paradoxically, there has been a *No Logo* craze. The book's very title sounds like a slogan. Despite its author's insisting that she does not intend it as a call to political action, it is what is sticks in the mind. The book's cover is particularly carefully designed and conceptual, and presents the title in the form of what could be called a "minimalist" logo (the designer obviously could not resist playing on the paradox). The composition, in red, black, and white, subtly recalls the constructivist posters and revolutionary agitprop of the 1930s. The book was launched simultaneously in several languages, supported by careful marketing campaigns. Designers and advertisers rushed to buy the book. Will the T-shirt with the *No Logo* logo, worn by a child in an illustration in the book, become a bestseller itself? We will have come full circle. Of course irony, provocation, and double meaning are at work. But hijacking is ineluctable, which is proof of the vitality of the system. The book, which tends to oppose brands, has managed to create a new one, whose name is *No Logo*.

This takes nothing away from a successful book whose ideas, in our opinion, are better than the approximations of them one hears circulating in urbane conversation. For example, we have often heard it said that *No Logo* argues for doing away with brands. This is simply not true. On the contrary, the author feels that the major brands, determined to defend their notoriety, constitute ideal interlocutors and adversaries for activists and consumer associations. We fully agree with that analysis.

The distinction has to be made between the serious work Naomi Klein has done and the superficial trend it has inspired. In writing this book, we wanted to respond to certain stereotypes that seem to be circulating since the publication of *No Logo* – in particular that brands are inherently evil; that they are the foundation of a system of hegemony and alienation; that by attacking them, one is attacking the heart of the "capitalist machine."

Our purpose is to plead not guilty to those charges. We see brands as authentic factors for social, economic, and cultural progress. Our *Pro Logo* tries to illustrate why, and under what conditions, these positive aspects can come fully into play.

Brands exist and are neither good nor evil in themselves. They can be criticized, but calling for their abolition is absurd. They are and will remain an essential tool of marketing, international competition, and contemporary social life. It's impossible to imagine that supermarkets would suddenly begin selling exclusively generic products. If that were to happen, the need for differentiating these products would immediately arise – and brands would reappear, or else the store's name would take their place. In fact, there is no such thing as a world without brands.

Brands are part of a phenomenon that is like that of technological innovation or the development of advertising, which are often both the cause and the consequence of evolutions in our society. They are irreversible. All we can do is to try to strengthen their positive aspects and reduce the ones that are deleterious to human development.

But for brands to be seen as a true force for progress, they must first be well managed; and second, consumers must involve themselves in the dialog in a serious way. It's important to remind both corporations and consumers of their responsibilities.

This implies showing corporate managers how to create, defend and develop their brands while adhering to their values and respecting the dignity of their partner in the exchange. We will point out the anomalies of the system and the excesses brand management can be guilty of, without indulgence. But our critiques will lead to concrete proposals for improving the process.

This also implies encouraging consumers to practice responsible purchasing. All transactions constitute a moral choice on the consumer's part. They must make known what qualities they expect from a product, along with their opinions on manufacturing conditions, communication, and the brand's values as a whole. Consumers, after all, are the ones who decide – through the exercise of their purchasing power and the principle of competition – whether a brand lives or dies. They have a right to vote that they must use effectively, by encouraging brands that express values they support. Consumers can influence the decisions managers make. We will give examples.

If everyone plays his or her role, products will move towards excellence, in terms of both tangible benefits (physical comfort, for example) and intangible ones (esthetic pleasure, a feeling of security). Consumers will benefit in terms of time, comfort, health, and culture. They will be able to put these benefits to use to carry out their responsibility as citizens more effectively – for example, making sure that the products they consume are produced under the best possible conditions as regards both ethics and quality. In this context, the more powerful a brand is, the more it will be obliged to ensure that production conditions are perfect, since the risk of consumers abandoning it will be that much greater. In this way, the chain of excellence can be self-sustaining and contribute to the progress of all of human society.

This book, then, will develop a simple thesis: brands are a force for progress to the degree that they are well managed and that the consumer behaves responsibly.

These are the considerations that motivated the plan of our book. In its first part, we describe the universe of brands and attempt to characterize it. We point out the objective failings of the system and attempt to analyze their causes. Finally we explain why these brands are powerful forces for progress.

This general discussion is applied in the second part of the book, which is devoted to general principles of brand management. We discuss the concept of brand identity – which we feel is fundamental – at length. We introduce several methodological tools, which we have used ourselves "in the field," to approach brands in an objective and relevant manner.

Finally, in the last part, we will concentrate on the role of the consumer, which we see as central to the system of exchange of which the brand is the instrument. We try to show how and under what conditions consumers can intervene to improve that exchange.

Our conclusion will discuss the problems raised by the role of brands in the complex process of globalization, and an epilogue will suggest how a beneficial system of commercial transactions might operate, gravitating around the interests of human beings.

This book, then, is intended both for brand managers and for consumers. We hope that it will contribute to encouraging the meeting of these two worlds and dissipating the misconceptions that are becoming prevalent on both sides, and create a necessary dialogue.

If we can convince consumers determined to defend their rights that brands are not *The Enemy*, and companies that they have everything to gain by making their customers' point of view a priority, then we can feel that we've attained the goal we had set for ourselves.

I

The World of Brands

Imagine a world without brands. It would be one in which the most familiar landmarks of our daily life had disappeared. We would continue to be surrounded by products and services, of course, and that would pose no problem as long as we were not faced with the need to make a purchase. But without those reference points, how would we buy our morning coffee, a bar of soap, an automobile? The principle of choice is inseparable from the way we relate to the act of consumption.

One environment comes to mind: the former Soviet Union. But even there, brands were marginally present. There was the Beriozka store chain, reserved for tourists, or the automobile makes Neva, Lada, and Zil. All of these names identified different origins or production plants, particular commitments in terms of comfort, and above all, a style of performance linked to specific segmentations. Brands and strong brand identities were able to prosper in the socialist-bloc countries, often associated with values like ingeniousness or no-nonsense technology. As proof of that, some of these products have today become cult objects and signs of mutual recognition for urban consumers bent on setting themselves apart. The little East German Trabant car has its passionate devotees, and the Lomo camera is available at Colette, the 'in' store on the chic Rue Saint-Honoré in Paris.

Would a world without brands be made up exclusively of generic products? That notion makes no sense. A generic product can only exist in relation to a group of brands. Without them, it loses its *raison d'être*.

In fact, the only place where there would be no more brands would be a desert island where a lone Robinson Crusoe would himself make everything he needed to eat, to clothe himself, and to survive. From the moment individuals need to acquire a product or service they have not discovered or harvested, they need to rely on a brand. It can be a name by which a merchant backs up his products; a brand identifying livestock; a mark on an amphora. From the earliest identifying signs used by potters in ancient times to our modern logos, an unbroken line of parentage extends through the history of exchange between human beings.

In a manner of speaking, the brand is the initial system of consumption, the medium for the guarantee between the consumer and the producer. It is also a component of relations among several persons, that is, a consequence of social life.

In their contemporary context, brands can be characterized via this notion of commercial exchange and social communication. For the consumer, the world of brands is first and foremost the "signals" he or she encounters every day. In 1968, Raymond Bauer and Stephen Greyser[1] estimated the number of advertising contacts an American was subjected to daily at 80. Today that figure is thought to be of a different order of magnitude, perhaps as many as 20,000. This means that the consumer must define his or her own way of dealing with these solicitations, and determine an attitude towards the purchase of a given category of products.

For the corporation, the brand is an essential component of its cumulative value and its long-term strategy. It imposes certain constraints. It requires choices to be made involving coherence and consistency with specific values. It is a fundamental asset of the corporation.

Interbrand, a consulting firm, publishes an annual ranking of 100 of the world's most valuable brands. The ranking is determined as follows: Interbrand calculates the present value of future profits engendered by the brand's power alone – such as, for example, the advertising savings resulting from the brand's name recognition, and the advantage the company may derive from selling its product at a higher price than if it bore an unknown brand. By this method of calculation, for the year 2003, the value of Coca-Cola – the brand considered most valuable of all – is US$70.45 billion, ahead of Microsoft at US$65.17 billion. The third-ranking brand, in terms of intrinsic value, is IBM with US$51.77 billion, ahead of General Electric and Intel.

It's no surprise that all the best-known brands of today are in this list. If you look at the list of the 500 leading companies worldwide published each year by *Fortune* in the United States, or *L'Expansion* in France, you will note that nearly all the names of companies are brand names, or a condensation of brand names – like KJS, whose acronym intertwines the initials of three of the group's brands: Kraft foods, Jacobs coffees, and Suchard chocolate. Though

---

1 Raymond Bauer and Stephen Greyser, *Advertising in America: The Consumer View*, Cambridge, Mass.: Harvard Business School, 1968

FIGURE 1.1			
Estimation of the financial value of brands by Interbrand, in US$ billion*			
1993		*2003*	
Marlboro	39.4	Coca-Cola	70.45
Coca-Cola	33.4	Microsoft	65.17
Intel	17.8	IBM	51.77
Kellogg's	9.6	General Electric	42.34
Nescafé	9.1	Intel	31.11
Budweiser	8.2	Nokia	29.44
Pepsi-Cola	7.5	Disney	28.04
Gillette	7.1	McDonald's	24.70
Pampers	5.9	Marlboro	22.18
Bacardi	5.4	Mercedes	21.37
Winston	5.2	Toyota	20.78
Levi Strauss	4.8	Hewlett-Packard	19.86
Newport	4.5	Citibank	18.57
Motorola	4.1	Ford	17.07
Kodak	4.1	American Express	16.83
Camel	3.6	Gillette	15.98
Nike	3.5	Cisco	15.79
Campbell	3.4	Honda	15.63
L'Oréal	3.4	BMW	15.11
Hennessy	3.3	Sony	13.15

Source: 'The Global Brand Scoreboard,' *Business Week*, August 4–11, 2003. Data by Interbrand Corp., J. P. Morgan Chase & Co., *Business Week*. This list covers only companies who export at least 20% of their total business volume and whose financial data are of public record. The BBC, Mars, Visa International, and Ferragamo, for example, are excluded.

it's true that there is virtually no such thing as an anonymous product or service, it's just as rare to find companies whose name is not, for consumers or for industrial or institutional customers, for all intents and purposes a brand.

The Interbrand list calls for several comments.

First of all, among the 20 leading brands, only two products are sold in food supermarkets (Coca-Cola and Gillette). The great majority of the others belong to the high-technology sector: Microsoft, IBM, General Electric, Intel, Nokia, Hewlett-Packard, and Cisco. Five of them are automobile brands: Mercedes, Toyota, Ford, Honda, and BMW. Finally, several correspond to services: Disney, McDonald's, Citibank, and American Express.

Note that the textile sector – from which Naomi Klein draws a good many of her examples – in fact plays a fairly modest role in this list. Not until the 36th place, with Gap, does it make an appearance. Nike is 33rd; Louis Vuitton is 45th. Slightly farther behind are Gucci, in 53rd place, and Chanel, in

61st. Finally Levi's, Prada, and Polo Ralph Lauren are respectively 77th, 87th, and 95th. However, with few exceptions these brands correspond not only to products, but also to the many stores that operate under the brand name, and who are therefore more or less retailers. We have taken care not to exaggerate the importance of these products in our analysis.

Interbrand publishes its ranking each year. We thought it would be interesting to compare the 20 leading brands of 1993 with those of 2003. Of the 10 leading brands in 1993, only three remain in the 2003 list (Coca-Cola, Marlboro, and Intel). Of the seven others that topped the list in 2003, none was among the leading 20 in 1993.

It's possible that Interbrand has broadened its research base. But in any case we can conclude that the presence of a brand at the top of the list is never a sure thing, and that the competition is always wide open and very unpredictable. A brand must be constantly worked on and engaged in a process of development, and has to be constantly enriched and imperceptibly changed, or else it falls into decline and can die.

In this first part of our book, before developing our thesis, we would like to describe the dynamics of the world of brands.

First of all, they are the instrument of a system of exchange whose two poles are closely interrelated. As a result of this process, the brand becomes a symbol of confidence for the consumer, and a commitment to quality and compliance with certain rules for the producer. The latter, as it honors those commitments, gradually builds up that capital of confidence, of behavioral habits, on the part of the consumer. It can be thought of as corresponding to the concept of goodwill. This is what we have called the contractual dimension of the brand. We will also discuss historical, sectoral, and social aspects, as well as the area of brand names and logos.

Second, we take note of the fact that abuses exist. We make a point of identifying them without pulling punches. At times we may even be more critical than certain theses we are opposed to. But there is such a thing as reality, and it is essential to know it and analyze it. We will also show to what extent these problems are not related to the nature of the phenomenon of brands itself. On the contrary, they are always the result of a kind of negligence or disinvolvement regarding responsibilities on the part of one of the partners in the exchange.

This brings us to the third section of this first part, where we develop the principal thesis of our book. We feel that, when the abuses are contained, when each of the partners fully assumes his or her responsibilities, brands, like any considered cultural fact, become authentic factors of progress. This book should be read with that in mind.

1 | What is a brand?

> Mouret was spending three hundred thousand francs yearly on cata-
> logues, advertisements, and posters. For the launch of the sale of his
> new summer items, he had sent out two hundred thousand catalogues,
> including fifty thousand abroad, translated into all languages. Now he
> was having them illustrated with engravings and even accompanying
> them with sample swatches, glued to the pages. The displays of his
> goods poured from those pages; Au Bonheur des Dames sprang forth
> before the eyes of the entire world, and was seen everywhere: on walls,
> on the pages of newspapers, even on the curtains of theater stages. He
> believed that women are helpless in the face of publicity, and that they
> must go and see what is being talked about.
>
> (Émile Zola, *Au Bonheur des Dames*)

Emile Zola's *Au Bonheur des Dames*[1] published in 1883, tells the story of
the rise and fall of a great department store. The concept of 'brand' is not
yet present in the novel, but we do find practices that are still in use today
in the mass-retailing sector: economies of scale, accelerated rotation of
capital, lowered profit margins, advertising campaigns, product assortment
strategies, sales and end-aisle displays.

Above all we find two elements that might be considered characteristic
of the presence of brands in our contemporary world: the maintenance of
name recognition through advertising, and as a corollary, the affirmation of
a certain commitment made to the consumer, which makes use of that same
name recognition (in the novel, the commitment takes the form of a policy
of constant prices or money-back guarantees).

---

1 Published in English as *The Ladies' Paradise* and *The Ladies' Delight.*

Yet the book is not prophetic. Zola, who always took great care with the documentation of his novels, wanted to describe the "new commerce" that was beginning its conquest.

We chose to open this chapter with this passage in order to make it clear that the advertising invasion and concentration associated with the major brands today are not new phenomena in themselves. As we will see, brands and branding have existed at least since Antiquity. The Industrial Revolution, with its resulting expansion of exchange and communication, greatly increased their audience. That revolution had already begun in Zola's time and was already causing concern. We don't deny the accentuation of the phenomenon, but on the other hand it seems difficult to see it as the major upheaval or the great danger of our time.

Yet that is the kind of trend in public opinion that can be seen taking shape today, in an informal way, in the wake of books like *No Logo*[2] – often, we suspect, at the initiative of people who have not read them seriously. Putting specific pressures on brands in the context of commercial exchange is, we feel, a constructive attitude. But rejecting branding en masse seems to us to be the result of a superficial analysis. Of course, it is not what Naomi Klein advocates; one can, however, criticize her for taking certain shortcuts and assigning guilt by association in ways that do little to clarify the distinctions. The latent "fashion" of opposing branding, inspired by her work, is even more open to criticism. And in fact this kind of protest, lacking in substance, has been quickly co-opted by the very "communicators" it claims to combat.

/ Brands are not globalization; they are not all of commerce, and even less so all of capitalism; and they are not the Internet. /

A few distinctions do need to be recalled. Brands are not globalization; they are not all of commerce, and even less so all of capitalism; and they are not the Internet. They constitute a specific historical and social phenomenon, based on a specific type of commercial relation. This introductory chapter will be devoted to outlining its major characteristics. We will take a more detailed look at most of the ideas we discuss below in the following chapters.

The brand as contract

When one company purchases a competitor for an amount above the sum of its net assets, there is a line item called goodwill in the consolidated balance sheet following the merger. This term designates, in a way, the sum

2 N. Klein, *No Logo*, London: Flamingo, 2001.

total of the intangible, but extremely valuable, positive attitudes of consumers toward the acquired company and its products.

In the context of market uncertainty prevalent at the time of this writing, goodwill does not have good press. And yet, though evaluating it can be problematic, it is a genuine added value, built up gradually as consumers become convinced that a certain brand can provide them with a product whose quality is above that of its competitor.

In France, 81 percent of consumers at a display of instant coffee will buy a Nescafé or Maxwell House product; only 19 percent will choose a store brand, even though it is much less expensive.[3] This is because behind the concept of brand is the capital of confidence, which is accumulated over time and must not be betrayed.

In the perception of the customer, this capital is embodied above all in a name. At the beginning of the history of industrial brands, this was often the name of a person, intended to lend a familiar, folksy quality to a standardized product, but also to emphasize the existence of human know-how upstream of the chain of production. This seems logical. If, as we have said, a brand comprises first of all a capital of confidence, then putting his or her name on a product is, for the vendor, the simplest way of winning that confidence. We are dealing with a fundamental structure in a great number of human exchanges.

We could cite the example of Johnson. Johnson was an American flooring manufacturer who had developed a wax for his customers. The name "Johnson Wax" recalled its origin – the product of a wood specialist – to the consumer and was a guarantee of quality. Little by little, the brand's reputation expanded and the customers became staunchly loyal. Today, French or Japanese consumers don't know that the founder of Johnson was a flooring manufacturer, but they continue to buy the Johnson product.

As we will see, the name of a brand, or its logo, is an important visible part of a more complex reality. The name and logo provide the mediation between the essential values of a company – its identity – and the perceptions its customers have of it – its "image." But note that what the consumer is looking for behind the brand is the guarantee of a specific quality, generally considered to be superior. That long-term assurance forms the basis of the relationship between the consumer and the producer.

/ What the consumer is looking for behind the brand is the guarantee of a specific quality, generally considered to be superior. /

This holds for products, as above, but also for a particular sales policy. The Saks Fifth Avenue department-store chain has a rule under which a customer

---

3   Source: Neilsen, 1993.

can return any product purchased within the last six weeks for a refund, with no questions asked. For a long time, the Saks Fifth Avenue stores had Revillon departments. Certain customers bought fur coats there on December 15 and returned them at the end of January. The Revillon teams, pointing out that these customers were abusing the return policy to get a free fur coat every winter, tried several times to convince the stores' management to make an exception to the policy, which was difficult to apply to their products. Saks always refused, considering that even if it left it vulnerable to abuse, the return policy was part of the stores' ground rules, that it constituted a commitment, and that it was one component of its brand identity.

From the point of view of managers, it's common to speak of the brand as an expression of the company's "genetic program" – a stable structure, rich in potential, which concretizes the company's existence and can win customers' confidence, but which also imposes strict ground rules. This is an expressive image, but it is also a bit unclear. We prefer, for our part, to speak of "semiotic invariants" and of a brand's ethic and esthetic. As we will see later (Chapter 4), the manifestations of a brand can be seen as "meaning facts," and these invariants simply make up a basic grammar, a signature of form and content that allows the brand identity to come into being.

In fact, in terms of ordinary discourse, two brands like Dannon and Nestlé do not express the same values and have distinct brand identities. Nestlé has nutritional associations which apply to diversified products: condensed milk, chocolate, coffee. On the other hand, the Dannon brand is currently still strongly associated with dairy products: yogurt and cream cheese. In addition to the constraints of production, distribution, and storage inherent in this type of product, both brands must take into account the diverse representations with which they are associated in customers' imaginations. As a result they adopt slightly different strategies and positionings in order to be recognized and to win and keep consumers' trust.

This trust relationship is the foundation of any brand's history. And it is an idea that the book *No Logo* recognizes in its way. By showing how vulnerable major brands are to consumer criticism, Naomi Klein is only underlining the power of this tacit contractual dimension.

Whether through plebiscite or criticism, then, the brand continues to assert itself as a company's seal of guarantee, its code of values, and the assurance given to customers that they will be treated as they expect to be treated.

This is one of the ideas to which we are most attached, and which led us to write this book: a brand is a contract, one which is implicit in nature and which governs the relations between a given company and its customers. This relationship is two-dimensional: it is not only economic in nature, but also, over time, creates emotional ties which are sometimes very intense – with infidelity on both sides, momentary or permanent abandonment, and above all, a capacity for reciprocal influence on the behavior of the two contracting parties.

The competitive dimension of the brand can be included within its contractual dimension. The brand exists only because it differentiates itself from its closest competitors. This is one of the bases of its identity. The consumer chooses a brand for the specific qualities it offers and, in this sense, the differentiation of the brand is part of the contract between the two parties.

/ A brand is a contract, one which is implicit in nature and which governs the relations between a given company and its customers. /

Because it is founded on differentiation, which is the *raison d'être* of any brand, such a contract remains implicit. As such, it cannot be confused with the 'standard' regulations of laws governing commerce, which are the same for all. What the brand pertains to is a relationship of another nature: for example, the Saks' stores' automatic return policy. The brand implies the promise of superior quality and better service; in short, it guarantees added value.

Brands and time

The prolongation of a contract in time is intrinsic to the notion of guarantee. In order to exist, a brand must not only establish its reputation, but establish it durably. Thus the chronological perspective is fundamental to understanding brands.

We will begin with a short historical sketch. In looking at brands as abstract entities, we tend to forget that, behind them, there is nothing more than a vendor who is concerned about customers' keeping him or her in mind. And this concern is as old as commerce itself.

As early as 2700 BC, artisans were affixing a sign to their creations in order to affirm their originality.[4] In Classical Greece and Rome, merchants used generic symbols to designate the business they were in: a ham for butchers, a cow for creameries, and so on; 'individual marks' identifying a particular merchant made their appearance, in the form of seals, circa 300 BC. More than 6000 different seals used by Roman potters have been catalogued.

---

4 cf. *Des Brevets et des marques, une histoire de la propriété industrielle* (*Patents and Trademarks: A history of industrial property*), INPI (French Patent Office): Fayard, 2001.

As for a giant like France's Saint-Gobain, we might point out that its founding dates from 1665, when Louis XIV signed letters patent authorizing the establishment of a manufactory of glass for mirrors.[5]

The large-scale explosion of brands – that is, the emergence of the brand phenomenon as we understand it – is largely a result of the Industrial Revolution. Should we see this as a 'mercantilization' of the world? It's more a case of a transformation of commerce itself. As exchanges become standardized, it becomes necessary for producers to establish a relationship of proximity with consumers by other means.

The extension of industrial property to the concept of brand appears in Europe in the second half of the nineteenth century; the US Congress enacted the first federal trademark law in the late 1800s. To give an example, between 1850 and 1890 the number of patents granted each year in the major Western nations increased by a factor of ten![6]

/ The trend since 1990 has been toward concentration and reduction of the largest companies' portfolios of brands. /

The major brands as such underwent sustained development between 1900 and 1945, and the development accelerated between 1945 and 1990. On the other hand – and contrary to what their omnipresence in the media might suggest – the trend since 1990 has been toward concentration and reduction of the largest companies' portfolios of brands.

To understand these recent developments, we must look at things on a smaller scale. These fundamental trends, like the individual fate of a given business sector, can be explained by the differential between, on the one hand, the cost of maintaining and developing a brand, and on the other, the immediate or longer-term profits to be made from it.

The costs of conservation of a brand are related to all the actions necessary for maintaining its competitiveness, as well as to the notion of relevance (see Chapter 6). They include, of course, the renewal of registrations with the various industrial-property bodies, but this is always a modest amount for a single country.

For brands of products sold in the mass-retail arena, the real cost is affected above all by two components: the advertising budget, necessary for keeping the brand in the "major leagues," and the sales budget, to ensure that the product is present in stores – or, more generally, its availability to consumers.

Profit will depend on the price at which the product can be sold to the consumer (or retailer). Two products offered for the same price on a super-

---

5 *Des Brevets et des marques*, op. cit.

6. Austria-Hungary, France, German States, Great Britain, and United States. Source: S. Lapointe, for Leger Robic Richard.

market shelf don't necessarily have the same profitability for their producers. Let's take the example of Taster's Choice instant coffee. A grocer who did not stock Taster's Choice – the most requested product in its category – would give the impression that it didn't pay attention to his or her clientele and didn't have the products they want. Therefore grocers are obliged to offer the product. Nor can they sell it at whatever price they please. Consumers remember what they paid for the last jar. If the grocer were to put too high a price on the coffee, it would give the impression that prices are high throughout the store. The producer, Nestlé, knows this, and so will charge the retailer a high price for Taster's Choice. And the retailer will have no choice but to cut the margin in order to be able to offer the product to customers. The price it displays will be very close to that of an economy brand, though the latter might cost it half as much. With the economy brand, the retailer earns a decent margin; with Taster's Choice, it is earning an image. The paradox of retailing is that grocers earn the most money with unknown brands and the lowest prices.

This dynamic explains the variations in the number of brands. If advertising costs increase and retailers develop an advantage over producers, this number will diminish significantly.

The phenomenon of concentration that is specific to recent decades was particularly spectacular in the French automotive industry. Before the Second World War, French auto manufacturers of course included Renault, Citroën, and Peugeot, but also Simca, Panhard, Hotsckitsch, Talbot, Samson, Delahaye, Facel Vega, and so on. The explosion of this industry had resulted in a multiplication of auto makers in Europe. The Italians Isotta and Fraschini, for example, had started out as dealers for the Renault mini-car in 1899, before founding their own brand in 1902. In France, most garages handled not one but several makes of car. Sometimes, even, they were non-exclusive. They worked on Facel Vegas as well as Citroëns. In addition, each brand had a specific positioning – technical in the case of Panhard, with innovations such as air cooling; sporty and exclusive for Facel Vega; luxurious in the case of Delahaye, and so on. Today there are only three makes left in France, distributed by exclusive dealers (who are more capable of repairing their brand than others), and these brands have very high advertising budgets.

/ The phenomenon of concentration that is specific to recent decades was particularly spectacular in the French automotive industry. /

Another sector, luxury goods, underwent its explosion later, characterized by the emergence of the Italian brands beginning after the Second World War. Armani, Ferré, Moschino, Trussardi, and Versace emerged in the 1970s. During the same period, slightly older brands – Fendi, Salvatore Ferragamo, Gucci – experienced extraordinary growth. Certain provincial brands left Florence or Milan and were soon found everywhere in Italy, in Rome and Venice for example. They soon became international, generally with strong presence in the United States and Japan. So while French automobile brands were disappearing, the spread and development of luxury brands was booming in Italy.

/ While the luxury and fashion industry doesn't escape from the phenomenon of concentration of capital, the reduction in the number of brands is less evident there, perhaps because of the versatility of the markets. /

While the luxury and fashion industry doesn't escape from the phenomenon of concentration of capital, the reduction in the number of brands is less evident there, perhaps because of the versatility of the markets. The novelty effect is a determining factor in consumers' choices. The result is a permanent renewal of the available brands. And yet an analysis of the effectiveness curves of advertising shows the emergence of what is called a "threshold effect." Such studies show that advertising expenditures on a very broad target of consumers are only effective at upwards of US$3 million.

To sum up, the trend towards reduction of the number of brands is well advanced. Over the past 20 years, major brands have disappeared from the landscape: Kelvinator refrigerators, Miracle Maid cookware, DeSoto, Rambler. At Nestlé, while the headquarters in Vevey had registered in 1991 100 new brands, in 1999 this same headquarters filed for registration of only five. The goal is to reduce the proliferation of brands to a minimum and concentrate on the strongest brands, ones that are leaders or potential leaders in their sectors and that have realistic worldwide ambitions.

In the 1980s, companies producing goods for the mass-retail market allowed each country to develop its own brands, close to the market and to the consumer. S. C. Johnson, for example, launched an aerosol-starch product in different European countries. In Spain, the product was called Toke (the final touch in ironing); in Germany, Bügelglatt (the iron that glides); in the Benelux countries, Glad & Net (gliding and getting beautiful results). Each name was the product of a local marketing analysis. It sought to communicate the benefits customers were deemed to expect from the product. Today, such an approach would be prohibited by the group's headquarters. It implies diversified production, whereas the trend is towards centralization of production at a single European site. It also implies the production of country-specific, differentiated advertising spots – whereas, for reasons of economy, Johnson will try to use the same spot everywhere. Further, since consumers cross national borders more easily, they will find the product they're used to in any supermarket in Europe.

At Unilever, it wasn't until 2000 that a new program, "the Path to Growth," took aim at this phenomenon of proliferation of brands. The group counted some 1600 brands, and set the goal of reducing that number to 400 by 2005. That means that 1200 Unilever brands will be sacrificed in the space of five years. This decision is obviously the result of an in-depth analysis. The group's business volume being US$45 billion at the time, it was decided to concentrate on 36 brands with an individual potential of more than US$1 billion (among others, Knorr soups, Lipton tea, Hellman's mayonnaise, Magnum ice cream, and Signal toothpaste). Each of these international brands must obviously be provided with a colossal yearly advertising budget, always in excess of US$20 million and, on average, more than US$150 million.

But why aim at 400 brands and not just 36? Because the approach, while it is highly constraining, leaves room for what Unilever calls "local nuggets," brands that are firmly established and very profitable in the context of a given country. In France, these include Omo detergent and Puget vegetable oils.

The Unilever program is not only very ambitious and reactive, it also sets new standards for the competition. If, tomorrow, 36 Unilever brands are allotted advertising-promotional budgets of at least US$150 million worldwide, the competitors won't be able to lag behind. They will also have to concentrate their efforts on a few of their brands in order to earmark budgets of that size.

At Procter & Gamble (P&G), in the very early 1990s, CEO Edwin Artz had earned the nickname "Terminator." Each time he visited a subsidiary in a given country, he axed one or more local brands and required his teams to concentrate their advertising efforts on an ever-smaller number of world-wide brands. It seems that Procter & Gamble, an American company named for its two founders – one an Irishman, the other British – is conducting a strategy comparable to Unilever's, without really admitting as much. P&G has 300 brands in the world, but 12 of them, with business volumes of above US$1 billion (including Tide, Ariel, Crest, Pampers, Folgers, Downy), represented 53 percent of the group's total volume for 2001 (US$40 billion).

It might look as if P&G has already completed the cultural revolution Unilever is undertaking. But with only 12 truly major brands – compared with 36 for Unilever – can P&G count on the same growth perspectives? It may be that the group has analyzed the problem and feels it is possible, in the coming years, to multiply the business volume of its major brands by a factor of two or three. Whatever the case, a brand of consumer products that can't mobilize US$150 million in media advertising won't be able to hold on to its rank in the international arena.

/ A brand of consumer products that can't mobilize US$150 million in media advertising won't be able to hold on to its rank in the international arena. /

The major corporations are preparing for that eventuality. 3M recently created a special department, under the direct responsibility of the president, whose task is to manage the brands. This center, called Brand Asset Management, is solely responsible for the registration of new brands, and aims at concentration and rallying around the company's major strengths. The Diageo group recently announced that it wanted to rely on only nine principal brands for 70 percent of its profits. Jean-Marie Messier, then President of Vivendi Universal, said on February 27, 2001, "We have too many brands within Vivendi Universal; our strategy consists in keeping the strongest niche markets and killing off or selling the intermediate brands."

The costs of advertising and internationalization have clearly changed the rules of the game. Small brands will have to remain local or else disappear.

But history hasn't had the last word yet. As we explain in detail in Chapter 5, niche strategies can still be justified. And moreover, advertising is not necessarily everything. There are brands positioned on a specific market that manage, below critical mass, to develop name recognition without advertising. In certain highly federated markets made up of devotees, word of mouth is a powerful force, even more of an advantage than advertising. In the case of fashion, a small, highly innovative brand will sometimes be extremely well received by the press and magazines; fashion writers will adopt it as a favorite discovery; it will be talked about for its originality. On the other hand, middle-sized and older brands, already 'publicitized' but with smaller budgets than the competition, will have trouble staying in the race.

We would like to point out that we do not share the opinion of Naomi Klein, who sees April 2, 1993, "Marlboro Friday," as an emblematic date and a decisive turning point in the history of brands. On that day, an announcement by Philip Morris that it was lowering the price of Marlboro cigarettes by 20 percent caused the American stock market to plummet. According to Naomi Klein's analysis, since one of the best-known brands in the world was forced to cut its prices in order to compete with weaker brands, the entire industry felt that the end of the brand premium had arrived. We don't feel that the incident deserves to be given such importance. We see it as a high-profile episode of strategic revision, amplified by the sounding board that is the New York Stock Exchange. With the lowering of the cigarette pack price, the market simply discounted lower future cash flows than before the price measure. 1993 was a period of formation and growth for the major multi-brand luxury groups. It was also the period of growth and consolidation of Italian and American brands like Armani, Versace, Prada, Ferragamo, and Calvin Klein, Ralph Lauren, Disney, Apple, Microsoft, Nike, Reebok, and so on.

While it is true that the globalization of the economy, technological progress in the communications industries, and the volume requirements of the traditional production and distribution industries – both for consumer products and for capital goods – have made brands indispensable, stronger, and less numerous, we will show that their evolution also depends on the economic sectors in which the brands operate.

Brands and industrial sectors

Brands exist in all sectors, but with different modalities. The same effort is not brought to bear in promoting a brand of bread or rice as to sing the praises of a detergent or a skin-care cream. The industrial sector defines, among other things, the ways in which the brand can be differentiated and the modes of accessibility of the product. Rather than defining a priori classifications by sector, we will give several examples to aid in understanding this diversity.

/ The industrial sector defines, among other things, the ways in which the brand can be differentiated and the modes of accessibility of the product. /

The first criterion that is specific to the sector has to do with the possibilities of differentiation of a given product. Let's start with the example of the European chocolate-bar market. The chocolate bar is a product of recent invention (1850), whose production process is complex, and which therefore requires extensive mastery of the physico-chemical processes involved. Thus its history is closely linked to the major stages of industrialization and to control of the refrigerated distribution chain.

Forty years ago, there were major national brands on the French market: Meunier, Poulain, Suchard (though Swiss, it had become a quasi-national brand in France, with a plant in Alsace). There were also other, local brands: Cémoi, Delespaul-Havez, Omnia and many others. The market was expanding regularly and retailers went along with the regional brands, though still being obliged to also sell the national brands. The same system was reproduced outside France, with Perugina in Italy for example, or El

Gorriaga and Favor in Spain. Today the national brands have all been purchased by major groups (Meunier and Perugina by Nestlé), which use them as the "regional" expressions of a worldwide strategy. The market is divided among Nestlé, Suchard (which acquired Côte d'Or and Tobler), and Lindt in Europe, Cadbury (which bought out Poulain) in northern Europe, and Hershey in the United States.

In this often impulse-driven purchasing sector, the market has structured itself into an international oligopoly. The regional brands have disappeared or have been transformed into economy brands, without advertising budgets. The supermarket shelves in Paris, Hamburg, and Naples are strangely similar, often with very close positions for Nestlé, Lindt, Suchard, and Cadbury. In the majority of cases, as in Germany or in France, there are virtually no major national brands of chocolate. While the brands have kept a certain weak national identity (Swiss or British, for example), their image has become so neutral, so asepticized, that at first glance the market seems to have become very homogeneous.

Yet evolutions are taking place. As is often the case in the food products sector, they are driven by the rise in demand for quality and security on the part of consumers as a whole. In France, brands like Valrhona have carved out a place for themselves little by little, by selling products that are much more expensive and of much higher quality. They are re-segmenting the market from the top, by establishing a niche market for quality and selectivity.

For more than ten years, these outsiders have relied on the French bakeries and pastry shops, who prefer to sell Valrhona or Cluzel, rather than Suchard or Nestlé bars at a much higher price than the local hyper-market. But the concern for quality has become democratized, and quality brands are now beginning to be found in supermarkets, thus beginning a new era in their development.

Consequently the presence of major international brands, as uniform and standardized as possible, has not prevented the development of newcomers with tighter, more focused positionings.

In the instant and ground coffee sector, the situation is a little different. Fifty years ago there were still coffee roasters in each region, and in particular near port cities. These brands disappeared little by little and were replaced by national brands such as Maxwell House and Folgers, a brand sold first in the West and now, of course, nationally. Then there was the arrival of Italian coffee brands like Lavazza, Segafredo, and Illy. These brands play strongly on the connotations of an "art of coffee" as representative of the Latin lifestyle, introducing a type of segmentation into the market for this basic product.

For a long time, the communication of the major coffee brands concentrated on the quality of the product, or on exoticism simply as a guarantee of quality ("Our beans come from far away, from the very best plantations"). But now, exoticism as such is emerging as another criterion of choice. Coffee is tending to become a cultural product. As a result, most major brands have launched varietal products, offering, for example, "Coffees of the World" collections (from Brazil, Colombia, Ethiopia and so on) available in supermarkets. This has resulted in a fairly fragmented market, offering a great diversity of blends and packaging. As for consumption habits, they are tending more and more towards the coexistence of "table" coffee (the equivalent of table wine) and more exceptional coffees, strongly imprinted with exoticism and fantasy, reserved for festive moments. But for day-to-day purchases, the public's preferences remain fairly fixed, and supported by considerable advertising budgets.

It's hard to mention coffee without mentioning Starbucks. In 1971 it opened its first store in Seattle. In 1987 it had only 17 stores, but by 1997 it had 1412, and today has some 6000, with an objective of 10,000 worldwide in 2005. It started quite simply by selling a better coffee in a clean and pleasant environment. Now, as a result of a license agreement with Kraft Foods, Inc., Starbucks has launched its own coffee in 18,000 US supermarkets. Starbucks's annual report shows that the royalties it receives from Kraft for the use of its brand name in the supermarkets is around US$65 million.

If we now move to a sector like milk, approximately 75 percent of the market is made up of store brands or economy brands. For this product, consumers see little point in buying a more expensive product with an additional guarantee. They consider milk to be a product that is not highly differentiated. Here again, however, the burgeoning of the natural foods trend offers possibilities for segmentation. These are still not very significant at the level of the brands, considering that "Organic," since it is a certified label, tends to function as a brand in itself.

/ The brand is all the more effective to the extent that the product moves away from non-differentiation and offers something different, an undeniable plus for the consumer. /

There are many possible examples. Note, in these three cases – but this is a universal law for all brands – that the brand is all the more effective to the extent that the product moves away from non-differentiation and offers something different, an undeniable plus for the consumer.

The business sector also conditions the mode of distribution of the product and the role the brand plays. Let us look at a case of concentration: that of the luxury/fashion sector, where a trend towards "specific" distribution – in monobrand (or "mono-brand") stores – is tending to become the rule.

Louis Vuitton, for example, has a brand that is sufficiently strong for it to open new stores in all the main cities on the planet. Such is not the case for Furla or Desmo, smaller Italian leather-goods brands. Their brands lack the name recognition or the attractiveness to allow them to stock and profitably run their own stores in, say, Minneapolis or New Orleans. They can only open stores in very large cities and hope – because of the quality of the products and their originality, as well as the strength of their advertising communication – to increase their level of interest and their volume.

What is more, the current trend towards megastores (for example, Gap on the Champs-Élysées in Paris, with its 17,000 square feet of floor space and annual rent of over US$2 million, or the Nike Town stores in Chicago or New York) is more beneficial to the strong brands. Studies show that these large-area stores are more profitable for a monobrand chain than for multibrand chains with low margins.

In the case of products manufactured in large volume, for which economies of scale are essential at the production level (microwave ovens, vacuum cleaners, luggage, and so on), the trend is, this time, towards "dilution." This means imposing the brand in as many countries and with as many distributors as possible, while creating an image of quality and sturdiness. Instead of playing on the brand effect, the brand aims at being ubiquitous.

Thus we have two very different ways in which a brand asserts itself, both of them effective in their area, and clearly related to the intrinsic characteristics of a given business sector. There is no one practice and one single approach. Each sector uses brands to play a different role, but always towards differentiation and promotion of the values expressed by these brands.

/ Each sector uses brands to play a different role, but always towards differentiation and promotion of the values expressed by these brands. /

One is struck, however, in reading Naomi Klein, by the fact that her examples remain concentrated in the middle-scale textile sector. She says very little about large-volume, repeat-purchase consumer products, and very little about manufactured products with a high technological content or luxury products. What she says is true in part for the sector she has chosen, but her conclusions don't take into account the diversity of situations, sectors, and consumer perceptions.

To end, we would stress the fact that this phenomenon of promotion of values, in its varying modes of operation, is not limited to a small number of sectors. A service station or a bank must also attract customers and win their loyalty. Shell and BP are not perceived by the consumer in the same way in terms of content, trust, national origin, guarantee, or product quality. The same is true for banking: Citibank or Bank One are not the same as AmSouth. Each bank, in basing its communication on its name and asking all its employees, whether they are in direct contact with the clientele or not, to adhere to a charter of good conduct and a specific behavior, and has organized to provide a service that is differentiated and specific.

Companies who sell their products or services to other companies are not exempt from this phenomenon. For the IT director of a major company, buying a computer made by IBM or a small Korean brand is not quite the same thing. If a major problem arises with an IBM computer, no one will challenge the purchasing decision. If, on the other hand, the problem happens with the computer from a minor Korean brand, there is a good chance the director's competence will be questioned. The choice of the most prestigious brand is the one that entails the lowest personal risk.

This mechanism is reproduced in almost all industrial purchases. Even when the brand does not appear on the product or the component, it exists in the mind of the user. For a purchaser of automobile parts, there is a difference between buying windshields or wipers manufactured by Corning or Trico and procuring the parts from a small local producer who will not offer the same technical guarantee.

Finally, we often forget that if the brand plays a crucial role with consumers, it also does so where the organization's own employees are concerned. They are the ones who are in contact with the customers in service activities. Through the identity it develops, the brand obliges them to adopt differentiated behaviors, which may evolve over time.

From this quick overview of brands by industrial sector, we should retain two ideas. Brands are present in all sectors, but have different modes of operation. Their common objective is to introduce differentiation within a given sector, through the promotion of the specific values on which their identity is built.

/ The common objective of brands is to introduce differentiation within a given sector, through the promotion of the specific values on which their identity is built. /

In this sense, they are an unavoidable reality, and a positive one, of all commercial activities. They are a guarantee of quality, trust, and innovation. Brands have a tendency, in fact, to act as qualitative filters at the sector level. This is because the interplay of competition and differentiation always leads them to focus their offering on the best of what a given area of business activity can provide. And this is one of the reasons why we see them as an essential factor in industrial dynamism.

Brands and society

When we think of the presence of brands in our contemporary society, the first idea that comes to mind is not the quality of the products, but the intensity of the messages.

On his desert island, Robinson Crusoe would not have needed his name if Friday hadn't turned up. Brands exist only because we can recognize them. And we recognize them because we perceive the messages they send, their specificities, and a certain constancy over time. We will have occasion to mention these components – communication, differentiation, and duration – throughout this book.

The communicative dimension of brands operates in two ways. First, the brand sends its messages to the consumers it targets. This is at first a shot-gun type of relationship, where a wide net must be cast to be sure of pulling in the targeted consumers. Second, signs, like money, circulate. Brands, too, display this phenomenon.

Let's imagine the reaction of extraterrestrials who arrive on Times Square in New York, on the Ginza in Tokyo, or in the via Montenapoleone in Milano. The logos and brand names on the buildings and on the clothing worn by the passers by would probably loom large in their first impression. They would discover a civilization where brands play an important role in social communication. They would also be discovering, by comparing different places, the multitude of global brands, their systematic presence in the most famous shopping streets, and the apparent homogeneity they impose on lifestyles.

/ The explosion of brand communication our civilization is now experiencing would never have happened were it not for the crucial social role brands now play. /

The explosion of brand communication our civilization is now experiencing would never have happened were it not for the crucial social role brands now play. The three stripes on running shoes, the polo player embroidered on a shirt, the 'swoosh' on the cap or the Kelly bag – not to mention the car someone drives or the restaurants he or she goes to – often say more about the personality of the individual who wears them than his or her curriculum vitæ.

It shouldn't be surprising, in a society characterized by exponential growth of communication in all its forms and contents, that brands should be at the heart of contemporary life. They guide the purchases we make, influence our judgments about products and persons, and force us to position ourselves in relation to the values (or counter-values, or the absence of values) they communicate.

These effects are not limited, of course, to the isolated moment of communication (the glimpsed billboard or spot). The way in which brands circulate, are copied, worn, or co-opted shows the extent and depth to which they affect our society. In fact, they have changed our way of living.

First, by claiming a conspicuous share of commercial and communication space, they have contributed strongly to the transformation of our urban landscapes. We will return to this in Chapter 2. Further, brands convey values. We will see, in Chapter 4, that the brand's identity is made up of invariants which express its vision of the world, the values it believes in and attempts to promote. Nike is the pursuit of excellence in athletic performance, Hermès the aristocratic life, Armani relaxed elegance in the Italian style. Brands oblige us, through their presence in the commercial circuits, to position ourselves in relation to these values that they stand for. The offering of products and the values associated with them has grown strongly in recent years, giving us a choice our parents could never have dreamed of. We can choose temporary lifestyles as we see fit, and reflect our moods in the way we consume.

Finally, brands are at the origin of numerous actions of solidarity. Whether under the influence of consumers or under the leadership of enlightened managers, they have greatly increased their commitments to causes in the general interest. Again, we will return to the mechanisms and the consequences of such commitments. As we will see, they are closely linked to the communicative dimension of the brands. At this early stage in our examination, we have simply touched on these tangible effects on our society.

The brand and its signs

With these initial analyses, we have tried to characterize the broad outlines of a brand's presence. What are the signs through which that presence asserts itself? They are of several orders, in fact, though often closely interlinked. To express itself, the brand uses these different elements, which are not interchangeable but are complementary.

The most important among them, of course, have to do with the name of the brand itself. The logo, now an unavoidable part of our urban landscapes, is what comes to mind right away. However the name, in its "literal" and onomastic dimension (how it sounds to the ear), is also given much time and close attention by the brands.

We will consider this literal dimension first before focusing on the phenomenon of the logo, and then move to consider other mechanisms of recognition.

Brand names

The name remains the first sign of recognition of a brand. It is never neutral, and today its choice must not be left up to chance. As proof of its importance, often, in the history of the major brands, the name has evolved towards a more incisive simplicity. When the brand bears the name of its founder, at some point the first name is dropped (Ford, Johnson, Hoover, Philips). Or the brand can be reduced to its acronym (IBM, BMW). Or again, it can be purged of elements that had provided details on the company name: "Source Perrier" became simply "Perrier," and "The Great Atlantic and Pacific Tea Company" A&P.

/ The name remains the first sign of recognition of a brand. It is never neutral, and today its choice must not be left up to chance. /

The brand can also choose to mimic colloquial usage. Realizing that the products of the Gap Generation brand were simply called "Gap" by their consumers, the brand's managers removed the "Generation" from the labels. Coca-Cola (as early as 1941) also adopted the omnipresent abbreviation "Coke." However, the fact that the name also designates cocaine in slang, the scandal that resulted in the 1980s from the introduction of a new formula for the soft drink, and the resounding failure of the Cherry Coke version of the product have attenuated the tendency towards reform.

Many brands, at the start of the twentieth century, were given the first name and surname of their founders. At times they have attempted to free themselves of it, in order to survive that person's death. Sometimes also, they have succeeded in assimilating the founding personality as a value, a durable component of their identity. The most emblematic cases are doubtless Henry Ford automobiles and the Walt Disney Company, who have simplified their brand name but perpetuated the memory of their founder in both their internal and external communication. Clearly, the charisma and reputation of these historic figures are large factors in such choices. Note also that the name of a person immediately introduces a reassuring human dimension in the relationship between the brand and the consumer. And it is here, as we pointed out above, that the brand returns to its most primitive dimension: that of a personal commitment on the part of the vendor.

For luxury products, the first name, since it identifies the creator, remains an indispensable part of the excellence and creativity of the brand. Saint Laurent never comes to mind without Yves, or Ferragamo without Salvatore. Yet there are exceptions, which have existed in their present form from the brand's origins: Gucci, the name of whose founder – Guccio – would doubtless result in an awkward alliteration; Coco Chanel always preferred to use only her surname.

When a brand name has taken hold of the collective memory, beware of ill-advised changes. The change of the brand Marcel Rochas to simply Rochas was not at all lucky for the business. In the early 1990s, an attempt was made to re-adopt the first name by opening a men's clothing store called Marcel Rochas in Paris, but the attempt was soon abandoned.

In the field of management of brand names, one of the most interesting phenomena to be observed today is the progressive disappearance of the first name of Christian Dior. Until 1995, the products and the advertising always bore the complete signature. Then, the name "Christian" progressively disappeared. For a long time, it was not shown in full size on the advertising, but on the baseline of the ad and on the packaging. Today, the brand appears more and more often without the first name, for example on the signs of the new stores and in all the advertising material. How should we look at this emancipation? Some will think that the company's directors are playing a dangerous game, and are in danger of progressively diminishing the affective component of the brand and cutting it off from its roots. But the brand's excellent results, up to now, seem to prove the contrary. The future will tell.

In the history of brand creations, the name of the founders or the regional origin (Pittsburgh Plate Glass) have given way little by little to more symbolic names. Very attached to the poetics of evocation as regards brands, perfume makers set the tone in the 1920s: Shalimar (Guerlain, 1925); Shocking (Schiaparelli, 1931). In the 1930s, the importance of the name given to new products became a preoccupation of industry as a whole, in particular for consumer goods. More and more compound neologisms were sought, whose overall effect is intended to evoke all the qualities, both concrete and abstract, of the product. (Often, this neologism extends to the producer's brand itself.) For an artificially refrigerated food locker, Frigidaire; for a fabric softener, Snuggle; for a tissue paper, Kleenex. The goal is to create names that are easily retained, full of immediate and powerful significance.

This increasing concern for evocativeness leads to a gradual distancing from the concrete realities of the company and its industrial sector. For a perfume maker, stressing the imaginative element seems only natural. On the other hand, in the case of Apple Computers, in 1976 – in a milieu dominated by acronyms, and over which loomed the shadow of the venerable International Business Machines – it represented innovation.[7] The fairly nonchalant abbreviation "Microsoft" (from "microcomputer" and "software") is part of the same trend: These names, in themselves, suggest the expression of a demystified attitude towards the machine, which was to characterize the microcomputer. The name had become a crystallization of a value, a "brand spirit," more than of the qualities of a product or service.

The break with the real went so far as to include the invention of fictional names. These were plausible names, where the neologism was not apparent, and which appear to hark back to an origin which is in fact not at all that of the brand. Häagen Dazs connotes (falsely) Scandinavia; Sony suggests an international brand; Bridgestone is the literal translation of a Japanese surname.

The phenomenon of concentration in recent years has been accompanied by the emergence of two trends. The first is for companies with a serious and conservative image – in particular in the European banking sector – to turn towards evocativeness. The other is that the names they choose are often neologisms, with a concern for geographic neutrality and a certain tendency towards abstraction. The sonorities often suggest the ancient Greece of the philosophers: the brand identity has moved from reality to concept. The name no longer connotes a founder or a region or the qualities of a product or service. Its indeterminateness is a federating force. Further, as a neologism, it celebrates creativity of action. Dexia, Natexis, and Thales fall into this category.

The choice can also be motivated by more pragmatic considerations – for example, finding a name that hasn't already been used or registered. We've also noticed that in inventing a name, there is a perceived advantage to choosing one that will put the company at the very top or bottom of the stock-quotations list. After the precursor, Axa, we've seen the appearance of Vivendi, Vivarte, and Areva.

The case of Accenture is a little different. When the two companies Arthur Andersen (the accounting and auditing firm) and Andersen Consulting were separated, the courts forced the latter to change its name. A contest was held among the employees for suggestions. The new name had to begin with "A," with a second letter coming before "N." That way,

---

7 We should point out that at the time, the name "Apple" connoted above all the Beatles' famous publishing company.

clients looking for Andersen Consulting in the telephone directory or on the Internet would find the new brand a little higher on the list. It also had to be the same length as "Andersen," so as to resemble it. A Scandinavian employee suggested "Accenture," a synthesis of "accent," "adventure," and the AC of "Andersen Consulting."

In conclusion, what needs to be remembered is that there's no ideal name. If there were, it would be the name of a person, easy to remember in all languages, that evokes the qualities of the product or service offered, that suggests the company's philosophy, connotes intelligence and creativity – and begins with the letter "A" or "Z" to stand out in the listings.

The fact remains that the name, in itself, constitutes a vital asset. It is a source of much worry and enormous investments for companies. If we revise our criteria to be a bit more realistic, we can say that a well chosen name has two characteristics: it's easy to remember; it has a significant emotional component or rational element. Yet in these two areas, the best is to be found alongside the worst. But such judgments of course imply a high degree of subjectivity. For that reason, we won't presume to give examples. We're reminded of Juliet's lovely speech in Shakespeare: "What's in a name? that which we call a rose / By any other name would smell as sweet." That may be so for the name of a flower, but certainly not for the name of a brand.

> / A well chosen name has two characteristics: it's easy to remember; it has a significant emotional component or rational element. /

Logos

"Logo" is the abbreviation of "logotype." It contains the Greek *logos* (speech, discourse) and the suffix "type," which in this case suggests the process of impression (as in typography). Originally, for typographers, this word designated a group of signs which were printed all at once, that were all part of the same typographical character. Later, the term began to designate any fixed group of graphical signs representing a brand, a product, or a company.

Codification is an essential component of a logo. To be easily recognizable, it must present an invariable visual grammar, where the shape of the characters, the size of the symbol, and the colors used are rigorously defined and protected by patent. Also note that the simple fact of codifying the spelling of the name of a brand, even without accompanying visual symbols, already constitutes a logo.

The logo, then, is not the brand, but a particular way of writing the brand. It is the heraldic shield of modern times – a combination of letters or signs, an image, an ideogram, or a group of graphical elements.

The functions of the logo

The logo, a unique and recognizable sign, has always served to mark an object, a work, or a building as belonging to a specific category. Logos appear to have always existed. Stone carvers placed their mark on their work, as did the great cabinetmakers. Roman slaves were tattooed with their masters' signs, and aristocrats and armies used escutcheons or standards. The word "brand" originally stood for the mark burned into the hide of cattle with a hot iron.

Communicating via symbols – language, mathematical signs, road signs – is one characteristic of humans. Logos are to modern communication and consumption activities what numbers are to mathematics or words to language: they constitute a new typology of conventional signs. In a way, logos are the new alphabet of an "overcommunicating" society, the symbols of our time.

/ Logos are to modern communication and consumption activities what numbers are to mathematics or words to language: they constitute a new typology of conventional signs. /

The logo plays a role in social relations for two complementary reasons: on the one hand for the informational content it communicates to the consumer before the purchase; on the other, for the perception it will create of this same consumer after the purchase, when he or she will be associated with the logo.

It's not surprising to see logos occupying such a preponderant place in our overmediatized society. They often fill the need for communicative synthesis pushed to its extreme: a maximum of information in a minimum number of signs. The synthetic expressiveness of signs as different from each other as the Nike "swoosh" and the Christian cross is remarkable; independently of their referents, they accomplish an analogous semiotic function! In a few strokes, a maximum number of values or a vision of the world are summed up.

It is difficult to draw up a strict typology of logos, since they borrow from a great number of expressive processes. One of the founders of semiotics, the philosopher Charles Sanders Peirce, proposed a classification of signs into three categories: icons, indices, and symbols. Each of the three evokes a particular type of relation between the sign and the thing it represents.

The icon, Peirce says, is a representation of a "literal" type, based on the notion of similarity. For example, to represent an apple, we draw the contour of an apple.

Indices correspond to a relationship that is more mental, yet extremely strong, between the sign and the thing. An index is a trace, an effect, or an element of the thing, which designates its presence without the slightest ambiguity. For example, if we see smoke on the horizon, it does not literally "draw" fire, but signifies its presence very strongly ("Where there's smoke, there's fire"). In this case the association is based on objective correspondences, in the sense that they are guaranteed by laws that are identical for everyone: in Tokyo and in New York, fire generally makes smoke.

Symbols, finally, correspond to the establishment of an arbitrary link between the sign and the thing: for example, a lion for the Republic of Venice. The force of the symbol rests on the establishment of a common culture. There is no graphical similarity between one and the other, nor is there an objective link of a physical or logical nature. A foreigner confronted with the symbol would not be able to decode it; on the other hand, for all the members of a given community, its meaning is obvious. We could say that a symbol is a federating element. In Greek, *symbolon* designated the fragments of a clay tablet that had been broken. These pieces were then distributed to the members of a group, who reconstituted the tablet at each of their meetings. When Nike issues a sports advertising spot which it signs only with its "swoosh," without even giving its name or slogan, it is obviously playing on the symbolic and federating dimension of its logo as well as on its reputation.

These categories are abstract. In practice logos are often hybrid, making use of all three at the same time. It might be better, then, to speak of the different functions of the sign. Let's take the example of the original Apple logo, which Jean-Marie Floch has analyzed in detail by comparing it to IBM's logo.[8] It can be called iconic, since it represents an apple; indicial (extrapolating a little), since the hollow in the outline clearly indicates that a bite has been taken out of this apple; and above all, symbolic: The bitten-into apple is laden with rich suggestions, and the rainbow of the original logo also connotes the cultural blend that is California society.

Nevertheless, the symbolic function is by far the one most called upon. This is not surprising. To say that a logo functions as a symbol for a brand is to describe this notion of consumers belonging to a special and prestigious club. Note that logos that are purely typographical (a very specific way of writing the brand – font, letter size, spacing, and so on) also participate in this

---

8 Jean-Marie Floch, *Identités visuelles*, Paris: PUF, 1995.

symbolic function. In fact, they rely on a set of visual conventions. For example, a serif character 11 will tend to connote Classicism or Neoclassicism, as in the case of Bulgari; a sans serif font will connote modernity (Lancel).

/ To say that a logo functions as a symbol for a brand is to describe this notion of consumers belonging to a special and prestigious club. /

Ideally, a logo also seeks to take on the indicial function. The brand's dream, of course, is for its logo to represent it in a way that is as elementary as the way smoke signifies fire – even though such an ambition is utopian. Very interesting examples of this indicial function can be found on the boxes of matches given away by cigarette producers in France. Very strict regulations prohibit the display of their name, their brand, their slogan, or any other distinctive sign on the box; but they've still managed to develop very abstract visual grammars, derived from their logos, which still carry meaning. It's a kind of graphical guessing game, and trying to decode them "blind" provides a good indication of a brand's graphical reputation.

A few forms of logo

In this rapid overview, we claim neither to be exhaustive nor to propose a coherent typology. We devote the bulk of our efforts to logos that are strongly graphical, in an attempt to suggest the diversity of this universe.

Like the seals of the ancients, most logos consist of an image or of intertwined letters.

In the past, certain logos expressed themselves in three dimensions. Rolls-Royce chose the Winged Victory of Samothrace; Michelin opted for the Bibendum character, made up of tires of different sizes, which was at home both in mannequin form and on billboards. Jaguar used the Leaper – a metal statuette of a leaping jaguar – as a hood ornament on its sports cars. Today logos are most often two-dimensional, an exception being the latest Renault logo which shows the make's traditional lozenge shape in relief.

Certain logos have a more iconic function. The logo of Poulain chocolate (a frisky colt – *poulain* in French) of course connotes youth and enthusiasm, but above all the surname of its founder, Victor Auguste Poulain, through the immediate graphical similarity.

In the category of images, the most frequent are those of animals. This harks back to the heraldic tradition, where animals were a prime source of inspiration for the escutcheons of the aristocracy.

Most often, we will find ourselves in the symbolic register, where the animal is an allegory for virtues that are assigned to it by convention. The choice of the brand name Jaguar, with its stylized but representational logo, is obviously associated with the aspiration to such virtues. And the list is long. There is Ferrari's rearing horse, an expression of indomitable vitality. The emblem was given to Enzo Ferrari by the family of a national hero, the aviator Francesco Baracca, who was wearing it on his plane when he was shot down over Montello during the First World War. For energy and speed, there is the greyhound used by Greyhound and Trussardi; Peugeot's lion; Merrill Lynch's bull (which also plays on the idea of 'bull market'); the shark of Paul and Shark; the elephant of Côte d'Or chocolate and Hunting World. For perseverance, Morabito's tortoise; for toughness and intelligence, the Lacoste crocodile.

Many other representative images exist: Hermès's coach, Ralph Lauren's polo player, Shell's scallop shell, the three keys of UBS, the blue star of the Crédit du Nord bank in France.

Another very widespread category draws more from the history of writing and the signature. These are "monogram" logos, made up of the brand's initials and its derivatives. What comes to mind first are obviously the two intertwined C's of Chanel and Cartier; Gucci's G; Yves Saint Laurent's YSL; Loewe's "crab," with its L reflected in two axes; or McDonald's "golden arch."

Some of these logos use already-existing symbolic conventions in the service of the brand rather than establish their own. An example is the Greek letter omega for the brand of the same name – a powerful denotation, but charged with a certain elitism; or the "Q8" of Kuwait Petroleum International.

Finally, we will look at logos of a more abstract nature, where the arbitrariness of the symbol predominates. This is not a new phenomenon. As with the choice of brand names, abstraction has been a trend for some decades. This is so with Tommy Hilfiger, with its red-white-and-blue rectangle, an extrapolation of the American flag, or Bally's red and white square. The automotive sector has always favored this type of logo. There is Chevrolet's "bowtie" – which the company's founder said he found in the wallpaper of a Paris hotel room – Citroën's chevrons, which originally represented gears, the Renault lozenge, Mercedes's three-branched cross, or the three intertwined circles of Toyota.

The logos of BMW and Alfa Romeo are immediately recognizable; but despite their relative formal simplicity, is it possible to draw them from memory? At Fiat, the five oblique stripes, deemed too complicated and unbalanced, recently gave way to the name of the brand inside a circle. It remains to be seen if the new logo will be more effective.

Regardless of the choices made, a good logo should have the power to express and synthesize the characteristics of the brand, symbolic force, and ease of retention, through a certain formal simplicity. Achieving all this is not as simple as it might seem, but success gives a brand a considerable competitive advantage.

/ A good logo should have the power to express and synthesize the characteristics of the brand, symbolic force, and ease of retention, through a certain formal simplicity. /

Managing logos

Formal fashions change. The graphics creators in companies, who are more sensitive than others to such issues, often ask for the transformation or rejuvenation of a logo. They rarely win out. This issue is a manager's nightmare. Many brands prefer to make do with a logo that is seen as somewhat dated rather than take the risk of damaging their customer awareness. The graphical evolutions of logos, at major brands, extend over entire decades, and each stage of the process is often almost imperceptible. One of the best examples of graphical evolution is that of Shell's logo, the "Pecten." Since 1900, when it consisted of a mussel shell symbolizing the young company founded by Marcus Samuel – which imported oriental seashells – it has evolved into the well known red and yellow logo, a stylized representation of a scallop shell, through nine progressive transformations (see Plate 8).

/ Many brands prefer to make do with a logo that is seen as somewhat dated rather than take the risk of damaging their customer awareness. The graphical evolutions of logos, at major brands, extend over entire decades, and each stage of the process is often almost imperceptible. /

Examples abound. The British brand Burberry's decided to alter its name to make it more accessible to an international clientele, and in general make the brand more competitive by giving it more modern connotations. This involved removing the apostrophe and the "s" of the possessive. This form is extremely widespread in English in the names of brands and restaurants, but it is less easily perceptible for other cultures. In France, for example, "McDonald's" is often pronounced "McDonald" in ordinary speech, and has rapidly become "Macdo" (phonetically "macdough"). Thus "Burberry's" becomes "Burberry" (see Plate 10). Removing the apostrophe and the "s" implies a change in the lettering as a whole, modernizing the brand, doubtless internationalizing it, but perhaps slightly destabilizing part of its Anglo-Saxon clientele. These are not the kinds of decision that can be taken lightly.

Our last example is the new advertising campaign for Gaz de France – a national gas utility and also an institution in France. In November 2002, it announced the change in its logo in these terms:

> Why change logos?
> The world is changing, markets are internationalizing,
> and competition is intensifying. Energy markets
> are also affected by these profound
> changes and new realities.
> In our leading position among
> European gas-supply groups, we must extend
> our scope more and more on the international level
> and to all business areas involving natural gas
> and the associated energy services.
>
> To symbolize this new destiny,
> we needed to change our logo. Modernise it.
> Attached to our name, which remains unchanged,
> we now have a distinctive, strong,
> and easily identifiable symbol.
> It conveys our fundamental values,
> in particular respect for our planet,
> its inhabitants, and different cultures.

We can think of no better way to sum up the importance of a logo in promoting a brand's new strategies and values.

Logos are always extremely sensitive to manage. Their creation, their esthetic evolution, and their utilization must be precise and organized to correspond to the general strategy of the brand.

What happens when there is no logo, or at least no graphical emblem? This is the case, for example, with Armani, Tiffany, Ferragamo, Bulgari, Coca-Cola, and others. Generally the company looks for one, but in the case of an already-established brand, with a rich history of existence, this is not easy.

Ferragamo, in the early 1990s, wanted to stylize the name of the brand to shorten it and make the founder's signature more legible. Also, the founder's baroque logo was very dated and was not used much any more. It also wanted to attach a graphical emblem. Numerous trials were made. A design with six horses, recalling the founder's six children, was studied, and also a drawing of the Feroni Palace, the company's headquarters. But the best intentions are not always successful, and the brand continues to use the Salvatore Ferragamo signature, whose calligraphy, and above all whose length, contribute to easy recognition.

Certain brands simply have no emblem and get along without one. The name of the brand, with its colors, graphics, and even sometimes its calligraphy, is still the first sign of recognition of a brand. The loops in the "C" of Coca-Cola, the Pirelli "P" with its elongated head, or the pointed Bulgari "U" have such strength that they make the search for an emblematic logo superfluous.

Logomania

Are logos omnipresent? Perhaps. In any case, disseminating these "totems" in all the registers of communication is an easy way of universalizing the representation of the brand. They are visible on products to the point where they become, in particular in the fashion sphere, concrete signs of added value.

Logomania is also a cyclical fashion phenomenon. The last craze dates back to Spring 2000. Already by fall–winter 2002, collections showed a marked decrease in the number of products that were covered with logos. The overexposure of signs always has the effect of partially demystifying the brand and making it a fashion element. This has implications that must be faced: fashion changes every season and can make obsolete an element that is strongly attached to the identity of the brand itself.

As for logos of public or private sponsors, they have proliferated in the past few years on posters and billboards for sports and cultural events. Their presence on the poster, and very often their size, are contractually imposed. Graphic artists often complain about this, pointing out that these additional signs, to which they are sometimes required to devote as much as 20 percent of the total display area, have a negative impact on the relevance of their communication. There's no denying that they have a point.

/ Logos, as symbols, presuppose a cultural community. Taking local specificities into consideration appears to be a determining factor in establishing a threshold of tolerance. /

We have said that logos, as symbols, presuppose a cultural community. Taking local specificities into consideration appears to be a determining factor in establishing a threshold of tolerance. Perceptions vary greatly from one country to another. Logos are much better received in Japan than in the United States or Europe. While a majority of Europeans refuse to wear a necktie printed with the acronym of a brand, Americans have no problem with it, and the very same necktie would become a genuine fad in Japan.

The majority of brands that have global ambitions have integrated these cultural differences and have the wisdom to take them into account. Louis Vuitton, for example, offers its Japanese clientele strongly monogrammed bags; on the other hand, for European consumers, the brand offers a fabric in identical colors, but with a checkerboard pattern, or else Épi or Taïga leather, where the monogram only appears episodically. Consumers in Paris as well as in Tokyo are very happy with their Vuitton purchases. They've made the effort of acquiring an expensive product and feel that a prestigious logo, one which reflects positively on them, is the reward for that effort, provided that it remains below their own particular tolerance threshold. They feel that by carrying the bag in public, they are affirming the values they seek (a certain elegance) without the risk of suggesting those they shun (bad taste).

The logo, as the ultimate synthesis of the brand's communication, must appeal to the eye, to the heart, and to the intelligence.

A logo is not a necessary and sufficient condition of success. However, not to have an adequate logo is to miss an incredible opportunity to communicate more effectively.

Other signs of recognition

Signs of recognition don't end with the name of the brand or its logo. Certain brands or products have succeeded in appropriating another element of recognition and differentiation, often by chance or through repeated usage. Yet they manage this additional element closely.

A first example is cult products that become emblematic of a brand, such as the Hermès Kelly bag or Gucci moccasins.

There are also certain distinctive characteristics of a product: the triangular section of Toblerone chocolate (the packaging is patented), or the shape of the Coca-Cola bottle, which has remained virtually unchanged since its origin. Color is another element. A red sports car has to be a Ferrari. Ferrari's monopoly on the color is so strong that it looks a little presumptuous to buy a sports car of another make in the same shade of red. Ducati has done the same with the color red in the motorcycle sector. Even sound can be an identifying element. Porsche, Harley-Davidson, and Ducati take great pains to maintain a very specific engine noise for their products, which they have even attempted to patent.

Finally, certain advertising slogans can be so often heard and repeated in association with the brand that they become extensions, fixed syntagmata operating like synonyms: Nokia's "Connecting people," HP's "Invent," or

Sony's "Go create." The clearest example is probably Nike's "Just do it." Slogans generally have a shorter life span than logos do, but renewing them also requires prudence. Take the example of Coca-Cola, a company over a century old (1886) and very active in terms of communication. Since its creation, the company has used 65 advertising slogans in the United States, and since 1966, only 13. The latest (the globalized "Always Coca-Cola"), true to its implicit message, celebrated its ninth year of existence in 2002. It has now been replaced by the "enjoy" campaign.

/ A brand's signs must first of all be identifiable, expressive, and easy to remember. They must create a feeling of closeness, familiarity, and even humanity. They must communicate a message of belonging, not only to the brand (at the first level), but also to its universe and its values. /

Whether names, logos, or other elements, a brand's signs must first of all be identifiable, expressive, and easy to remember. They must create a feeling of closeness, familiarity, and even humanity. They must communicate a message of belonging, not only to the brand (at the first level), but also to its universe and its values. This last point is what will distinguish between a brand that projects meaning and one whose significance is vague. Finally, they must stay in their proper place, not be a nuisance, and never give themselves over to semantic inaccuracy, which would involuntarily complicate decoding. Their primary role is to "speak" the brand and its universe with elegance and conciseness. It is the brand's responsibility to keep a close watch over its signs, their nature and their frequency – failing which they could very well turn against it.

2 | Anti-brand communication

> These images shock, but do not trouble; photography can "shout," but
> it cannot wound. I page through it, but I don't recall it.... I'm interested
> in it [the way I'm interested in the world], but I don't like it.
>
> (Roland Barthes)

You have surely been struck, as we have, by the proliferation of hostile graffiti on advertising posters and billboards in the street or in public transportation. "Subvertisement" – the *détournement* of advertising – is becoming an unavoidable component of our urban landscape. Contemporary artists see it as an esthetic principle. Satirists, on television, regularly subvert familiar spots to make fun of some celebrity or other. Organized activists make wide use of this process to disseminate their boycott calls.

What is new is that the street is doing it now. A few years ago, people scribbled "Feed me" on Calvin Klein's emaciated adolescents. There is a burgeoning of graffiti which seems to be spontaneous, showing a state of disorganized exasperation on the part of the public. In certain cases, these proliferate in the wake of the anti-brand campaigns that have recently drawn much publicity – calling, for example, for a boycott of Danone or the destruction of McDonald's restaurants. In other cases – and this is what is most troubling – the motives of the graffiti writers remain confused, if not obscure, and seem to show nothing beyond a generalized hostility.

What is behind this phenomenon? Clearly, this resentment is not aimed at a product (can a T-shirt engender scandal?), or even at a brand in the commercial sense of the term (can a vendor of T-shirts, as such, cause outrage?). It is aimed at a brand as an issuer of advertising. What is being targeted, with varying degrees of brio, is a communication strategy, and the most visible brands, those that provide resources for the most ambitious or provocative communication, are the first victims of these attacks.

This visible rise in the level of exasperation is one of the arguments of *No Logo*. For opponents of globalization, the major brands are only the tip of the iceberg. Naomi Klein stirs passions against powers that are gigantic, and which we seem to be supporting each time we buy a pack of Marlboros or a can of Coca-Cola.

We share that analysis – while stressing the fact that, in spite of the confusion between them that Naomi Klein's book propagates, it is not brands that are being criticized so much as their communication. Nevertheless, we part ways with her in that to us, the act of purchase is a civic act, one through which the consumer restores the balance of power.

We will return in more detail to the issue of consumer power. We want first to look over the different criticisms of brands that arise today. We feel that they fall into three major categories. First of all, there is the gap between the cultural models transmitted by advertising – a fantasy world – and the day-to-day reality of the purchaser. This phenomenon is not new, of course. Fantasy has been an element of brand promotion for a long time, and often the consumer enjoys it. However, the extensive use of advertising and the constant raising of the stakes have intensified the problem and are engendering an increasing number of undesirable side effects.

Then there is the more and more frequent use of provocation, be it in violent or sexual form, and of the most shocking forms of expression. This ceaseless clamor brings forth understandable reactions of rejection.

And finally, there is the "bad manners" of certain brands that deliberately move away from what consumers expect of them in the normal context of commercial exchange. Discretion, humility, and honesty are precious values. If a brand makes itself omnipresent, or takes on a moralizing role the public perceives as inappropriate – often leaving itself open to accusations of hypocrisy – or ignores professional ethics in its relations with its clients, its subcontractors, or its competitors, it calls attention to itself in the eyes of consumers, who interpret these as signs of arrogance.

It's not a good policy to think that all is fair in business. Many companies have taken greater and greater liberties with consensual rules for development of and communication about their brands. There's no doubt that some have benefited from them, and perceptibly increased their sales. But all these individual behaviors, these attempts at increasing insolence, placed end to end, have produced a type of pollution that only feeds hostility towards the general phenomenon of brands.

We want to be clear about this: we disapprove of these practices. As citizens, we are at best indifferent to them, and at worst indignant; as marketing professionals, we consider them to be ultimately counter-productive. These are niche practices, which make sense only within a very limited space and time. As soon as people get tired of them or the "scam" comes to light, they spell the decline of the brand that makes use of them. They contribute to the ethical impoverishment of our world and to increasing instability of employment.

Our goal in this chapter is, using examples, to show the scope of this phenomenon, to stop the flow of images and slogans, and to look at certain topics that have entered the public arena, to be digested and then – in the case of some – forgotten. Finally we try to show that such strategies are not viable in the long term.

Models under protest

Is it permissible to encourage people to fantasize about anything and everything, with no holds barred? The danger appears when fantasy advertising begins to take on reality.

Fantasy against life

Brand communication offers models that do not correspond absolutely to what people experience in their daily lives. This is particularly true where women and the fashion sector are concerned. The first challenges to this departure from reality were launched by American feminists 40 years ago. It would be an understatement to say that brands in general, and fashion in particular, are not very responsive to the criticism. Whether they continue to promote canons of beauty totally removed from reality, or defend a kind of cheap hedonism for commercial purposes, the hostility of the public is the same. It has continued to grow through the decades, and has now become associated with a more general resentment of the "mercantilization of the world."

This is no doubt a sign of the times, but it is also proof that brand managers have been slow to deal with this problem. The public likes fashion; it contributes greatly to building the trends that the brands then take up and prolong. Nothing justifies these tensions, except a certain indifference on the part of some communicators and brand executives towards the social implications of their messages.

For the philosopher Hegel, clothing is an intermediary through which our bodies "tell something," project individuals as a whole to themselves and to others. Fashion is a way for our bodies to enter a world of fantasy. But what happens when the fantasy ideal no longer has any relation to who and what we are in reality?

Just as classical statuary influenced traditional criteria of beauty for centuries, the unrealistic silhouettes offered by fashion designers after the Second World War marked several generations.

Of course, extravagant dressing is not a historical novelty. However, despite all their excesses, even the *merveilleuses* of the Directoire period after the French Revolution had a choice between the short Grecian tunic or the ample Roman toga, depending on whether they were svelte or pleasingly plump. Today, artificial beauty canons are getting farther and farther away from the average morphology of the Western women of today (see Plate 13).

Gilles Lipovetsky mentions that the average measurements of beauty-pageant contestants in 1950 were 5.6 ft and 121.25 lb.[1] In 1983, they had reached 5.8 ft and 116.8 lb. As an indication, the measurements of Kate Moss, during her Calvin Klein period in the mid-1990s, were 5.6 ft and 97 lb. It's true that it's easier for a couturier to dress a tall, slim young woman.

The new canons of corporeal beauty reflect the influence of the designer/media tandem in our time. The designer defines the silhouette, the media serve as sounding board, industrial production follows suit, and women can no longer find anything over a size 6 (European 38) in brand-name stores. Of course, they feel attracted by such images. They project themselves onto the advertising they see, and in many cases buy the products they are offered. This is not surprising. The most inaccessible dream is also the most seductive.

/ The new canons of corporeal beauty reflect the influence of the designer/media tandem in our time. The designer defines the silhouette, the media serve as sounding board, industrial production follows suit. /

Yet encouraging such an image is not without its consequences. Brands continue to promote a model wherein youth, health, slimness, and androgyny are the rule. This esthetic of the female body excludes 95 percent of women, negates "normal" femininity, and obscures motherhood. The distance between dream and reality produces frustrations on a global scale, and extreme reactions multiply.

Should we condemn fashion, and are the brands entirely responsible? Probably not. This is a game with two players, between the supply of and

---

1 Gilles Lipovetsky, *L'empire de l'éphémère: La mode et son destin dans les sociétés contemporaines*, Paris: Gallimard, 1987.

demand for fantasy, and often all the brands do is follow the trend. Yet the weight of their communication is cryingly obvious in certain extremes. There were 700,000 plastic-surgery operations performed in the United States in 1999; in 1997, 15,000 operations were on young women under the age of 18. In Africa and Asia, a fashion for "light skin" has resulted, since the 1980s, in a craze for skin-whitening products, which can be particularly harmful and often leave behind irreversible lesions.

It's impossible not to associate the development of anorexia nervosa with the explosion of advertising and magazines for adolescents. Anorexia is a disease that has developed very rapidly in wealthy countries, and whose growth is only exceeded by that of AIDS. This disease, which is a form of voluntary starvation, has reached epidemic proportions. It is estimated that between 0.5 percent and 3 percent of the world's population is affected – and in 90 percent of all cases, the victims are adolescent girls. In Spain, the Spanish society of endocrinology and nutrition indicates that the disease affects 0.5 percent of the population. In 1999, in Madrid, 32 percent of girls between 15 and 16 thought of themselves as too fat, and 27.5 percent had dieted to lose weight. In their desire to emulate the diaphanous figures of top models, too many girls sacrifice their health, and sometimes their lives.

The initiative of the Spanish Minister of Health, Jose Manuel Romay Beccaria, in March 1999 is a good example of an institutional reaction to such out-of-control effects. The minister promulgated a plan to combat anorexia in collaboration with representatives of the apparel industry, families of victims, psychiatrists, pediatricians, advertisers, modeling agencies, and consumers' associations. Among the objectives it has attained are above all the recommendations made to clothing manufacturers to produce sizes above 6; to brand-name clothing stores for teenagers to stock sizes 10, 12, and 14 in their locations; to advertisers and marketing firms to be sensitive to the problem of anorexia, by beginning to show images of models "who reflect social reality."

One of the most effective reactions has been the appearance of brands (for example, Lane Bryant, Tomatsu, Jenna Lane, Zana Di, and Delta Burke in the United States, or Marina Rinaldi, of the Max Mara group, in Europe), stores, and magazines (for example, *Mode Magazine* in the United States) dedicated to tall, full-figured, and normal people. However, this is a niche positioning which unfortunately does not have the same media weight as the luxury and fashion industry.

As was to be expected, certain brands have also responded to the wave of protest, and have gotten into the act of challenging the dominant esthetic. This is the case, for example, with the Body Shop, an English retailer of beauty and hygiene products, which bases its brand identity on the values of protection of the environment, the use of natural ingredients, and above all the promotion of its customers' self-esteem, by declaring, "We like you just the way you are." The Body Shop presents its famous Ruby doll, red-headed and plump, the anti-Barbie, accompanied by this slogan: 'There are 3 billion women in the world and only 8 top models' (see Plates 13 and 14).

The case of Kate Dillon ("the muse of plump women," as Fabienne Reybaud called her in *Le Figaro* in November 2001), a model for Marina Rinaldi, is exemplary. Anorexic at age 16 , Kate Dillon modeled for Chanel, Fendi and so on. One day, she couldn't take the pressure of the business any more; she realized that she herself was contributing to the perpetuation of this artificial image of women. She began eating normally, gained weight – and lost her job. Until the day Marina Rinaldi contacted her.

Then, thank God, Laetitia Casta arrived. A modicum of good sense had returned. There is in fact the start of a change in attitudes. The return of *zaftig* women to the movies (*Bridget Jones*) and the arrival of reality TV seem to announce a return to real people.

Cultural counterfeiting

Beyond indifferently supporting the esthetic values of the moment, brands are also criticized for the influence wielded by the cultural model they in part construct and largely contribute to disseminating: fascination with labels and, in models of communication, promotion of values that are materialistic, egocentric, and hedonistic, and also encouragement of drug use.

The example of the Japanese students who engage in prostitution to pay for a Louis Vuitton, Prada, or Gucci bag remains, we hope, an extreme case. But it clearly shows the nefarious power brands have over persons who are easily impressionable, in a society where brands have a much greater social significance than in the West.

This is what theologian Giuseppe Angelini, in his book *Le ragioni della scelta*,[2] calls the "Phariseeism" of fashion. This is an attitude that compels consumers to blindly follow what they think to be the rules of behavior. The most susceptible are individuals with weak, uncertain, or under-asserted personalities, who find in fashion an easy refuge where appearances hide substance, and where the judgment of others becomes more important than one's own.

---

2 Giuseppe Angelini , *Le ragioni della scelta*, Magnano: Edizioni Qiqajon, 1988.

Here again, it is less the brand itself than its management that is in question, through a certain indifference to negative side effects and a lack of restraint in communication, which end up turning against it.

Nowhere, perhaps, is this phenomenon more visible, or does it pose a direct threat to the brands, than in a tolerance for drugs, or even a concealed defense of their use. This dangerous game remains limited today to the fashion and showbusiness milieux, which are quicker than other sectors to co-opt all the codes that can signify a marginal lifestyle or an appealing difference.

/ It is less the brand itself than its management that is in question, through a certain indifference to negative side effects and a lack of restraint in communication, which end up turning against it. /

"Heroin chic" is also an invention of the world of fashion and showbusiness. Certain artists and creators have used drugs or alcohol to encourage their creative processes, or simply as a way of dealing with their overweening sensitivity. From Baudelaire's artificial paradises to the Beatles' *Sergeant Pepper* album, the examples are numerous, and so are the victims – direct and indirect.

For reasons to do with the prevailing culture, but also with difficult working conditions, fashion designers haven't escaped from this phenomenon. And it's not surprising to see elements of their lifestyle spill over into their creations (products, advertising, and fashion shows). The first victims are often the young models who can't always stand up to work that is extremely difficult physically and mentally. The top models don't escape, either. The British press love to show shots of these unfortunate young women leaving drug-cure centers.

Here again, resistance is becoming organized. The anti-narcotics organization of the United Nations has always been very critical of the fashion, media, and showbusiness industries, exhorting them to behave more responsibly and refrain from promoting the idea that recreational drug use is part of people's normal lives. In England, associations like Designers Against Addiction are active in promoting a drug-free lifestyle for models.

Yelling to be heard

Made popular by radical artists in the early twentieth century (Dadaists and Constructivists), large-scale provocation has since successfully moved into advertising. We have in mind a Dadaist leaflet that was handed out in Paris in the 1920s: "You can't see, but think of people who can." The *détournement* of people's compassion for the blind, a blow against common sense, a taste for absurdity – legitimate creative fantasy, yes, but through a violent form of communication. Such practices, adopted by the brands for commercial purposes, have been proliferating.

/ Provocation means proposing a representation that infringes on a consensual pact of communication between the issuer and the recipient. It is saying things that no one expects to hear you say in a given communication situation. /

Provocation means proposing a representation that infringes on a consensual pact of communication between the issuer and the recipient. It is saying things that no one expects to hear you say in a given communication situation – a billboard, for example. It also means using words that no one expects to hear you use. The violence of the real world (as in the famous Benetton campaigns, for example), the bad taste, and the erotico-pornographic connotations fashion brands are fond of are the privileged themes of such techniques.

Why this fad for provocation?

For consumers, advertising represents fantasy, and anything that departs from the real or the ordinary can contribute to feeding that fantasy. Eroticism and transgression are obviously a privileged medium for fantasy. They are the most direct means of signifying that we have left day-to-day reality behind. As long as the provocation does not go beyond a given individual's tolerance limit and is not drowned in a flood of similar audacities, it may well find a receptive audience.

From the point of view of the brands, there appear to be three types of motive. First of all is the understandable desire to follow the Zeitgeist, to ride the trends, to communicate with the words and values of today. This is basically the argument Oliviero Toscani, the brains behind the most famous Benetton campaigns, which many feel are "scandalous," uses to justify his strategy.

More subtly, there is also the desire to structure a market, to create a niche of consumers federated by common values. Exclusion is an easy but powerful tool to do this. All it takes is to set people against one another and play on their differences. To target young people, for example, make fun of old people; to get to women, go after men; to home in on men, point the finger at women. Provocation, because it draws battle lines between those who can tolerate the message and those it scandalizes, serves this purpose perfectly.

If such societal or ideological objectives aren't reached, there remains, finally the most cynical argument of all: that the one who yells loudest has the last word. One thing is certain: whether it pleases people or not, provocative advertising never goes unnoticed. The impact rates are always very high, and are multiplied by word of mouth.

Video captures

Historically, one of the first forms of provocation in advertising is based on the surprise effect, the "teaser." In France, two famous campaigns illustrate this trend: the launch of the Elf brand, with its mysterious slogan "Les ronds rouges arrivent" ("The red circles are coming"), and the striptease by the model Myriam for Avenir Publicité in the early 1980s (a beautiful girl baring her breasts in a large-print ad, saying "Tomorrow I take off my bottom" – and then later being shown naked, but from the back).

With the Myriam striptease, the surprise effect was reinforced by explicit erotic connotations. Transgression, until then limited to what is ordinarily expected of advertising – that something is being sold in an immediate way – now extends to the domain of morals. The difficulty of this exercise is in jarring spectators without going beyond their threshold of resistance.

Back in 1971, the couturier Yves Saint Laurent caused a scandal by posing nude for the launch of his perfume. He was seen as a precursor. Throughout the 1970s, eroticism became a commonplace of advertising. The appearance of video was greatly increasing the audience for pornography, and brands, eager for transgression, pushed back the limits of provocation. The teaser campaign "Tomorrow I take off the top" by the Avenir Publicité agency contributed to defining the new advertising order. From that point on, in order to surprise, the ante had to be upped, and to project an avant-garde image, transgression was necessary.

/ From that point on, in order to surprise, the ante had to be upped, and to project an avant-garde image, transgression was necessary. The lesson is easily learned and applied. /

The lesson is easily learned and applied. The Diesel brand built its notoriety on particularly outrageous campaigns: for example an old lady, seen from the front, sitting on a bench near a companion whose private parts she is grabbing (see Plate 16). The directors of Diesel responded to the numerous letters of protest by saying that their philosophy of communication was based on provocation and irony.

Fashion is a milieu that thrives on fantasy. A wave of 'porno-chic' swept over it in the late 1990s and was accentuated in 2000 and 2001. The trend is waning a bit today. Italian brands were the first to cross the line separating an eroticism of suggestion and unambiguous pornographic connotations. We'll give just a few examples:

- Gucci, in its Spring 1998 campaign, showed a couple where the young girl's head is located in an unmistakable way between her partner's legs.

- Cesare Piaciotti presented provocative young models wearing visible, flimsy panties sitting on tombs in a graveyard.

- Exte, and to a lesser degree Sisley, specialized in representations of female couples who apparently don't need the opposite sex to satisfy their impulses. Christian Dior followed suit in Spring 2000, before adopting grease-monkey and manga styles. The same is true for Gucci, in their fall 2000 campaign, though Tom Ford denies it: "This is neither a photo of lesbians nor is it not a photo of lesbians. It's an image that speaks to people and that is why we chose it," he told *WWD* in September 2000.

The French, defending their reputation, weren't to be outdone.

- YSL returned to scandal with his Opium perfume, with an ad showing an absolutely naked Sophie Dahl. There was also the campaign showing a scantily-clad young woman, surrounded by naked men in a shower which seems to be in the locker room of a soccer team.

- A few seasons ago, Ungaro decided to destabilize us with high-quality photos showing young women languorously embracing statues. In the following campaign (Spring 2001), the statues gave way to magnificent dogs.

In Spain, every year *Elle* magazine dedicates its May edition to the female buttocks, with explicit front-page titles like "especial culo" (see Plate 15). The domain of pornographic provocation is not exclusive to the luxury industry. The campaign for Lee jeans showing a woman's leg wearing a high-heeled shoe placed against the posterior of a prone nude man with the text "Put the boot in" was in especially bad taste. The English brand French Connection had so much success with its "fcuk" campaign that it used it as a logo for a line of clothing. In December 2001 the coffee brand Lavazza launched a billboard campaign in Germany showing a frontal view of a naked woman, with stickers with the name of the brand stuck to her skin.

It is in this area of pornography that institutional mobilization is most effective, though it may itself be a reflection of local cultures. Europe seems to be much more permissive than the United States, certain Asian countries, and of course the Middle East, where nudity is illegal. Brands have learned to deal with these different sensibilities. Catalogues are often censored by the companies themselves; provocative photos are replaced by photos of products or logos.

In the United States, where Puritanical tradition makes transgression easy, Calvin Klein continues to cultivate equivocation about androgynous youth. The fall 1998 campaign, showing teenagers in suggestive poses in a basement, was removed from New York bus stops after the company was accused of promoting child pornography. There was another scandal in February 1999 when, under pressure from Mayor Rudolph Giuliani and the *New York Post*, Calvin Klein was forced to remove – five hours after it was installed – a giant billboard on Times Square showing scantily-dressed children, because it was considered "sexually implicit." The brand was reportedly under FBI surveillance at the time.

Fashion shows are ideal platforms for staging the most outrageous provocations before a specialized audience (the fashion and daily-newspaper press, buyers for department stores, showbusiness and society personalities).

Since nudity has lost its effect through overuse, other techniques are being tried: the evocation of decadence, of female homosexuality strongly tinged with male voyeurism, and sadomasochistic practices:

- Alessia Merz bathing in ass's milk for Coveri in Milan (winter 1999 collection)
- the Sapphic kisses of the brand Piano Piano Dolce Carlotta
- graffiti on the nude torso of an American model for Swish.

Creators themselves have spoken out against these provocations – which, they feel, only show up the creative poverty of certain designers. Gianfranco Ferré disapproved of "the theatricality which is now a part of fashion and of our time." According to Romeo Gigli, "Collections are made to be looked at, not spoken about like a society event." In France, the advertising verification bureau (BVP) – a self-policing entity made up of agencies, advertisers, and support professionals – does attempt to control the most obvious excesses. The Weston ads in early 2001, which showed a nude woman dominated by a man whose shoe only was shown, had to be changed after the bureau stepped in. The British Advertising Standards Authority, late in 2000, outlawed 500 Yves Saint Laurent billboards for Opium perfume which showed the pale nude body of Sophie Dahl.

Provocation is not limited to the sexual domain. The sacred is also a favorite object of attack. Everyone remembers the Pirelli ad showing soccer star Ronaldo in the pose of the statue of Christ over the bay of Rio de Janeiro (see Plate 28). In France, in February 1998, Volkswagen waited until it had lost a lawsuit brought by the bishops' synod before withdrawing the launch campaign for the new Golf, which made use of the image of the Last Supper. Diesel, once again, met with numerous protests over its campaign showing four nuns and the Virgin Mary in tight-fitting jeans.

Does provocation sell?

Does provocation increase sales? Sometimes, at first, and better if it contains a modicum of humor. But as everyone begins using these methods, they become less effective. In the general brouhaha, for provocation to remain effective, it must become more excessive. The process contains its own end within it.

/ In the general brouhaha, for provocation to remain effective, it must become more excessive. The process contains its own end within it. /

The Benetton brand, above all during its collaboration with publicist Oliviero Toscani, has made a specialty of this type of shock campaign. Its campaigns fall into two categories. On the one hand there are undifferentiated attacks on a whole gamut of ideologies presented as so many forms of discrimination (racism, suspicion against homosexuals or AIDS sufferers, the denial of mortality, but also sexual abstinence among Catholic religious). Then there is the appropriation of the most violent current events, for the promotion of positive values, world peace, and the blending of races and cultures (see Plates 22 to 27).

Managing the gap between the high-mindedness of the message and the prosaic nature of the product is sometimes a high-wire act, and these campaigns, by dividing opinion, have gotten a lot of press. But has this strategy, with the graphical violence that accompanies it, increased Benetton's sales? According to store managers, this type of communication systematically increases traffic at the points of sale, but entering a store is not buying. The association of German Benetton franchise holders – that is, the individual proprietors of stores under the Benetton brand – recently sued Luciano Benetton. These vendors feel that the brand's provocative campaigns affected their sales and caused them losses. Are they justified in complaining?

We have figures for France of the impact scores of an image from the 1991 Benetton campaign. In the image, a Catholic priest is kissing a nun on the mouth (Plate 26). The impact of the ad in France is summed up in Figure 2.1.

What strikes one first of all in these results is the fact that in terms of appreciation of the campaign (like it, don't like it), the ad received scores very close to the mean for the advertising tested by the survey agency, Ipsos. The appreciation is stronger, however, among young people (65 percent liked it, 29 percent didn't like it) than among the 35–55 age group (58 percent as against 41 percent). Also, the recognition of the communication is 48 percent higher than for a standard ad. Obviously, the campaign didn't go unnoticed... As regards attribution (I've seen this ad and it's an advertisement for Benetton), things are even clearer: The overall impact of the campaign was 3.28 times higher than for a normal ad campaign. But we have to go farther and compare overall attitude with intention to purchase (see Figure 2.2).

What do these new figures show? When we question the public on its intentions of purchase, the results are reversed: Over a third of the persons who liked the ads (23/59) say that they don't make them want to buy the products. The photograph amuses them, no doubt; but in the perspective of buying Benetton products, the technique is no longer amusing at all. And this trend seems to accentuate as these consumers' income bracket becomes

FIGURE 2.1					
Impact of the 1991 Benetton campaign (percentage by age group)					
	Recognition	Attribution	Like	Don't like	Indifferent
Overall sample	64	59	59	38	3
18–24 years	65	63	65	29	6
25–34 years	67	65	60	36	4
35–55 years	60	53	58	41	1
Ipsos standard	43	18	59	36	6

Source: Christian Pinson and Vikas Tibrewala, *United Colors of Benetton*, INSEAD, 1996.

FIGURE 2.2				
Impact of the 1991 Benetton campaign (percentage by income level)				
	Like	Don't like	Indifferent	Makes me want to buy	Doesn't make me want to buy
Overall sample	59	38	3	36	61
High	56	43	1	41	55
Medium	66	30	4	36	60
Low	48	48	3	21	79
Ipsos standard	59	35	6	–	–

lower. You get the feeling that they don't want to be taken in. You can't call it an active boycott, but clearly the campaign is not achieving all its sales objectives.

We can draw the bottom line on advertising of a provocative nature like the one showing the priest and nun kissing. The impact is three times greater than that of a normal ad; but at the same time, 61 percent of consumers are being discouraged, either rejecting the brand or stopping short of making a purchase.

It remains to be seen if the strategy is a winning one. In estimating the score of a normal advertisement in intentions of purchase at a proportion of 75 percent of respondents who attributed the brand for and 25 percent against, the bottom line becomes as shown in Figure 2.3.

In the final analysis, the ad campaign with the priest and the nun produced a desire to purchase that is 57 percent higher than the standard, while eliciting rejection or boycott among 36 percent of the target.

In a certain way, this "pollution" among 36 percent of the population is not significant compared with the 21 percent of convinced purchasers. The ad, though provocative, had a kind of playful irreverence that was a far cry from the bloody campaigns that followed. But these figures don't legitimize the claims made by the German Benetton franchisees. In the short term, at least, provocation sells. It results in a growth of impact by a factor of three, elicits intentions to purchase two times greater than normal advertising, and on the downside, causes a negative reaction among almost ten times the number of people who would have been sensitive to a standard ad.

FIGURE 2.3				
Comparison of the 1991 Benetton campaign with the Ipsos standard				
		In percentage of the overall population		
	Campaign attributed	*Want to purchase*	*Don't want to purchase*	*Don't know*
Ipsos standard	18*	13.5**	4.5	–
Benetton	59	21.2	36	1.8

Notes:
* Ipsos
** Author's estimate.

But there are serious doubts as to the viability of such a strategy in the longer term. In any case, Benetton and Oliviero Toscani have since parted ways. After several successive campaigns, the cumulative number of rejections was becoming problematic. Added to that is an escalation in the violence of communication that is likely to alter the results we have just seen. The very aggressive campaigns showing HIV tattoos, dying AIDS victims, and the bloody T-shirt of a Bosnian soldier may have won over some spectators, upon reflection, with their "ethical" connotations, but one doubts that the majority found them "nicer" than a kissing priest and nun. The latest campaign by the photographer James Mollison, in February 2003, entitled "Food for Life" and showing a man with a metal spoon replacing his amputated hand, is following the ethical direction initiated with Oliviero Toscani in the exact same vein.

Our opinion is that these practices tend to trap the brands in a vicious circle and that they necessarily lose in the more or less long term. The system operates only if the provocation constantly increases. If the psychological tension the new campaign creates is less than that of the preceding one, it goes unnoticed and the balance of consumers who resent the brand for it becomes

/ Provocative advertising tends to trap the brands in a vicious circle, and they necessarily lose in the more or less long term. /

very high. Provocation in advertising works once or twice, and maybe more; but it stops working of itself when escalation becomes impossible.

In order to last, a brand needs a precise identity, different from that of its most direct competitors, easily perceptible by the target customers. How can it differentiate itself when the only dimension it projects is the same as for most of the others? How far should it go? Once all the taboos have been transgressed, what is left is the creator's real responsibility: to offer original products, that have their own personality and that clearly express the values potential customers identify with.

Arrogant brands

A third complaint against brands is very widespread today among consumers. It has to do with the idea that they "don't stay in their place," that is, that their visibility goes far beyond the borders of a consensual commercial exchange accepted by both parties.

This argument contributes greatly to the case Naomi Klein makes in her book. Brands are colonizing our geographical, cultural, and political territory; they have become imperialist powers which threaten our public spaces, our artistic expression, our freedom of thought as citizens, and the sovereign independence of our governments.

To our mind, this argument lumps a good many issues together. Although it appears comfortable and modern to develop a thesis based on the simple phrase, "Everything is a brand today," we don't see it as a revolution compared with traditional critiques of capitalism. The concept of "cultural space" sounds good, but we don't know exactly what it includes, and how such a "space" can be "colonized." The "political power" of Nike remains to be demonstrated, and we don't see why all sponsorship efforts or any ethical claims made by a company should be condemned on the grounds that they are necessarily examples of corporate hypocrisy.

These questions of course deserve to be raised; we don't have all the answers to them, but we haven't found them in *No Logo* either. It has to be recognized, though, that Naomi Klein succeeds in grasping a certain contemporary spirit, singling out the rising tide of hostility towards what might be called the "arrogance" of brands.

We use this term in its primitive sense, which comes from the Latin *arrogantia*, and which signifies "to make undue claims to something," arrogating a right or a station without being entitled to it. This arrogance consists in not remaining in one's place, in not remaining in one's "normal" role – or, to a certain extent, not fulfilling that role.

Whether because of brands' excessive presence in the urban environment, their desire to achieve a certain insincere complicity with the consumer, or their failure to adhere to a normal code of professional ethics, both towards their customers and towards their competitors, certain companies sometimes come to the public's attention because of abuses. Do they realize that in so doing, they discredit all of commerce and hurt their own brand image?

Brands and the urban environment

Brands and labels are inexorably invading our public space. On the periphery of cities, the countryside is dotted with billboards. In our finest downtown streets, the places we have loved, the most picturesque restaurants are giving way to stores or fast food outlets with garish signs.

We've all known nostalgia for a place that has disappeared, an urban landscape that has been transformed, and we've all felt resentment towards city officials who are too modernistic, or towards a department-store chain. But today, in the busiest public places, brands are what stand out above all, and often the same brands. How can they fail to understand that this accumulation and homogenization are causing rejection reactions?

Lease costs have become so high in the most famous shopping streets that only groups with enormous budgets or a few old brands that are still under favorable lease contracts can afford to be present there. The result is a feeling of uniformization that is tiresome to the eye. Downtown areas are full of brands, and they're always the same ones.

Admittedly, the demand for prestige locations has exploded. First, there are the major groups that want a single-brand showcase. And these centrally-located spaces exert a growing attraction on emerging brands (Nike, for example) or those that aren't generally associated with the luxury world (like Levi's). All of them want to cash in on the undeniable prestige of having a location near the top luxury brands and the foot traffic they generate.

Success creates success. A strong brand, capable of generating annual sales of above US$3000 per square foot, can locate just about anywhere. The real-estate market aligns itself with the performance it knows the major brands are capable of. A few minor brands do set up in a few choice locations and write off their losses to the communication budget. The others choose adjacent streets with less traffic, or settle for areas where rent is lower, where their true competitors are.

These trends are part of the vaster phenomenon of the "metropolitanization" of the planet, to use an expression taken from the work of George Cavalier.[3] For over a century, the movement towards urbanization has

---

3 'Les villes, acteurs de la mondialisation,' in Ramses, *Les grandes tendances du monde*, Paris: Dunod, 2001. The statistics presented in this paragraph are taken from this book.

undergone unprecedented expansion, at once the cause and the consequence of economic growth. Today, for the first time, city dwellers are more numerous than rural, whereas they represented only 10 percent of the world's population at the start of the twentieth century. Humanity has built as much in the last 30 years as it did in its entire prior history. There are now 19 cities with more than 10 million inhabitants in the world (compared to two in the middle of the twentieth century) and 22 with between 5 and 10 million inhabitants. This trend is now more concentrated in the Southern Hemisphere, which has 33 urban areas out of the total 41 that have more than 5 million inhabitants.

/ The city is the stage where the major evolutions of our societies are played out. The city offers not only economic opportunities, but also greater freedom and possibilities of expression, self-assertion, and for superior social relations. /

Such growth makes cities the ideal setting for a transformation of lifestyles and behaviors. It is the stage where the major evolutions of our societies are played out. The city offers not only economic opportunities, but also greater freedom and possibilities of expression, self-assertion, and for superior social relations.

In this scenario, the megabrands are at center stage. They are the ones that have the resources necessary to occupy the most prestigious retail locations. Unfortunately, they contribute to accentuating the social gap between the center and the periphery. However, should the brands be held responsible for the degradation of the urban landscape? All they are doing, really, is taking advantage of vacant pieces of real estate and a certain vacancy of political will. Solutions exist. For example, in the historic centers of Italian cities, in Rome and Florence, McDonald's restaurants exist, but must have very discreet signs, designed for each location to respect the harmony of the surroundings.

When brands moralize

A major trend in the last decade of the twentieth century was that brand communication, after having gone through stages where they promoted incorporeal values, then concepts, finally entered the field of ethics. The issues are the same as for provocation: promoting fashionable values and affirming new modes of consumption; a desire to federate consumers; the need to differentiate themselves from the market as a whole.

Naomi Klein condemns this attitude in harsh terms, calling it pure cynicism. We fail to see, however, how the affirmation of positive values, even for purely commercial purposes, can be harmful to the common good. It is true that ethical values are not just a sales gadget, and that if a brand is going to hold itself up as an authority, it had better be beyond reproach itself if it doesn't want to be a target for angry consumers.

What we have in mind is the difficulties brands like Nike had over the media coverage of the sweatshops where its products were produced. But the problem was related to the much vaster one of globalization, and involved almost all the major producers of sporting goods. There are even more striking cases where poorly-managed communication on the part of brands in the field of ethics has earned them a certain reputation for cynicism among a wide audience.

There's the case of the Spanish cigarette brand Fortuna, which caused a scandal, in 1998, with its campaign "Now, with Fortuna, 0.7% goes to an NGO." On the billboard was the face of a teenager and "0.7%" written in smoke (plate 31). It turned out that at the time of the launch Tabacalera, the then owner of the Fortuna brand, had not yet made any agreement whatsoever with a non-governmental organization. The committee of five experts that was to have made the selection had not even been formed. This caused an outcry in Spain. The General Director of Public Health, the anti-tobacco campaign committee, certain NGOs, and a majority of the press protested loudly over this apparently Machiavellian practice, which uses young people's feelings of solidarity to incite them to use products that are dangerous for their health. Since then, Tabacalera has merged with France's Seita, in December 1999, to form Altadis. The experts' board has been formed and the funds collected are really being used for specific solidarity projects.

/ Selling goods by getting up on a soapbox is acceptable only if you do it with humor or if it aids an important cause. But as soon as the shadow of cynicism falls over the orator, he or she meets with general indignation. /

Even if we leave this extreme example aside, the exercise is all the more perilous when it's accompanied by a radical type of communication. The problems associated with provocation arise: selling goods by getting up on a soapbox is acceptable only if you do it with humor or if it aids an important cause. But as soon as the shadow of cynicism falls over the orator, he or she meets with general indignation. The more you moralize, the more you run the risk of having other moralizers turn against you.

We've already mentioned the provocations of the Benetton brand, one of the first to enter the ethics field. It's clear that the ethical argument also served as a rationalization for highly visible campaigns based on images of exceptional violence. A lesser-known initiative was the redistribution campaign launched in 1997 in the United States. The ad showed a nude Luciano Benetton saying, "Give me back my clothes. Empty your closet!" The project consisted of collecting old clothes for redistribution to the disadvantaged. But it was also, of course, a particularly innovative way of improving traffic in the stores. Attentive observers did not fail to point this out.

In the face of these experiences with "charitable" communication, the trend seems to have diverged in two directions in recent years. In the wake of the forerunners, the majority of brands adopted ethics, but did so using more general values and less violent forms of communication. Here are a few examples of slogans from Kenneth Cole's summer 1999 campaign featuring products or models (see Plates 29 and 30):

For every dollar a man makes, a woman earns 76 cents. Change, please.

65% of Americans have more success making their outfit work than their marriage.

At least two people are found innocent prior to their execution each year. How many are overlooked?

[After the September 11, 2001 terrorist acts in New York] On September 12, people who don't talk to their parents forgot why.

One might doubt the effectiveness of a campaign that adopts so many different issues, mentioning all the possible problems of American society. Yet Kenneth Cole is an emerging brand with a strong rate of growth.

The avant-gardists, on the other hand, move to the next stage: subverting the codes of this ethical communication. There has been a spate of mock "humanitarian" ads for consumers who didn't buy Product X. In a similar spirit, on the theme "We know you're not taken in," Nike planned a campaign in which it would feature some of its own critics, in their usual discourse of denouncing the brand.

At Calvin Klein, the slogans have an ethical flavor and color, but are only an empty shell around a total absence of values, with assumed irony. Take the ad for the CK Be perfume, where the text, under a picture of a teenager, reads, "Be good, be bad, just be." And from Moschino: "Whatever." These messages are characteristic of the state of mind of too many creators. Nothing original to offer, the absence of a personal point of view, and a lack of new ideas which is masked by trying to make that very void itself into an idea. It reflects certain defects inherent in the current state of Western civilization: relativism, nihilism, facile glibness, superficiality, materialism, egocentrism – in short, postmodernism.

The brands probably find more credibility in controlled sponsorship programs, in which they give up the moralizing role in favor of backing some concrete action. Pepsi-Cola, for example, has made agreements with the NGO Médecins Sans Frontières. That organization's code of ethics requires that manufacturers not use child labor, exploit their employees, pollute, or support totalitarian regimes. Producers of alcohol, cigarettes, and drugs are automatically ruled out.

More credible also is the 2002 initiative by the telephone operator Orange, whose billboards in Switzerland and on its web site promote its long-term agreement with Unicef. The documentation on the site explains that the brand believes in a future where people will communicate more to exchange ideas and feelings. The commitment to Unicef stems from the idea that education is considered the foundation of mutual comprehension. For each new subscription, the brand donates 12 Swiss francs to a project to build 130 schools in India.

Capitalism makes use of all moods. If consumers are more socially responsible today, the brands pick up the cue and offer them the possibility of consuming with a clear conscience. Is this pure, scandalous cynicism? Again, the reactions of the general public show that what shocks consumers is excess: words that are not followed by actions, naked promotion – in short, ideological arrogance. But there is still room for initiatives that are more modest, at least in the way they're promoted, provided that the brand stays in its appropriate role and doesn't overstep the bounds. A well-managed humanitarian effort has proven to be more beneficial, for the community as well as for the company, than attempts at scandal for its own sake. Sales do better under a cloak of ethics than with gratuitous provocation.

/ Brands have both the desire and the resources to encourage good-citizenship initiatives, and because of their commercial nature, they remain subject to the general expectations of consumers, which guarantee the balance of power. /

The undeniable advantage is that values are promoted. They are widely discussed, which contributes to raising consciousness. Despite the hypocrisy of numerous brands who use this mode of communication, there is still a world of difference between such commitments and the pursuit of facile pornography. It results in actions that contribute directly to humanitarian causes and the adoption of ethical behaviors encouraged by the agreements with NGOs.

So let's not be too demanding. Look at where we're coming from. There's no point in condemning brands; they have both the desire and the resources to encourage good-citizenship initiatives, and because of their commercial nature, they remain subject to the general expectations of consumers, which guarantee the balance of power. It seems to us that everyone benefits.

Today, all or nearly all the major brands include support for social action in their global strategy. They are active, in a more or less visible way, out of conviction or out of need, in promoting major causes with a social dimension. We will cite a few examples (and apologize to the numerous brands active in the humanitarian area who are not mentioned):

- Levi's against AIDS

- Axa for the development of disadvantaged rural areas

- Air France's support for underprivileged children

- Timberland in community services

- Shiseido in financing retirement homes and orphanages

- France Telecom on behalf of autistic children

- Avon against cancer

- Shell for environmental protection

- Dow Chemical, also for protection of the environment

- Procter & Gamble for sustainable development

- L'Oréal, who, in collaboration with UNESCO, started the "For Women in Science" project to recognize and encourage women's participation in scientific areas at all levels.

Many of these came about as a result of pressure from consumers or associations like Greenpeace. The latter's actions against the dumping of the Brent Spar platform, and its worldwide echoes in the press, have influenced the awareness of Shell's directors. These are positive examples of combined action among consumers, associations, and the press that lead to the raising of awareness and to socially positive actions on the part of directors of brands. We will discuss this in more detail in Part Three.

Breaches of professional ethics

There is also arrogance in the liberties taken by certain companies with their commercial ethics. This code, often stricter than the equivalent legislation, is where the real pact between the vendor and the consumer is set forth. It is through it that the brand differentiates itself and builds its image. Infringing it amounts to the brand stepping out of its role by flouting the rules of commercial exchange. Alert consumers react immediately: The brand "thinks it can get away with anything."

Under the category of what might be called the ambient pollution that results from certain marketing actions are false advertising or exaggerations that push the limits of legality. When consumers are encouraged to buy a product and find out they've been more or less swindled, they always feel justifiable anger. And that anger can easily extend, without nuance, to producers, retailers, and advertisers as a whole.

Producers of repeat-purchase products (detergent, for example, or chocolate bars) do all they can to avoid misleading advertising. In their case, this concept is very broad, covering any and all promises about the product's qualities that they can't necessarily keep, or that certain consumers may feel they can't. Purchasers compare the claims that have been made with their experiences as consumers. Any feeling of having been lied to can result, overnight, in a decision never to buy the brand again. Consequently, managers of this type of company police their own advertising for such excesses, which they call "overclaim."

On the other hand, where single-purchase products are concerned, some producers do engage in full-scale deceit. Such is the case with rental vacation homes that are "only steps away from the beach," and insurance contracts that are much cheaper than the competition's but don't necessarily cover the same risks in the same way. It's also true of advertisements for contests where everybody wins.

These practices are particularly prevalent in mail-order sales. The magazine *Capital*, in April 2002, catalogued a few such misleading promises:

- "Your gift," as the caption under a collection of superb articles. Barely visible in a corner of the page is a tiny pizza slicer – which of course is the real gift being offered.

- "Your weight in gold," which – instead of the customer's weight in pounds – turns out to be a tiny scale.

- "You win if there are yellow silks with red dots in the picture." In the picture it's the jockey's cap that's yellow with red dots.

■ "You are a winner if your number starts with a double 00." The number
you are sent starts with 00, but not a "double 00" – in other words, four
zeroes.

Such tricks may seem to be amusing, or to show the extraordinary creativity of marketing people. Such practices surely increase the response rate for
a mailing. But the extension of this dubious type of communication
contributes greatly to maintaining a climate of mistrust of companies in
general on the part of consumers.

Imitation and plagiarism are indirect breaches of the implicit pact of
trust that governs the relations between producers and consumers. Origi-
nality and innovation are essential aspects of a brand's image. Unlike false advertising, plagiarism hurts the competition above all. But it's a mistake to think that the discredit to the brand will remain confined to the narrow circle of producers, and not reach the general public. When a major brand stoops to this kind of practice and the plagiarism becomes known, the sanctions in terms of brand image can be harsh indeed. Here again, the oppro-brium can feed an undifferentiated resentment of all commercial activity.

/ For an enterprise to resort to a deontological code comes back to leaving its role and no longer respecting the rules of commercial exchange. With the consumer warned, the sanction is immediate: the brand "believes it can do anything." /

Again, we take some examples from the luxury industry – while noting that wherever
creativity is crucial, creators are in danger of being influenced, consciously
or unconsciously, by their peers' success models.

One has to admit that it must not be easy to create a new collection of
ready-to-wear and accessories twice a year – or even four times, with the
pre-seasons, or six if you add the haute couture collections – and never
stumble on a model someone else has already invented. In the early 1990s
Ferragamo neckties, with their ethnically inspired, animal, and sports
motifs, were quickly successful with the label's admirers, to the chagrin of
Hermès, which cut off all relations with the family and major directors of
the Florentine brand. To the untrained eye, the patterns could indeed resemble those used by the French label. Yet the Ferragamo motifs were the
result of authentic creative work and were in fact inspired by Persian
carpets.

There are several examples of successful lawsuits. In 1998, Abercombie
& Fitch sued American Eagle Outfitters for systematically and intention-
ally copying the brand and its catalogues. In January 2001 a Paris court

required Gucci France to pay more than a million francs in damages to the Berluti company and to Olga Berluti for having counterfeited two models of shoes created by Olga Berluti. In February 2002 Nike brought a lawsuit against the Sega Corporation, accusing it of copying the sequence, tone, atmosphere, rhythm, music, and characters of Nike's famous 1996 spot in which Michael Jordan scores for the Chicago Bulls in slow motion.

Even the promotion of noble sentiments is not exempt from legal battles. In May 1999, Reebok published an advert in the magazine *Men's Health*, showing a shoelace crossed to imitate the red ribbon of the fight against AIDS, with the caption, "Human rights: unconditional, inalienable, without limits. Do you feel it?" But Kenneth Cole had already created that shoelace image in 1994, with the slogan, "What you stand for is more important than what you stand in." Kenneth Cole had the intelligence to give his lawsuit symbolic value, and asked Reebok to make a donation of US$100,000 to a charitable organization. The press did not report on the result. Generally, these conflicts are settled out of court between the companies.

Plagiarism, or to a lesser degree a lack of originality, is an accusation that is especially feared in the fashion world, where differentiation is above all based on the individual creativity of a designer. Yet there are general fashions and trends whose origin would be difficult to attribute to a single individual. This does not keep consumers from looking behind the general expression of the trend for the specific "stamp" of a creator they like. Rather than speaking of plagiarism, it would be better, for the fashion sector, to talk of common and simultaneous inspiration, and esthetic or stylistic convergence.

Roland Barthes, in his time,[4] underlined how close this paradox is to what linguists and grammarians call the "language/speech opposition". Language is a tool, a system of values shared by all and which must remain general, without which people would not be able to understand one another; speech is the way each individual uses language to communicate an individual message. At the same time, we all contribute, through our own speech, to the evolution of the language. This is what happens with famous authors or the press – for example, through certain inventive expressions that catch on and end up becoming part of the language. This also holds true for trends and the "stamp" of the creator. The latter follows fashion while at the same time contributing to its evolution.

For example, why, in spring 2000, was there a sudden explosion of products covered with logos in the press and in display windows, and then being worn by the most fashionable people? Logomania had struck

---

4 Roland Barthes, *Système de la mode (The Fashion System)*, Paris: Seuil, 1967 (English trans. University of California Press, 1990).

consumers. The ultimate in chic was to be dressed in initials, or other recognizable elements of style. Christian Dior led the pack with a new stylized "CD," Gucci brought back its old snaffle bit, Bally invented its "Busy B," Céline came out with a monogram, Louis Vuitton printed its "LV" on a new leather, and the Burberry plaid signaled the brand's relaunching (see Plates 6, 7 and 35). In fall 2002, the fever suddenly broke. The proportion of luxury products sold plastered with logos fell from 40 percent to less than 15 percent.

In the past few years, specialization and horizontal concentration in the sector have led to the creation of "trend agencies," whose only purpose is to prospect all over the world to deliver to creators the styles, colors, materials, and even values that will make up the fashion of tomorrow. This phenomenon, widely covered in the media, may have given the false impression that all of fashion depends today on the diktats of a small number of decision makers, ruling out any real originality. This is likely to further encourage paranoia towards the major brands and accusations that they manipulate consumers. Some see it as another demonstration of arrogance: fashion presents as original creations what are in fact preformatted products, all alike, dictated by the influence of powerful economic interests.

/ There is no "empire of the brands" that dictates fashion. The general volatility of the sector and the very rapid renewal of the dominant brands in this field are proof of that. /

This view is not very realistic. It fails to give credit to the extraordinary fertility, the complex interactions, and the reactivity of the sector. The recent phenomenon of concentration only makes it more apparent that a mechanism of "cross-pollination" has always been at work in the formation of trends. There is no "empire of the brands" that dictates fashion. The general volatility of the sector and the very rapid renewal of the dominant brands in this field are proof of that. The structure of the industry hasn't fundamentally changed the way fashion is created: through a series of interactions which take place at all stages of the production process, and of which trend agencies – whose function, let us not forget, is purely prospecting – are only one component.

Other aspects of the system which contribute to the convergence of styles could be cited:

■   First of all, the professional trade fairs, which launch the start of work on the collections – Première Vision in France, for example, where textile producers present their latest products, or Idea Biella and Combipelle in Italy.

■ Producers and subcontractors, who very often, especially in Italy, work for competing brands and among whom a lot of information circulates during the phase of sample development.

■ The simple fact that creators and their teams know each other, go to the same places, read the same documents, and exchange ideas.

■ The close ties between the entertainment world and that of the brands. The world of fashion brands uses actors' and actresses' power to rapidly influence people. Madonna in low-waisted pants at the Oscar ceremony is enough to create a seasonal fashion.

■ The *prontomoda* system. These companies specialize in rapidly marketing what the major brands present in their fashion shows. Using a highly effective logistical apparatus, they can reproduce the articles that make the best impression in less than two weeks.

■ The evolution of tastes among the members of a society that go to the same schools, are submerged in the same advertising, watch the same TV programs, and read the same newspapers and books. Convergences are bound to appear. But each time homogenization becomes too strong, a counter-trend always emerges, and then is absorbed by the system in its turn.

All these factors contribute to producing fashions. Consequently, we are dealing here with a societal problem, one of a general nature, for which the brands alone cannot be made to bear all the responsibility. On the other hand, what can be criticized is a lack of creative boldness, during a period that is obsessed with everything "vintage," with "revivals" of fashions of the past, taking flea markets as inspiration. The recent launches of the new Mini Cooper and the Volkswagen New Beetle are two examples of restyling which point up the current lack of innovation and the defensive withdrawal into baby-boomer nostalgia (see Plates 55 and 56).

The implicit contract that governs the relations between brands and consumers requires brands to be attentive to consumers' expectations, but also to be authentically creative, and to behave properly both towards their customers and their competitors. Any infringement of this code exposes them to well-deserved sanctions; in today's context, it may also throw undifferentiated discredit on all commercial activity and lay an entire system open to blame for abuses that are really only episodic. Taking care not to leave themselves open to this kind of guilt by association is the primary responsibility, both professional and civic, of brand managers.

Conclusion

In the face of the excesses we've been condemning throughout this chapter dealing with the virtual image of women, provocation, the commercial exploitation of solidarity, mendacious advertising, and so on, it seems appropriate to quote part of an essay by the Archbishop of Paris, Jean-Marie Cardinal Lustiger, published in the daily *Le Monde* on February 7, 1998, in response to the use of an image of the Last Supper to launch a Volkswagen car.

> What do you respect? Does money justify everything? Don't you think that in hurting us, in a premeditated way, you are betraying yourselves? ... When you advertisers tout a product, you do it to convince us that it is worthy of us.... We ask you, do you think that your work can reconcile advertising and dignity ...

The key words have finally been spoken: respect for the dignity of others.

In taking us for mentally unstable voyeurs riddled with complexes, believing in nothing but the frantic quest for our own pleasure, brand managers, advertisers, and the media betray their own idea of consumers and of themselves. The archbishop takes advertisers to task. In fact it is the entire chain of decision that's under accusation: creators, designers, and artistic directors, directors of communication or marketing, company CEOs, advertising agencies, and the media.

The sad fact is that there is still too little sensitivity today to the dignity of the public at the level of that chain of decision. This indictment, with particular emphasis on the luxury brands sector, is not intended to be systematic denigration of a world known for its frivolity, but rather a way of throwing light on certain failings on the part of the principal players in the system. We are convinced that it is not permissible to incite the public to fantasize about just anything and by whatever means, and hope we have pointed out approaches that can correct these failings, which must not become an inevitability or an epidemic.

/ The sad fact is that there is still too little sensitivity today to the dignity of the public at the level of that chain of decision. /

Generalization must be avoided. There are numerous brands that regularly show the respect they have for their customers. There are many examples of creative ads and commercials, full of humor and good sense, which promote the ethical and esthetic specificities of the brand. To cite a few:

- The Eram campaign showing a chair with shoes on the two front legs and the caption: "No female body was exploited in making this advertisement" (Plate 32).

- The Burberry campaign showing Kate Moss and a judge, with its strong sense of English modernity (Plate 35).

- The ad for Lightware, showing its new projector with a stuffed monkey and the caption, "We fired our celebrity spokesmodel and passed the savings on to you" (Plate 33).

- The advertisement for the Audi A4 TDI V6, showing a camel and a jaguar rubbing noses to symbolize speed and low fuel consumption.

- The Ducati people 2002 campaign which shows genuine Ducati owners and the very personal and emotional link they have with their machines (Plate 34).

We would add that the role of advertising is probably overestimated today. The main function of many magazines is to distract people in the dentist's waiting room. The explosion in the number of publications, the increase in the number of pages of advertising, the constant competition to provoke, which alienates the majority of people, the emergence of new media like the Internet and advertising on building scaffolding and on vehicles – all contribute to diminishing the relative influence of each medium.

Zara is a fine example of a successful brand, positioned in the intensely competitive clothing sector and gamely giving Gap, H&M, Mango, and Kookai a run for their money. Zara has an annual sales volume of more than US$2 billion after less than 20 years of existence, without advertising (except for sale promotions). The mythical Ferrari is another example of a brand that never advertises.

The evils we've listed in the preceding pages illustrate above all the lack of a sense of responsibility and, sometimes, of proper professional training on the part of the major players in the brand arena – creators, communicators, managers of brands and media, copywriters, publicists, retailers, and also buyers. These criticisms are not aimed at all the brands. The extreme practices of some are far from being statistically significant. But it's necessary to denounce the abuses of some to avoid their spreading and worsening the general conflagration. As Jean-Paul Gaultier told the weekly *Panorama* (Italy), "Natural selection happens on the basis of the clothes, not the transgressions." And we needed to take a hard, objective look at this world of brands, whose virtues will praise in the next chapter of this book.

3 From value to progress

Progress is man's mode of existence.... The collective stride of the human race is called Progress.

(Victor Hugo)

The current of anti-brand activism we see emerging today has a paradoxical side. On the one hand, critics denounce the brands' hegemony in the contemporary world; on the other, they point to their increasing vulnerability – the result of growing reputation coupled with their dependence on consumers. The more a brand becomes visible, the more it leaves itself open to public bashing and consumer backlash. This being the case, it's difficult to see where the hegemony really is.

Naomi Klein is quite conscious of this paradox. She even sees it as reason for a certain optimism, which sets her apart from the crowd of anti-globalization critics. The "overexposure" of the brands, which she assimilates with globalization in general, becomes, for her, a powerful tool of protest. We share her opinion that there is a balance of power; we ourselves harshly denounce the reprehensible and counterproductive brand-management abuses we cited in the preceding chapter; we salute the efforts of responsible consumers, whose part Naomi Klein takes. But on a more theoretical level, we are not convinced by the analysis.

/ The more a brand becomes visible, the more it leaves itself open to public bashing and consumer backlash. This being the case, it's difficult to see where the hegemony really is. /

First, it seems to present brands as being systematically turned against the real life of individuals and their communities. This a priori judgment seems to be seen as justification, in and of itself, for their becoming the enemy in a holy war. Second, Klein implies that brands themselves are not affected by the globalization of exchange and of communication, but rather are its deliberate instigators.

With the Internet and Coca-Cola lumped together, the "hope for citizenship" the author talks about, the mobilization she issues a call for, seem to be the result of a kind of historical stroke of luck. Citizens and consumers have nothing to do with it. Passive victims of the "conspiracy" of the brands, they are only using the weapons they forge against themselves. As for corporations, outside the cynical pursuit of mercantile interests, they can have no role to play in the universe of citizenship or in social progress.

This model of a world divided in two is a very static one, where the only interaction takes place through mutual antagonism. We don't accept it. It's the kind of trap fallen into by all simplistic analyses that insist on cutting commerce off from real life. The central thesis of this book, on the contrary, consists in maintaining that brands, in a context of good management and faced with responsible consumers, are real factors for social, economic, and cultural progress.

We are speaking here of brands in particular, and not companies generally. It is our view that brands, in terms of progress, represent an advantage. As we have tried to show, the notion of the brand is founded on that of differentiation. And there can be no differentiation without promotion of values – be they qualitative, hedonistic, or ethical ones. It is up to all the players concerned to see that these values are positive, and in many cases that is what happens.

Nike, for example, is a favorite target for Naomi Klein, in particular in her denunciation of the working conditions prevalent, during a certain period, in the "export processing zones" in certain developing countries where Nike – among other companies – locates its production. Nike has answered these attacks via the press. Its main objection, while it admitted the accuracy of the facts reported, was to say that it had ended such abuses through energetic measures, well before the publication of *No Logo*. In fact, the controversy over these so-called "sweatshops" has forced the major brands in the category to implement programs of controls to ensure that their products are manufactured under conditions that are beyond reproach.

Let's suppose for a moment that these major brands don't exist. Suppose that in the sweatshops of the Third World, millions of pairs of unbranded, undifferentiated shoes were produced, under execrable working conditions, before being sold via a network of anonymous operators. How, then, could pressure be brought to bear on these hundreds of small producers? It is precisely the existence of a brand like Nike that provides a means of action and progress. The brand has committed an error? Undeniably; but because of its very reputation, the cost of not correcting that error would be too high.

Once again, Naomi Klein is conscious of this paradox; yet our conclusion parts company with hers here. Because to us, the reputation of the brands is not only an antidote to their negative influence. If Nike, or some other brand, did not exist for consumers to demand that it show itself worthy of the image it projects – sportsmanship, youth, solidarity, multiculturalism – these values would simply disappear from the commercial arena. To us, this story is not the illustration of mercantile cynicism. It shows that Nike has freely chosen certain values to represent it, and that such a covenant entails certain constraints. Because it implies the promotion of values, the notion of the brand allows progress to be made, at all levels of the chain of production and distribution, towards a more equitable world. We see brands as a positive force for progress, and not simply an incidental effect.

This chapter is devoted to the exploration of this idea. We feel that brands can exert a positive influence on society in five ways: They create wealth; they encourage the processes of innovation and creation; they perfect markets; they favor multiculturalism and the understanding of diverse cultures; and finally, they put people in a position to generate progress individually, in their own situations.

The generation of wealth

Brands create wealth for everybody. It is their most immediate contribution to social progress. Of course they have no monopoly, but today they seem to be ahead of other companies. Unbranded business consists principally of small or medium-size companies, the majority of them service providers, retailers, dealers in generic products, and developing brands. The development of branded activity in the service industries and its continuing growth in the area of products contribute to accentuating the phenomenon.

Companies that own brands and that prosper create wealth for all the stakeholders involved: their employees, their shareholders, their subcontractors, their consultants, their service providers (banks, auditors, insurance, advertising agencies), the tax authorities, social-protection entities, and so on. This is an obvious reality, but it is being obscured today by the rise of resentment and protest against brands. Isn't the protest aimed at the wrong target? Brands, with their clear identities, bear the blame for all the ill effects of a globalized economic model. Doubtless they are more convenient targets than the system as a whole, to which no clear alternative is visible.

Recalling the role of brands in the creation of wealth is an opportunity to respond to three prejudices. The first consists in saying that brands amass wealth without redistributing it. The opponents of globalization often cite as an example the wages prevalent in the relocated production units of multinationals. But clearly, the brands are not at the center of this problem. On the contrary, in most cases, the wages paid by the major brands are higher than the average wage in the countries in question, and are accompanied by various benefits. Taking the concept of intangible value into account, the brands' motivation goes beyond profit alone. Quite often, the image of a brand is at stake in the code of conduct that governs its relations with the whole of its economic environment: suppliers, subcontractors, employees, customers, and competitors.

/ Isn't the protest aimed at the wrong target? Brands, with their clear identities, bear the blame for all the ill effects of a globalized economic model. Doubtless they are more convenient targets than the system as a whole, to which no clear alternative is visible. /

Another prejudice is related to the preceding one: the idea that all brands use their reputation and power to exert pressure on their suppliers' prices. In France at least, what come to mind are the major supermarket chains and their relations with suppliers of agricultural products. A corollary to this idea is the notion of homogenization of products, of "downward" standardization, of the disappearance of the specificities of individual artisans. This is a negative side effect of the mechanisms of concentration, but can it legitimately be blamed on brands? As we will see later, this phenomenon is most often associated with the distribution of unbranded products. On the contrary, the quest for value can lead brands to seek out, and to pay for, excellence in their suppliers. This is why certain luxury brands – we have in mind Hermès, Loewe, Daum, and Baccarat – continue to offer products of close to craft quality, and enable the perpetuation of rare trades and skills: bootmakers, shoemakers, tailors, saddlers, glass blowers and engravers. Without them, these skills would have already disappeared, left behind by the mass market and the industrial imperatives of volume and rapidity.

The last prejudice claims that the brands exact a high price for the wealth they distribute – for example, by taking over control of information or culture wherever they exercise their power, through sponsorship or advertising. This argument is accurate in part. In the financial balance of a magazine, for example, advertising revenues generally account for over 50 percent of total business volume. Is it realistic to think that the publisher of a specialized review will not instruct the writers to put on velvet gloves for a client that represents between 10 and 15 percent of advertising income?

In women's magazines in certain countries, there is an unspoken rule that an advertiser that pays for a page of advertising promoting perfumes, fashions, or cosmetics is entitled, more or less officially, to an editorial page mentioning his product. In other cases, the reporters are the ones who must be attracted and won over. At certain fashion shows and new-product launch meetings, gifts to journalist are de rigueur.

Gratitude has its limits, however. All individuals have their way of dealing with these pressures. Fortunately, they don't rule out the exercise of journalistic free choice. There is always room to maneuver in the face of what amounts to a form of lobbying. No, the brands are not in control of editorial departments. We can cite the example we have both encountered in our own careers, of journalists at the *New York Times* who systematically send back valuable gifts to the companies in compliance with their newspaper's code of ethics. This attitude is tending to spread in the American media, and also in Europe. A few years ago, the critics at a French daily were astonished at being presented, at the screening of a Hollywood super-production, with a cell phone "featured" in the film. They returned the gift and blew the whistle – in a humorous vein and without attacking the film – on this dubious marketing practice.

In presenting the press as being enslaved by the brands we tend to forget that, without brands, there would be no advertising and therefore no (or very little) independent press, radio, or television. The brands are behind the burgeoning of advertising, and this is what supports the pluralistic, diversified, and innovative dissemination of information and culture. The multiplication of advertisers is also a guarantee of the balance of power.

Promotion of the process of innovation and creation

Brands encourage innovation. There are two motives for their doing so in a systematic way. The first is inherent in the concept of the brand. In order to exist, a brand must cultivate its own identity, must differentiate itself. Innovation is a powerful means of achieving this.

The second motive is contingent on the first: the race for novelty. We live in a period where cycles are shorter and shorter. Competitiveness is based more and more on ever-greater rapidity in developing new products. In sectors like luxury and fashion, where this dimension is not yet sufficiently developed, it is replaced by a frenzy of esthetic creativity. Novelty tends to become a value in itself, and becomes more important than the real advantages of the products offered.

Whatever the results, these considerations make brands powerful catalysts for innovation. They stimulate creative and innovative forces which are expressed not only at the level of products and services, but also in all other aspects of companies' operation – communication, distribution, logistics. Thus they contribute to constant innovation in the technical, scientific, industrial, organizational, and esthetic fields. In this sense, they are a factor for social progress.

/ Brands contribute to constant innovation in the technical, scientific, industrial, organizational, and esthetic fields. In this sense, they are a factor for social progress. /

Today, the intrinsic quality of the products is often criticized. This is explained in part by the nostalgia for "old-fashioned quality." It can be seen as the other side of the coin of innovation, but also proof of its dynamism. In cars, for example, wood and metal have been replaced in part by plastic and fabric. In houses, stone has been replaced by cement blocks. Hand-polished wood slabs have given way to molded plastic objects. We all witness these daily changes, and we get the feeling that we live in a world that discards its reference points. It's explained to us that cement is stronger than stone and that in many cases, honeycomb plastic is stronger than metal, but that leaves us feeling dissatisfied. We're told that today's cars may look less solidly built than 30 or 50 years ago, but they're much more reliable. But we're not entirely convinced.

The phenomenon is fairly new. One or two generations ago, consumers and producers were united in their pride in the industrial innovations ushered in by product standardization: lower costs, higher quality and so on. Today, volume production is seen above all as alienating us from craft, where the work of the human hand could be seen in the curve of a car fender or the polish on its bodywork. People's direct influence is no longer so visible. The marks are more difficult to identify. And that is precisely what brands help us do.

The objection might be raised that the innovation brought about by brands is of a secondary order, that often it should not be confused with the real progress made by fundamental research in science, or experimentation in art; that what it produces above all are useless products, sold through high-pressure marketing which creates needs that are non-essential. Obviously, all innovation is not done by brands. But they have such a need of it that they encourage it well upstream. The ways in which the private sector contributes to scientific research may be open to criticism, but the association of the two has proven itself.

The discovery of a new technology is no guarantee that it will change the lives of a majority of people; often, the brands are the ones that will innovate and invest considerable resources in democratizing it. Innovation then moves into the fields of production, logistics, distribution, and sometimes the modalities of commercial exchange itself. The vendor's perspective can, in this area, prove to be much more dynamic than the scientist's. The explosion of microcomputers was less the result of pure invention than it was of the ambition to democratize an already existing technology for applications which remained to be created. This required that someone take up numerous technological challenges (in order to lower production costs). At the origin of this revolution were above all vendors and visionary brands.

/ Often, the brands are the ones that will innovate and invest considerable resources in democratizing an invention. /

Finally, the idea of "non-essential" products can be challenged. Take the case of Évian water spray. This is an aerosol that many women use to refresh their faces. At first glance, this seems to be a typical example of a useless product. It is used in the same way as tap water – and anybody can spray his or her face with that. To the extent that the product is not ingested, its purity, guaranteed by Évian, does not seem to be a determining factor. Yet the spray was a notable success. Users of the product find the contact with the thousands of tiny droplets extremely enjoyable. So the Évian brand did create a new need, one that could be called non-essential. But above all it created a new pleasure. Is this negligible? We don't think so. We feel that brands are factors for progress when they give people the means to engender progress themselves. And happy people are better at doing that than others. In this sense, a small pleasure, a small gain in terms of comfort, represents progress at its level.

There are also more high-profile innovations, such as the cellphone – probably the most influential innovative phenomenon of this new century. The sudden emergence of these devices in everyone's daily lives is a significant factor of progress in communication between persons. It contributes not only to perfecting markets, but also to enabling people to generate progress.

Interestingly enough, at the introduction of this technology, few people predicted the incredible expansion it would undergo. Here again, it took an ambitious network of brands and vendors to invest in the democratization of a complex tool which at best seemed reserved for a handful of executives who are constantly traveling.

To us, the movement towards innovation is never negligible. Of course, many useless gadgets have been created and forgotten, and will continue to be, but the price to be paid is low compared with the extraordinary fertility of a dynamic which is also inspired largely by brands. Innovation, when it is authentic, is one of the activities that best characterizes the human race, and is without doubt the most humanistic aspect of the world of brands.

/ Innovation, when it is authentic, is one of the activities that best characterizes the human race, and is without doubt the most humanistic aspect of the world of brands. /

Perfecting markets

Brands make transactions between all the participants in the market more effective. They have concrete advantages for economic players, be they direct or indirect producers, distributors, or consumers. Let's look at our example of Évian spray again. The seductiveness of such a product is largely based on the brand's guarantee, which ensures the consumer of irreproachable quality. For retailers in a tiny niche market, this is the product that has to be stocked. The same product with no brand, or under a store brand, would not offer the refinement consumers expect of it.

Further, the retailer knows that if, for one reason or another, the product did not sell as well as expected, resulting in an insufficient volume of sales for the shelf space devoted to it, the Évian brand might well decide to launch an advertising or promotion campaign to move the product. This means that the profitability of the shelf space devoted to the product is ensured; in return, the producer knows that it has a product in which it can invest and that it can promote. These investments will be all the more useful as the product acquires, little by little, a real *raison d'être*, and can't be easily copied.

It might be objected that the Évian spray is a niche product for a marginal market. It is true that, for basic products that are used frequently, where differentiation is neither easy to obtain nor very necessary – butter or milk, for example – the brand plays a less determining role. In this case, each of the players acts in a less harmonious way. Consumers don't make a distinction as to brand, or in any case, don't remember it. They have a tendency to buy the least expensive product. As for retailers, they must have significant space to devote to the sale of butter or milk, but can't sell these products at a very high price. In this case, it's the price put on these items that will determine the consumer's choice, and which, in his or her mind, will position the supermarket in relation to its competitors.

The retailer will therefore keep prices low. It will ask the producer to also lower its wholesale price, in order to earn a minimal margin. At all stages of the process, margins will be reduced; as a result, relations between producers and retailers are often more conflictual. The brand, on the other hand, thanks to the added value it commands at the level of retail price, federates the complementary interests of consumers, retailers, and producers.

/ The brand, thanks to the added value it commands at the level of retail price, federates the complementary interests of consumers, retailers, and producers. /

This is a good illustration of how brands make markets more effective. This influence is brought to bear principally in the areas of communication and distribution.

Influence in the field of communication

The explosion of brands has revolutionized communication around commercial transactions. We have identified three areas where decisive progress has been made. First of all, there is the establishment of relations of greater transparency between consumers and the brand; then, the contribution of brands to promoting a cultural identity; finally, the impetus they have given the communication industries, with positive fallout that goes well beyond their specific domain.

On the consumer side, brands fulfill their primary function – that of a commitment: purchasers know they are not buying just any product. The brand is the incarnation of a set of intangible values, qualitative or ethical, which guarantee certain conditions of exchange.

The brand allows a customer to place a product in a known context and deduce certain characteristics, whether tangible or purely imaginary. It provides differentiation amid the proliferation of offerings of competing brands. Its visibility and its identification extend the episodic contacts of commercial exchange into a prolonged relationship between the brand and the consumer, an implicit covenant of exchange which it is important to respect. If this pact were broken, the backlash would be immediate, in the form of a single non-purchase, or worse, adverse publicity or rumor – an advertisement of consumers' disappointment.

Salvatore Ferragamo, a designer of genius, was also a clever merchant. He said that losing one customer is losing all the women in a group in a living room or at a dinner. This clear covenant or pact, a dimension of the brand we refer to as "contractual" in Chapter 1, is the most concrete advantage brands give the consumer. The brand must prove at all times, and everywhere where it has chosen to be present, that it is consistent with itself, true to its identity in ethical, qualitative, and esthetic terms.

It is in the area of quality that this effect seems most perceptible. Without brands, producers would not be mobilized as they are to maintain constant quality, in line with their identities – and therefore with consumers' expectations. When, in the United States, Ralph Nader casts doubt on the safety of a particular car model (General Motors' Corvair), sales of that model collapse overnight and the brand is profoundly affected. The organization puts in place teams of engineers who must immedi-

/ The brand must prove at all times, and everywhere where it has chosen to be present, that it is consistent with itself, true to its identity in ethical, qualitative, and esthetic terms. /

ately go to work to find solutions and solve the problem. It's hard to imagine what would happen if all cars were produced by undifferentiated, unbranded plants. Neither the urgency nor the extent of what is at stake would be taken into account in the same way.

The brand creates a transparent relationship with its consumer. Also, brands express the cultural environment from which they arise. Through their communication and distribution activities, they disseminate their own cultural reality on a very wide scale.

The phenomenon also has an educational dimension; we shall return to that. The brand speaks with a differentiated voice – for a group of persons who share common values and a common culture. This influence is found in its advertising communication as well as its sponsorship operations. Brands are faithful donors, which generally make a point of promoting, with constancy and in the context of long-term relationships, events that are organically linked to their identity. Support for national cultures, a favorite area for airlines, is a good example.

Finally, as we have said, brands made enormous contributions to the development of the press, radio, and television in the twentieth century. Their investments in communication in all its forms are the essential factor in building and expanding brands and their identity. In return, the brands have participated significantly in the emergence of free and pluralistic information, and in the progressive structuring of the communications industries.

These influxes of capital and creative resources have been the driving forces behind decisive progress. The efforts and the creativity of advertising, for example, have nourished cinematographic art and contribute to renewing its grammar. The director Stanley Kubrick was frank about his admiration for television advertising. He mentioned in particular the famous Nescafé "slice of life" spots, which, he said, managed to tell a complex human story with extremely condensed resources. And some of the major filmmakers of today are products of training in advertising.

Influence in the area of distribution

Brands have also profoundly influenced all forms of distribution of goods, and transformed urban and suburban landscapes. There are stores – like Aldi in Germany and Lidl in France – that sell almost exclusively unbranded food products. These stores focus on the competitive dimension of price. For example, they will sell cookies of an unknown brand, which can vary depending on the contracts the retailer enters into. Consumers buy these products for their price; they are often happy with them, but they are never sure of finding the same product on the shelves on their next visit to the store. In this case, the brand is only there to indicate the origin of the product and identify its producer. The store itself and the chain it belongs to provide the guarantee to consumers – a global and little-differentiated guarantee.

If, on the other hand, we go into a more traditional supermarket, we are struck by the diversity of products, the quality of the packaging, and the presentation. Innovation, diversity, and sophistication are the impressions that dominate. This is competitiveness in action; each brand tries to outdo itself and differentiate itself from its competitors. For example, we won't find a single pack of chocolate-sandwich cookies or fig bars as we would at Aldi, but many types of cookies – with jelly, shortbreads, brownies, ladyfingers, sugar cookies and so on. We are in the domain of diversity, difference, excellence, and choice. That diversity is the direct result of the presence of brands in this department, and of the competitive dimension they introduce.

Here, competition is has free rein and is merciless, all to the benefit of the consumer. Products appear nearly every month. They try their luck, aiming to gain the interest, then the preference of purchasers. If they don't succeed, they disappear from the shelves. The rapidity with which this system has responded to the increasing demand for "natural" products among consumers is proof of its reactivity. Take the case of eggs, which originally were a fairly non-differentiated product: All retailers today offer eggs from free-range chickens or with an "organic" label. Thanks to brands, product offerings in the mass retail sector are in a process of unin-terrupted change, and the consumer calls the shots. This diversity and quest for quality and innovation is what the supermarket will use to try to attract and hold its clientele.

The objection could be raised that, in the last few years, a fashion for generic products has arisen in mass retail. In fact, certain chains have launched campaigns with "white" or "free" products. The objective was to provide, alongside products from major brands with high advertising budgets, products that were just as good, cheaper, but unbranded.

/ Thanks to brands, product offerings in the mass retail sector are in a process of uninterrupted change, and the consumer calls the shots. /

Make no mistake about it: the brand concept remains present in this initiative. The product the consumer buys bears a brand, if only the name of the store itself. And just as for a major producer's brand, the retail chain had to support the launch of these products with a large advertising budget, in particular stressing its rigid selection criteria. In these products, customers appreciated the quality and efficiency of the retailer, who is delivering a seal of quality. The product therefore has a brand, a guarantee, and quality requirements. Customers' experience with these products directly influence their perception of the chain.

To sum up, the "generics" phenomenon must be understood as being an attempt at substitution of a store brand for a producer brand. For all retailers who develop their own products, these products that don't come from major brands are a source of discrimination, an additional factor in the consumer's evaluation of the store chain.

To gain independence from the major brands, retailers now know that they have only two choices: either substitute "private labels" – proprietary brands like Roebucks for Sears or Towncraft for J C Penney, which they outsource to a manufacturer – or else market products under their own name. Mass retail cannot escape from the brand system. The Darty appliance stores in France understand this. For years, they've focused all their communication on their "contract of confidence," a fundamental dimension of the relations between the brand and the consumer.

Without brands, the major retail chains would not be able to have a diversified, complete, adaptable product offering. They would have to compete with each other on the price variable alone and on service. The competition would then become one-dimensional; it would work to the detriment of the wealth of choice offered consumers.

Mass retail has also remodeled the urban landscape. There is a real problem of urban "pollution" in areas with low population density today (the peripheries of cities, rural areas) because of the anarchical proliferation of budget stores and supermarkets, but the phenomenon of brands raising the value of commercial space is not at work there. Still this is an issue managers need to deal with. In downtown areas, on the other hand, the major shopping streets have witnessed the arrival of numerous fashion and luxury brands. These brands have progressively taken the place of small, non-branded businesses, and also of banks, whose presence and level of service have decreased in urban areas. These newcomers have all attempted to set up in the heart of the downtown shopper flow pattern, preferably with single-brand stores, near the locations of long-established luxury brands.

Admittedly, customers have lost the charm of small cafés and storefronts selling fruit and vegetables in these neighborhoods. But they have gained in the choice of brands of clothing, shoes, accessories, jewelry, eyewear, perfume, and so on. The concentration of the businesses and their quality make shopping easier. In addition, this phenomenon contributes to the dynamism of urban renewal. The impact on values in the real-estate markets of the world's most chic thoroughfares has also been a prime factor (US$400 to 500 a year per square foot in New York, Milan, or Paris for a lease, and staggering additional amounts for key money). Since the major streets have become unaffordable for most emerging brands, other districts are beginning to develop.

Airports are a good example of the progress brands have been responsible for in terms of choice and accessibility of branded products, whether in duty-free areas or in traditional stores. No international airport has been built in the last 20 years without a boutique space being part of the plans. Duty-free is a business that deals in brands.

Promotion of multiculturalism

As we mentioned earlier, brands often reflect the cultural environment of their principal decision-making center, generally the place where they came into being. Frequently their identity borrows the values of the region or country in which they developed. Christian Dior will always represent a certain idea of Paris, independently of whatever designer is in charge. When Giorgio Armani retires, his products will continue to cultivate a neoclassical style reflecting a certain typically Italian nonchalance that is specific to the brand. Mercedes will be German; Coca-Cola, Gap, Marlboro, and Chrysler will be promoters of American lifestyles.

The increase in the media bombardment, above all on the part of the international brands, contributes to promoting cultures specific to other regions. We feel that this phenomenon of raising awareness of other cultures is fundamentally positive. It encourages better comprehension of different values. It nurtures respect for difference and the possibilities of solidarity.

Thus it's only logical that we find the brands that are most involved in this multiculturalist effort behind promotions of a cultural or humanist nature. We've already pointed to the dangers of abuse in this area, but at the same time the real progress certain brands have fostered by disseminating their cultural identity must be recognized. In the developing countries, music, literature, theater, and film are generously supported by national brands – airlines, but also other types of brands.

Brands promote the values of their specific cultures not only through their planetary distribution and communication, but also by the simple fact that a culture can be "tried on" or consumed, thanks to these brands, which then become a factor for more intimate understanding of cultural diversity. The construction of the European Union has been concretized, in supermarkets, by numerous campaigns introducing consumers to a neighboring culture and cuisine, and they have met with a very favorable reception by customers. This openness to other consumption choices is also based on the brand system, and it seems to us that everyone – consumers, producers, retailers – stands to gain from it.

Progress engendered by consumers

As promoters of values, brands influence the excellence of products. That excellence, in turn, often means concrete use benefits for the consumer. As we have already said, we feel that this is no small advantage. We feel that brands can make a positive contribution to public life. Through the benefits they bring consumers, they can be true factors of social progress.

This phenomenon is not automatic; but, in the framework of a covenant of exchange which is well understood by both parties, with well-managed brands and responsible consumers, we see it as inevitable. In order for brands to stimulate social progress, they must motivate in men and women – consumers and employees – the qualities that are conditions of progress: confidence in one's abilities; curiosity, inventiveness; a sense of action and of risk; a desire for conquest, a taste for hard work; esthetic sensitivity; solidarity and respect for difference.

/ In order for brands to stimulate social progress, they must motivate in men and women the qualities that are conditions of progress. /

We believe that if individuals, men or women, are at ease, feeling attractive, and sure of themselves, if they have developed a certain sense of beauty, a sensitivity to other cultures, then they can be considered to have reached the summit of Maslow's pyramid of needs.[1] The chances are better that such individuals, having satisfied their most immediate needs, will find the time and the peace of mind necessary for altruism; will become aware of responsibilities regarding environmental problems; will make efforts of one kind or another to improve their world; will promote humanist values of solidarity and respect for others.

Brands, we feel, participate or can participate in this movement towards higher values. Many of them are already working – whether directly or indirectly, tacitly or explicitly – in this direction. They succeed by improving consumers' physical, psychological, or moral comfort; in so doing, they lead them to take a position in relation to the perceived values of the brand's identity. Let's look at how these mechanisms work.

Increasing consumers' physical comfort

The intensity of competition and the demands of consumers who are increasingly well informed have led brands to considerably improve the concrete benefits to be derived from their products. The contemporary frenzy of innovation, where often the best is to be found alongside the most frivolous, tends to make this less obvious. Yet a modicum of historical perspective clearly shows that the gains have been enormous in terms of quality. The common prejudice which holds that "life was better before, at least in certain ways" needs to be challenged. Industrialization and the increasing competition to which brands are subject have caused our quality of life to improve in every way, and have put quality within everyone's reach.

Contrary to a certain stereotype, "good, old-fashioned fare" was not necessarily healthier. In many cases, the control of the refrigerated distribution chain and rigorous selection of varieties have revolutionized food quality, safety, and practicality. Excessive industrialization is doubtless a threat to the food chain; but in terms of distribution, it has brought undeniable progress while bringing about the disappearance of old culinary habits and simplifying food preparation. Few consumers still pick over their vegetables, wash their meat, or rub their butter with bicarbonate of soda. The reason is simple: they don't need to any more. The fashion of eating

---

1 The psychologist A. H. Maslow proposed a hierarchy of human needs organized as follows, from the most to the least immediate: physiological needs, safety needs, social needs, esteem needs, and self-actualization needs. See e.g. A. H. Maslow, *Motivation and Personality*, New York: Harper and Row, 1970.

raw fish, now spreading in the urban West, would have been unthinkable only 50 years ago in developed countries outside Japan.

This holds true in many areas. Comfort as it was known to the privileged minority of a century ago would seem Spartan to today's consumer. Innovation has not been limited to the introduction of new technologies and new needs. It has also affected the most prosaic objects. Shoes fit better, making it possible to shop all afternoon or dance all night without torturing your feet; car seats adapt to the driver's body type and clothing; suits stand up to air travel; ice cubes are dispensed directly through the refrigerator door; cellphones are increasingly replacing handheld computers and connecting you to the world and a world of services: These are all examples of progress, some less decisive than others, some less visible, but all of which contribute to an overall improvement in our quality of life.

Increasing consumers' psychological comfort

Brands also work to increase consumers' psychological comfort. They do this in two ways: by responding better and better to their expectations and values, and by letting them project these expectations and values towards the outside world – in other words, by communicating. Today's human beings swing back and forth between the need to belong to postmodern tribes – which are numerous, flexible, and easily changed – and the need to express an individuality that is their own, yet conditioned by the opinions of others.

/ By differentiating themselves, brands extend their vocabulary, making it possible to express to others identities that are more subtle, and in fact respond to the ever-keener expectations of their consumers. /

For the linguist Ferdinand de Saussure, language is always nothing more than a system of values.[2] To name is to classify and to organize reality. As a system of values, brands also constitute a language. Whether they connote a strongly identified style, aggressively proclaimed by a logo, or a certain protean discretion, brands always say something. By differentiating themselves, they extend their vocabulary, making it possible to express to others identities that are more subtle, and in fact respond to the ever-keener expectations of their consumers. No one escapes from this semiological function of appearances. Even unknown brands that play on more or less clumsy imitation of a famous model can

---

2 F. de Saussure, *Course in General Linguistics*, London: Fontana, 1974.

connote a nonchalant disdain for brand tyranny on the part of the wearer – who is nonetheless espousing a certain style.

We will see further on that many brands tend to become (successfully in the case of some) "lifestyle brands." We agree with Gilles Lipovetsky's vision of a "hypermarket of lifestyles."[3] The plurality of brands offers consumers greater freedom of choice; above all, it gives them the possibility of buying and wearing products which correspond closely to their mood or needs of the moment, by associating themselves with the values (or the absence of values) proposed through the brand identity.

At this point, an entire range of purchasing behaviors becomes possible. There is the appropriation of values or of a style that are not one's own, but which are fascinating and which one is happy to borrow. This is what is know as a "refuge" brand. There are also purchases which represent full support for the values proposed: the "personal expression" brand. There are impulse purchases of products the consumer "falls in love with." Finally there are purchases that could be called "combinatory," to the extent that the product is acquired with the intention of complementing other products, of different brands, in a specific ensemble whose totality will signify a particular identity. Brands lend themselves to any and all combinations, to elaborate juxtapositions of styles and values. In this way, they encourage the expression of the individuality and the creativity of each person.

What is true of the utterance (that is, purchasers' intention to project a certain image of themselves to others) is also true of its interpretation – the way that image is perceived. In their role as language, it is inevitable that brands function as elements in the classification of individuals.

That classification is less indicative today of belonging to a social class than it is of having an individual personality. The immense variety of choice, the permeability of social borders, the fashion of appropriating or *détourning* certain brands located at the extremities of the scale (for example, the Lacoste shirt, or at the other end of the scale, clothing from a flea market or secondhand store) have multiplied the expressiveness of the language of brands. A highly delineated appearance no longer connotes social determinism, but a persona, the voluntary projection of an identity within the framework of social rules. Despite its complexity, this language can be deciphered, often in an unconscious way. It is a vehicle for information about the persons who wear a certain brand or who are associated with them.

Like any sign of recognition, the brand language has positive effects on human relations. It is much easier today to get an idea of the personality of

---

3 Gilles Lipovetsky, *L'ère du vide, Essai sur l'individualisme contemporain*, Paris: Gallimard, 1983.

the people we encounter than it was in the nineteenth century. The result is greater clarity in initial exchanges.

Increasing consumers' moral comfort

The search for value and differentiation leads brands to be ever more attentive to consumers. It was perhaps inevitable, then, that they venture into the field of ethics, both to better respond to the intangible expectations they express and to find, in the promotion of such values, new ties of federation with their clientele. We have previously discussed the trend for certain brands to become promoters of social causes and the dangers of excess inherent in that strategy. But its benefits must also be pointed out.

The awareness-raising initiatives in the private sector, whether publicized by controversy (as in the case of Benetton) or less visible (we are thinking of Estée Lauder and its foundation, which is very active on behalf of breast cancer research), achieve concrete, often very positive results supported by the brand's reputation. Beyond these tangible benefits, it seems to us that the ambition of these brands, which is to renew their relations with consumers, is partly attained and is expressed in advantages of a psychological nature. By becoming involved in consumers' ethical concerns and in their life as citizens, brands have the opportunity to join with consumers in a common cause. Brands empower people to carry out actions that contribute to progress. In so doing they increase their moral well-being, commonly known as "good conscience," which also represents a not-insignificant part of their psychological well-being.

/ By becoming involved in consumers' ethical concerns and in their life as citizens, brands have the opportunity to join with consumers in a common cause. /

Conclusion

In this chapter, in the form of a plea in defense of brands, we have sought to go beyond the polemics fueled by books like *No Logo*. By distancing ourselves from the static antagonism they foster between brand and consumer, and consumer and citizen, we have tried to suggest another model. It is a dynamic, cooperative model which restores commercial activity to the public arena and is based on the conjunction or disjunction of interests between the brand and its consumers. We feel that it is the ongoing interactions between these two poles that maintains not only the balance of powers, but also the virtuous circle of social progress.

Attentive to consumers and committed to them, brands are full-fledged participants in that progress. They create and distribute wealth, encourage innovation, perfect markets, disseminate models of openness to others, and concretely improve the quality of life – the necessary foundation of any collective progress. But for such a model to work, brands and consumers must assume their responsibilities and honor their commitments, both to themselves and to their partners. This is why the question of good brand management presupposes an awareness of the global role brands have to play in public life – not only in terms of profits or treatment of employees, but also with their clientele and in public life generally.

The product offerings of certain brands or the content of their advertising show that that awareness is long in coming. No one is taken in any more by the messages of freedom disseminated by the producers of cigarettes, and the violence, provocation, and pornography certain brands promote are dead ends.

A major change is taking shape today in the relation between corporations and citizenship, in the role corporations must play and the commitments they must honor in social life. We feel that resistance to this change, through a lack of perspective, and simply through poor management, feeds the rise of latent resentment of brands.

The second part of this book will seek to study this more considered role of the brand that we have attempted to describe and the responsibilities of its manager in greater depth. It will also describe concrete tools for defining and implementing that role. For while certain commentators insist on seeing a definitive crisis between brands and consumers, we feel, for our part, that a reconciliation is possible, desirable, and that it has begun.

PART II

Brand Management

We have mentioned several French brands that have disappeared today: Facel Vega, Talbot, Panhard, and so on. Kelvinator, Miracle Maid, DeSoto, Studebaker, and Rambler are examples of American brands that have disappeared.

The history of the evolution of industry and the phenomenon of concentration that is indissociable from it is punctuated by such disappearances. But aside from occasions like these when a brand's fate is linked to cyclical fluctuations, the economic success or failure of a brand essentially depends on how it is managed. And in certain cases, it's no exaggeration to use the term "mismanaged" – by managers who want to play God, and unimaginative marketing. The aforementioned Studebaker is a good example, as are Jean Patou, Carven, and Fiorucci.

Other brands, however, are undeniable successes. Take Louis Vuitton, a company that went international beginning in 1977. During the period just after the Second World War, Louis Vuitton was vegetating in its shop on the avenue Marceau in Paris. At the time, sales of luggage and leather goods were so poor that the store offered a complete assortment of toys on its first floor in order to keep up business volume and pay the bills.

These failures and successes are not the result of chance. A brand must be managed and developed. It has to be constantly enriched and touched up to keep it in step with the times. Like a plant, it must be cultivated; it requires constant care if it is to stay alive, remain in fashion, and make a modern, likeable, attractive statement.

The history of these unceasing efforts is shown in company museums. Take the example of the Senegalese Infantryman of Banania, whose evolution is similar to that of the Betty Crocker, Aunt Jemima, and Uncle Ben characters in the United States. The Banania brand was founded in 1912 to market a breakfast-drink mix consisting of cocoa and banana flour. For a few years, the brand used the image of "l'Antillaise," a West Indian woman with European features. Then, starting in 1915, the Senegalese Infantryman made his appearance on the back of the box. This popular figure, realistically drawn, with his broad smile, prospered all during the colonial period. He permanently replaced l'Antillaise in 1935. With decolonization and the arrival of human rights movements, the character was stylized little by little, and finally reduced only to his smile (1977), then to his pompommed fez (1984), eventually disappearing completely. As for the yellow of the box, it gradually became more fluorescent.

Behind such evolutions is real, ongoing work. Between two successive packagings, the differences are almost always infinitesimal and the consumer never notices the difference. But over a long period, the impression is quite striking.

We're limiting our discussion to the packaging here, but the same thing could be said about its contents, because the product itself has also evolved – more or less sugar, a more or less pronounced banana or cocoa taste, and so on. In the 1950s, Banania had to be simmered in milk. Today the powder is spooned into the cup, and hot milk is simply poured over it. The formula had to be changed to adapt it to the different method of preparation.

Finally, the advertising approach has evolved even more than the packaging. To keep it up to date, Banania's managers have had to change their product continually. However the brand's fundamental values, associated with the family and good nutrition, have continued to be expressed as the product, the packaging, and the communication continued their ongoing evolution. "Vigor, energy, health, strength" were already Banania's watchwords in 1914.

This example is a good illustration of what brand management should be. It must constantly adapt to the changing conditions of the market in order to stay competitive and relevant and to generate wealth. But the adaptation must remain within the framework of the brand's fundamental values.

The task is a complex one. Tastes change; the competition is legion and better and better prepared; there is never room for improvisation or approximation. If we had to characterize brand management, we would have to say that it is relative, progressive, continuous, and focused.

It is relative, because it must adapt at all times to what the competition is doing. Marketing never takes place in a vacuum. It is the result of confrontation with the competition. To assess whether the advertising

budget of the Signal brand is sufficient, you do a historic analysis of budgets that have been devoted to competing toothpastes – Colgate, Aquafresh,
or Crest. An in-store promotion for a new brand of coffee also depends on
the competition's promotions. This relativity, the very *raison d'être* of
marketing, applies to the management of a brand at all times. A positioning
or sales pitch are valid only to the extent that they provide an advantage
over the competition. We will see, in Chapter 4, that beyond the operational
levels of management of a brand, its identity implies differentiation, and
therefore relativizing in terms of the competition. The brand exists only in
relation to other brands.

The management of a brand must also be progressive. It must follow
markets and changes in consumer attitudes closely. We mentioned this in
connection with Banania. When Remy Martin launched the first local
white wines on the Chinese market, it created very sweet wines to adapt to
a clientele that was not accustomed to these products. The learning process
Chinese consumers underwent regarding these first white wines, sold under
the Dynasty brand, was closely observed. Little by little, the sugar was
removed in order to reveal the more refined gustatory aspects of the wines,
which became richer and more interesting. Of course, the consumer was
never told about these gradual changes. Only expatriates, who had sometimes rejected these wines at the time of their launch, finding them too
cloying, were astonished when they tasted them again a few years later.

Brand management is an ongoing process. Any hiatus must be avoided.
Consumers don't like it when old friends change – unless, of course, the
brand's managers are consciously trying to change their clientele. This
effort towards continuity is endless. To remain in keeping with current
tastes, brands must ceaselessly change their products, their communication,
and what we call the manifestations of their identity, all without alienating
their fundamental values. When we look at the successive transformations
of the Shell logo (see Plate 8), the scope of the graphical evolution is
evident. The latest version is clearly an improvement (in stylization, in
expressiveness) over earlier ones. But there is no reason why the process
should stop.

Finally, the management of the brand must remain focused on what
constitutes its very soul: its identity. It is the fundamental reference point
of any well managed brand. To succeed in a context where everything
changes, brand evolutions are relative, progressive, and continuous. The
only stable element that remains behind this environment of multiple and
contradictory tendencies is the brand identity.

This last idea seems crucial to us. We see the brand identity as the keystone
of any rational management. That is why, in this second part devoted to

brand management, we will endeavor to describe it and introduce a series of tools suited to studying it.

In Chapter 4 we analyze the concept of brand identity. We said earlier that a brand needs continuity and permanence. This imperative, projected into the dynamic space of communication, and in tension with it, characterizes the unceasing dialogue between the identity of a brand and its multiple perceptions by consumers. When these two needs – to communicate a set of specific values and to endure over time – are combined, we find the definition of what an identity is.

In Chapter 5 we study the life cycle of brands, as well as the difference between local brands and international brands. We extend the famous life cycle curve from the product to the domain of the brand. This life cycle is so well known today that it is wrongly considered to have outlived its usefulness. We don't agree. We explain why this concept is at the very center of brand management. In particular, we show that the evolution along this curve is not ineluctable. A brand has to be relaunched at certain times in order for it to break out of what appears to be an approaching decline. We propose a new approach to the life cycle, one that makes it more than simply a deterministic descriptive element, rather a tool for development and action.

Finally in Chapter 6 we describe in detail how, in our opinion, a brand has to be managed in an operational and continuous way. In addition to a description of the principal factors of success, we felt it was useful to also propose a methodology for brand auditing that has been proven in the field. It can serve either to conduct a complete, in-depth diagnosis of a brand, or simply to throw light on certain issues or problems that management of a brand on a day-to-day basis can tend to neglect.

This second part develops, in an operational perspective, the general ideas we presented in the first part. We have endeavored to address both brand managers and a wider public. The former are addressed in order to recall a few simple truths of good management and suggest methodological tools, in a field where there is sometimes a tendency to delegate to instinct. The latter are addressed in order to explain that, in this process, there is no place for truncated, superficial, or dishonest reasoning, but on the contrary, there is a need for logical, responsible, and efficient practices.

4 Brand identity

Sir, a man may be so much of everything, that he is nothing of anything.
(Samuel Johnson)

What is the identity of a brand? Our first answer might be that it is what the brand "says" to consumers – making a distinction between what it says and how they understand it. The notion of identity is still too little used by managers, and that's a shame, because to our way of thinking it offers some very useful and concrete glimpses into the essence of the brand phenomenon itself. It constitutes the foundation and the federating element of all the activities we have designated as being manifestations of the brand.

We sometimes have a tendency to confine brand identity to the intuitive, affective sphere, which the company's concrete and methodical processes cannot influence. Yet tools for analysis do exist, originating in the field of semiology, with which this area can be at least partially rationalized and provide very concrete lessons about managing a brand. During our careers, we have had occasion to use them "in the field," from the pragmatic point of view of managers, and with tangible results.

In this chapter we want to describe the operational importance of the notion of brand identity in the light of our personal experience, and present a few simple tools for formalizing it. Of course, like any phenomenon that produces meaning, a brand represents multiple values, which can give rise to infinite interpretations. Yet it is in this latent set of values that the real source of its past and future reputation lies. If certain brands are "richer" than others, it's because their evocative potential is greater and more easily mobilized. To manage a brand well, therefore, we have to begin by understanding what it consists of, and separate its essence from the variable perceptions it engenders among consumers.

A still too unfamiliar concept

While the term "brand identity" is encountered frequently in professional jargon, it is nevertheless a fairly new one. It is probable that an in-depth and systematic consideration has been undertaken of the identity of few brands today. To formalize this concept a little more, we might refer you to Merriam-Webster's *Collegiate Dictionary*, tenth edition, which gives the following definition of "identity":

> 1 a: sameness of essential or generic character in different instances b: sameness in all that constitutes the objective reality of a thing: ONENESS
> 2 a: the distinguishing character or personality of an individual: INDIVIDUALITY b: the relation established by psychological identification
> 3: the condition of being the same with something described or asserted.

What we call the brand identity corresponds to an extension of the definition above, with a strong human dimension. But the term suits our purposes, because two necessary (though not sufficient) elements are present in it: on the one hand, specificity; on the other, permanence – or, if you will, "durability."

We may attempt a more precise initial definition of brand identity: the capacity of a brand to be recognized as unique, over time, without confusion, thanks to the elements that individualize it. One might think that an attachment to these criteria of individuality is somehow spontaneous with managers, but the history of brands is full of examples to the contrary, as a result of either ignorance, or else a voluntary disregard for the virtues of reflection on the identity of brands.

/ Brand identity is the capacity of a brand to be recognized as unique, over time, without confusion, thanks to the elements that individualize it. /

Take the case of Givenchy. The house of Hubert James Taffin de Givenchy dressed elegant, refined women, with a sophistication that was quintessentially Parisian. Audrey Hepburn, who was the creator's muse for 40 years, typified all its values. In 1996 Hubert de Givenchy retired. John Galliano succeeded him – for one season only, before moving to Christian Dior. Then came Alexander McQueen, a 26 year old Scottish designer. In 2001 a young Welshman, Julian McDonald, replaced him.

This revolving door for designers would not be so harmful had there been, at least, a concern for respecting the values that were at the origin of the brand's prestige. We don't mean to call the great individual talent of these creators into question, but it must be recognized that such was not the case. Consequently the "message" of Givenchy was clouded, its identity was dispersed by uncoordinated stylistic daring. The priceless capital the brand's reputation represented, instead of being preserved and prolonged by the innovations of these young talents, now has to be rebuilt. It is certainly possible to express elegance, femininity, and sophistication, and still be modern (Ungaro does this very well) – even if these three values are not sufficient to define an identity.

Another counter-example, which we have encountered in the banking sector, is a good illustration of the absence of consideration of brand identity in such important undertakings as the definition of a new graphical identity. Banco Sabadell is a bank of Catalan origin, extremely dynamic, which was successfully introduced on the Madrid stock exchange a few years ago. In 1998 the bank decided to transform its "corporate image," notably by adopting a new graphic identity. It called in Mario Eskenazi, an Argentinean architect based in Spain, the winner of numerous awards and the creator of several logos for major Spanish companies. He was put in charge of designing a new graphics charter, with a new logo to be used on all communication media, and also of redecorating the bank's agencies. Once the job was done, the designer gave an interview, which the bank itself published. Here is an excerpt:[1]

What does the new image of Banco Sabadell try to get across?

That's a very difficult question to answer without falling into excessively pompous phraseology. I think that, when you create a new image for a company, it's very rare that you start by considering what you are trying to communicate. It's very difficult for a corporate image, in and of itself, to transmit something. Its role is to facilitate clear identification of the company. In this sense, the new image of Banco Sabadell is not trying to get anything across ...

This may have been provocation on the part of the designer; it may have been his way of asserting the primacy of his "intuitive" creativity over the careful calculations of the communicators. Or maybe it was a way of discreetly expressing his disdain for the idea that a commercial brand can actually "produce meaning." Whatever the case, a statement like this one does a disservice to the extensive collaborative and deliberative effort that must be inherent in any renovation of a corporate identity. It shows that the notion of brand identity is not sufficiently widespread in the corporate

---

1 Banco Sabadell newsletter, first quarter 1998, no. 11. Translation by the authors.

world and in corporate communication. Otherwise such a statement, made in the name of the bank itself, would be unthinkable.

We recognize that the logo created by Mario Eskenazi is very original, graphically more modern (see the old and new Sabadell logos, Plate 36) and easily recognizable – qualities that many brands might envy. But what a loss of an opportunity to reflect on the specificities of the Catalan bank and create a corporate image that produces meaning!

The case of the French bank Crédit du Nord, on the other hand, is a good example of careful reflection on the identity of a brand. In 1984 Crédit du Nord, the fifth-ranking French banking group at the time, introduced a new image, involving redesign of the logo, the graphics of the name, the architecture of the branches, and advertising and public relations campaigns. The image is entirely founded on the concept of clarity. For ten years the bank had suffered from an indistinct image as an old, serious provincial bank. Its merger with the Banque de l'Union Parisienne, a business bank active in high finance, had not helped clarify the situation.

The detailed history of the development of a new logo and all the elements of communication, starting with the concept of light or clarity, has been recounted in a book by the semiotician Jean-Marie Floch.[2] In it he explains how the communication agency Creative Business, with whom he collaborated, developed, using semiological tools, all the elements of the new communication – beginning with the blue star, which replaced the orange cube as the brand's logo.

The concept of light, in the banking field, was analyzed as the choice of a certain type of relationship between the banker and the client. This relationship was based on the recognition of the competence and sovereignty of the client. The idea of light thus crystallized a value involved with the very essence of what any relationship with a bank should be: confidence. This concept led first of all to the choice of a code; that is, a style: a brand esthetic resolutely Classicist in nature, wherein the logo had to contribute to conveying frankness and personalized attention. The star was chosen because it represents a visible element in open space; it is also a navigational reference point with rich symbolic connotations. (See the old and new logos of the Crédit du Nord, Plate 37.)

In these last two examples, two approaches to graphical identity are in confrontation: the intuition of the creator alone as opposed to the intuition of that creator contained within the framework of an understandable discourse on the part of the brand.

---

2 Jean-Marie Floch, *Sémiotique, marketing et communication: sous les signes, les stratégies,* Paris: PUF, 1990.

To avoid formalizing the values that are to be expressed is to have blind faith in the graphic designer. And in no way should it be assumed that the latter is happy with such a situation. What such an attitude shows above all is a lack of real reflection on the brand's identity. Graphics designers and communication consultants know this and shy away from the unwieldy freedom left to them in such cases. They are the first to complain of the lack of substance in the briefs they're given – if they are even given any.[3] Too often, they say, clients express extremely imprecise intentions ("Our logo will be young and pleasant"), or provide purely technical specifications ("Our logo is to be 6 cm high and should reflect our values"). Instructions like these tell design professionals very little about the nature of the values to be communicated.

/ To avoid formalizing the values that are to be expressed is to have blind faith in the graphic designer. And in no way should it be assumed that the latter is happy with such a situation. What such an attitude shows above all is a lack of real reflection on the brand's identity. /

The creative function, like all other functions necessary to the a brand's operation, must be part of an overall strategy. The brand's identity is a major resource and a frame of reference for the development of that strategy. It influences not only creation and communication, but also logistics, production, distribution, human resources management, information processing, and so on. At all levels of its activity, a brand aspires to become what it truly is. And in fact concrete tools exist for apprehending and managing that individuality.

Tools for analyzing brand identity

We will present some of these tools here. Our intention is in no way to cover exhaustively all the existing tools for analyzing a brand's identity. The tools we will present have been used effectively by the authors at various points in their careers, and we would simply like to share them with our readers. Analyzing a brand's identity is a fairly new approach, one whose history is related to that of the concept of brand identity itself.

Naomi Klein rightly refers to the work of Bruce Barton – who was, incidentally, the creator of Betty Crocker. In the 1920s, this advertiser began to seek out the "corporate soul." Awareness of the fact that a brand can have meaning beyond the products themselves and the advertising

---

3 On this subject, see *Graphisme en France*, review published by the Delegation on the Plastic Arts of the French Ministry of Culture, 2001, on "La commande."

slowly developed, and the vocabulary was enriched with concepts such as the "essence," "*raison d'être*," "consciousness," "soul," and "genetic code" of a brand. But it was not until the 1970s that the word "identity" made its appearance in the specialized literature, generally linked to the concept of "corporate identity."[4]

The use of "brand identity" appeared in the early 1980s and spread quickly among professionals in advertising agencies.[5] Originally, the term designated, in a limited sense, everything that can identify the brand by linking it to the content of the advertising material. It soon evolved towards a real personification of brands. The use of the words "personality," "individuality," and "identity" became common. The French advertiser Jacques Séguéla speaks of the perception of brands through the intermediary of their physicality, their character, and their style. In 1980, he developed this new methodology under the name "brand person," which later became known as the "star strategy." The concept of identity began, in an indistinct way, to be joined with that of image.

In 1984 David Bernstein, in his book *Company Image and Reality*, devoted a chapter to brand identity.[6] Little by little, the specialized literature began to study this area. David Aaker attempts a classification, still quite heterogeneous, of "brand equity." This includes brand loyalty, name awareness, perceived quality, brand image and, finally, other assets.[7] The term "personality" appears briefly in the book, which also proposes the diagram reproduced as Figure 4.1, which was one of the first tools for analyzing a brand's identity.

This model, however, maintains a certain confusion between the concept of brand image and that of brand identity. This confusion remains common today. It is important to point out that, in our view, these two concepts do not coincide. The images (rather than "the image") correspond to the perceptions induced in the different consumers who make up the market segments. They are receptive in nature. The identity is the substance of the brand, expressed via all the methods of communication used by the brand. It is emissive in nature.

There is a difference between these two concepts. Imagine, for example, that you ask someone about his or her work. This person has a highly specialized profession or trade, about which you know nothing. He or she tries to explain it to you simply, but either because of a poor choice of words, or

---

4 Cf. W. P. Margulies, *Harvard Business Review*, 1977.

5 "Chrysler sharpens its brand identity," *International Business Week*, November 1983.

6 David Bernstein, *Company Image and Reality: A Critique of Corporate Communications*, New York: Holt, Rinehart and Winston, 1984.

7 David A. Aaker, *Managing Brand Equity: Capitalizing on the Value of a Brand Name*, New York: Free Press, 1991.

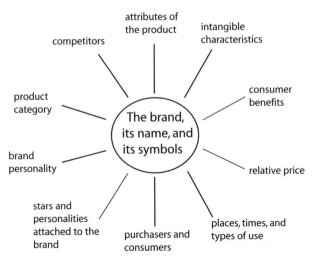

Figure 4.1 The dimensions of brand image

Source: David A. Aaker, *Managing Brand Equity: Capitalizing on the Value of a Brand Name*, New York: Free Press 1991.

because you yourself are not paying attention, you "get it wrong." Or, more exactly, having never seen this person at work, you form an image of the job he or she does that is more or less removed from reality, an image that does not correspond exactly to this person's professional identity. After all, it's not easy to describe that identity in "purely objective" terms. In any case, there is a palpable difference between what the person wanted to get across and what you actually understood.

> / The images (rather than "the image") correspond to the perceptions induced in the different consumers who make up the market segments. They are receptive in nature. The identity is the substance of the brand, expressed via all the methods of communication used by the brand. It is emissive in nature. /

To avoid misunderstanding, we avoid using the word "image." For us, the expression "brand identity," as we have just said, refers to a "substance." We will see what this substance, which can be expressed in terms of ethical and esthetic invariants, encompasses. On the other hand, when we want to refer to the representations induced by the markets, we will speak not of image but of perception of the brand's identity.

Let's return to our historical perspective. Jean-Noël Kapferer, in 1992, introduced the first fairly sophisticated analytical tool for dealing with the difficult area of brand identity: the identity prism.[8]

---

8 Jean-Noël Kapferer, *Strategic Brand Management*, New York : Free Press, 1994.

The identity prism

Advertising and creative agencies used and still use the graphics charter or "copy strategy" in developing campaigns or collections, but these tools have never really been able to identify a brand's ethical and esthetic constants. Kapferer's prism, on the other hand, allows a much more detailed approach to the problem. Its introduction represented a major step forward.

Here is how the interpretative diagram works. Six dimensions are positioned around a prism (see Figure 4.2). Let's look at the different elements of identity.

The "physique" of the brand corresponds to the concrete element that comes immediately to mind when the name of the brand is mentioned. It is a set of sensory and objective characteristics.

Aubade: women's lingerie.

Coca-Cola: the original bottle. A bubbly brown liquid.

Levi's: a pair of blue jeans, with specific labels.

Suchard: a chocolate bar and its purple wrapping.

Toblerone: a chocolate bar with a triangular section, in a yellow and red package.

Bally: a pair of shoes.

Todt: moccasins.

Ferrari: a red automobile.

Ducati: a red motorcycle with a tubular trestle frame.

Missoni: knitted fabrics or materials colored in a specific way.

Opinel: a pocketknife with a wooden handle, fitted with a safety catch.

Brand "personality" is apprehended by means of questions like: if it was a man, what kind of character would he have? Professional, esthete, performance-oriented? Original, like Audi? Colorless and odorless, like Opel? This is what is behind the intensive use of famous personalities who act as lasting incarnations of the brand's values in recent years: Kate Moss for Calvin Klein, Inès Sastre for Lancôme after Isabella Rossellini was dropped, and so on. These constitute easy short-cuts for giving a semblance of personality to

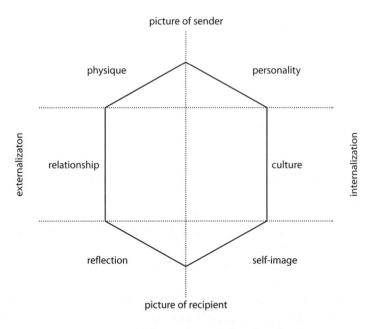

Figure 4.2 The brand identity prism

Source: Jean Noël Kapferer, *Strategic Brand Management,* New York: Free Press, 1994.

brands that may be a bit too weak, or too opaque as to their specific values. Fashion brands like Armani and Gucci, who have their creator to fill this role, don't encounter these problems.

The brand's "culture" is linked to the original values of its creators – often, the culture of the country, the region, or the city where the brand developed: Madrid for Loewe, Sicily for Dolce & Gabbana, Majorca for Majorica, Japan for Shiseido, and so on. But the geographical dimension is not the only one expressed: Hewlett Packard, for example, puts forward the "garage spirit," its two gifted pioneers, and the sprit of an American company.

"Relationship" is involved with the dimension of social communication of the brand. A brand with identity influences relations between individuals, first through signs of belonging to a group, and then well beyond. What do people think when they see me stepping out of my Maserati or wearing the latest Christian Dior swimsuit? Gucci strongly suggests seduction; Diesel, provocation; banks, confidence in general.

The brand's "reflection" describes the typical customer the market associates with the brand (the customer it imagines for it). This is not to be confused with the target customer: Kapferer is referring here to the market's perception.

The brand's "self-image" corresponds to the image consumers have of themselves when using the product. When a man lights up a Marlboro, climbs into a Porsche, or puts on an Armani suit, how does he perceive himself?

Figures 4.3 and 4.4 are examples of use of the identity prism, from Kapferer.

Kapferer's prism introduced a major innovation. It was a tool that, for the first time, made systematic study possible while showing the complexity of any approach to brand identity. Nevertheless, it does have certain limitations. Self-image and reflection – the "two sides of the mirror," as Kapferer calls them – are receptive in nature: they have more to do with the perception of the brand's identity than that identity itself. As for the "relationship" dimension, it belongs more to the cultural domain. Personality and culture overlap. After having used it ourselves numerous times, our judgment is that the prism is a useful tool but is tricky to use, in particular because of the lack of homogeneity in its categories.

The most enlightening parts of the prism are still "physique" and "personality." These two concepts were studied in greater detail with the semiotic approach of Jean-Marie Floch. In the late 1980s, the semio-linguistics research group directed by A. J. Greimas (at the École des Hautes Études en Sciences Sociales in Paris) was the hotbed where Jean-Marie Floch, then director of the seminar on visual semiotics, developed a

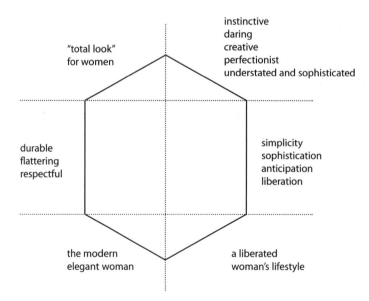

Figure 4.3 The brand identity prism applied to Chanel (early 2000)

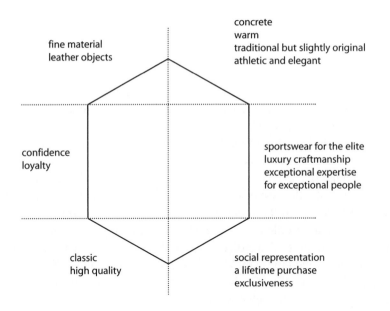

fine material
leather objects

concrete
warm
traditional but slightly original
athletic and elegant

confidence
loyalty

sportswear for the elite
luxury craftmanship
exceptional expertise
for exceptional people

classic
high quality

social representation
a lifetime purchase
exclusiveness

Figure 4.4 The brand identity prism applied to Hermès (early 2000)

certain number of tools derived directly from the methods of structural semantics, intended for analyzing the conditions under which meaning can be produced and perceived. In parallel, François Schwebel, founder of the Creative Business consulting firm, was also a pioneer with his launching of the concept "global communication." He maintains that everything is in communication, and that coherence among all these messages is provided by a federating concept, called "personality," at the time. One of the authors had the privilege of working with Jean-Marie Floch and François Schwebel on formalizing the identities of Ferragamo, Loewe, Bally, and some other minor brands.

Brand ethic and esthetic

Of all the tools available today, semiology is, in our opinion and based on our experience, the discipline best suited to aiding a manager in defining, prolonging, and defending the identity of a brand. From our perspective as non-specialists but convinced users, we would like to take a moment to discuss this discipline.

First of all, what is semiology? Imagine two no smoking signs, one of which gets its message across better than the other. Is it possible to describe exactly what makes one more effective than the other, without the discussion becoming simply a matter of subjective tastes? And to describe it in general terms, to aid us in designing another type of sign (for example, a no parking sign)? In broad terms, that is the project of semiology. Its aim (according to Greimas) is to describe, as objectively as possible, the process of production of meaning, and generally of all the practices of signification that make up cultures. But it can be extended, Jean-Marie Floch adds, to a certain disposition of the mind, curious about anything that has (or could have) meaning.

If we accept the validity of applying semiotics to the study of brand identities, we are making the following basic premise: brands are systems that produce meaning. The tools we present require a certain degree of formalization, so we should assure the reader at the outset of their operational viability. We have used them ourselves "in the field," and while they can't, of course, solve all problems, we feel that their usefulness is undeniable.

The first semiotic tool we discuss we call the "hinge." This is a simple framework developed by Jean-Marie Floch to bring out the different levels of analysis or definition of a brand universe. Let us briefly recall a few basic principles to better clarify our discussion. First, semiology studies any and all "discourse" or signal capable of being interpreted, that is, of producing meaning: text, music, film, photography. The concepts we will present, then, are not limited to a particular area of expression.

Second, in order to attempt to understand by what processes we manage to interpret a signal (text, sound, image), semiologists, following Ferdinand de Saussure, have introduced a distinction between the "signifier" and the "signified." The signifier is the material part of a sign; the signified is the representation with which that material part is associated. For example, for the Egyptian hieroglyph that resembles a wavy line, the signifier is simply a zigzag; the signified is a simple sound, the consonant "N." What is true of hieroglyphics is also true of our own writing and of all signs. The succession of letters "t," "r," "e," and "e" written on a blackboard corresponds to the mental image a reader of those letters produces – that of a tree, a woody plant having a trunk and so on.[9]

/ If we accept the validity of applying semiotics to the study of brand identities, we are making the following basic premise: brands are systems that produce meaning. /

However, these two dimensions are the two sides of a single coin, or as Saussure put it, a single sheet of paper: one side cannot be separated from the

---

9 Our examples are simplified. We are leaving out, for example, the acoustic image (the sounds I hear in my head as I read, before forming an image), which is itself a valid level of interpretation. The signifier/signified differentiation has been the subject of complex debates, but they take nothing away from the fruitfulness of the distinction made by Saussure.

other. A poet choosing one word rather than another (which might be an almost perfect synonym) to signify the same idea is playing on sound, transforming the beauty but also the meaning of the line. And no one can pretend to translate a book of poetry armed only with a good catalogue of correspondences between signifiers and signifieds (in other words, a dictionary). A sign is an indivisible whole, even if its twofold dimension is evident.

All signs, then, are articulated at a hinge between the signifier (or level of expression) and the signified (or level of content). The same is true, by extension, of groups of signs – and thus of the creations and physical manifestations of brands. This articulation also extends to criteria of invariance and variation. For example, as regards expression, the "pool" of the vocabulary, the principles of rhyme are the same for many writers, but the style of the poet is unique; as regards content, the poet's favorite themes – which remain the same from one poem to another – are not necessarily sufficient to describe the particular subject of a given poem.

The advantage of this methodological approach is twofold. First, it brings out the two fundamental levels of a brand's discourse, clearly separating content and container. Then it places the accent on the invariant elements of the brand. These invariants are precisely what make it possible for the brand to be recognized as itself over time. They constitute the very foundation of its identity.

Figure 4.5 shows the hinge principle applied to a brand universe. Looking at this diagram, one thing becomes clear: ethic and esthetic are the invariants on which the brand's identity is founded.

The use of the hinge is relatively simple. It aims at characterizing the brand's identity through its expression and its content – that is, at giving a formal definition of its esthetic and of its ethic. The esthetic study is fairly easy to put into practice, above all if the brand in question is a very "typed" one, where the colors, shapes, and materials are resolutely baroque or classical. In this domain the contribution of Jean-Marie Floch, who updated the work of Heinrich Wölfflin, has been essential.

Note that generally, the Northern European brands – Jil Sander, Ikea, Helmut Lang, BMW – and North American ones – Calvin Klein, Donna Karan, Coach – have an esthetic of the classical type, characterized pictorially by:

- clearly-defined lines and contours, emphasizing individually recognizable elements
- space divided into easily identifiable zones, each with its own autonomy
- closed shapes, visible in their entirety: planes

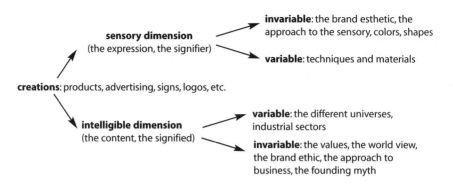

Figure 4.5 Levels of analysis or definition of a brand universe

- impressions of stability: symmetries

- saturated colors.

On the other hand, Mediterranean brands – Loewe, Ferragamo, Dolce & Gabbana, Rubelli, Majorica, Lamborghini, Versace, Roberto Cavalli – have a tendency towards the baroque, characterized pictorially by:

/ Ethic and esthetic are the invariants on which the brand's identity is founded. /

- lines delineated by shadow effects: curves and criss-crosses

- open forms, which can appear accidental

- each part losing its autonomy and taking on meaning only in association with the rest of the work

- movement treated in depth: volumes

- chiaroscuro and deep colors.

See Plates 44 to 53 for a few illustrations of logos and ads in the baroque and classical esthetics.

The study conducted on Loewe in 1996 by one of the authors, who was its president at the time, in collaboration with Creative Business and Jean-Marie Floch, led to the development and the communication of the concept of a "minimalist baroque" esthetic. These apparently contradictory terms met with much success with the press. In the late 1990s this Spanish fashion brand – a century and a half old and often referred to by the French as the "Iberian Hermès" – had good name recognition, associated with quality and a strong presence in Spain and Japan, but was still timid on the other markets. Struggling to achieve international status, and also suffering from the absence of a charismatic founder in its history – unlike Chanel, for example – Loewe had the appearance of a slightly "tired" brand. The characterization of the brand's esthetic effectively transmitted the message of a brand that was faithful to its roots (the baroque) and with a strong desire for modernity (minimalism, which at the time was still in vogue). That message was coherent with the recruiting of designer Narciso Rodriguez, who was himself a blend of modernity and respect for tradition.

The study of the brand ethic, on the other hand, is by far the more difficult, above all for brands that were not founded by a creator with a strong personality, or that have squandered their heritage. Certain brands are so clearly positioned that the task is easier. Take Nike, for example. Since the appearance of its initial slogan, "Just do it," Nike has cultivated the universal values associated with sports and the Olympic movement: surpassing oneself, determination, competition, accomplishment. Nike, remember, is the goddess of victory. This is where the brand's ethic, its vision of the world, and what it believes are situated; "what it stands for," to use Jean-Marie Floch's expression.

The launch of the controversial Mecca-Cola in France in November 2002 is a very significant example of a brand that directly communicates the values underlying the ethic of its brand identity. Its bottles and the opening page of its web site say, "No more drinking stupid, drink with commitment!" and "10% of our net profits, for Palestinian Childhood. 10% for [local] charity – NGO." This is clear to everyone, without the need for a semiotician to translate. See Plate 57 for the opening page of the web site (http://www.mecca-cola.com/).

In certain cases, setting about finding the permanent values the brand has expressed since its inception is a frustrating process. It sometimes leads – as was the case with Loewe – to a recognition of the non-existence of a brand ethic. Such a situation has an advantage in that it of course leaves a very broad field open for the choice of values, but it also shows that the brand has had no obvious permanent values over time, and therefore has been perceived in a very imprecise way up to the present.

Using a semiologist who is experienced in the study of the corpus of brands is an absolute necessity in this type of research. His or her role consists not only in finding possible meanings beyond the signs, but also in precisely determining the objective procedures to be used in constructing that meaning. By describing in detail the nature a brand's identity and the means of its expression, the semiologist will help the manager perpetuate that identity and prolong its life.

Figure 4.6 is an example of the use of the hinge approach in the case of Taurus. Taurus is a fictitious name for a real brand – in existence in Europe for over a century, designing, manufacturing, and retailing luxury products – whose real name contractual considerations forbid us to reveal. The brand's state in 1997 is represented on the hinge.

/ By describing in detail the nature a brand's identity and the means of its expression, the semiologist will help the manager perpetuate that identity and prolong its life. /

The recommendations that came out of the above assessment and the competitive conditions of the sectors where the brand was active are presented in Figure 4.7. As can be seen, these recommendations are expressed in concrete, precise terms, on the level of both esthetic and ethic. Real choices are made, ones that clearly define values to be cultivated and others to be shunned. The brand's identity is anything but a melting pot of fashionable values. On the contrary, it is structured by differentiation. These recommendations were the starting point for a series of briefs dealing with all aspects of the company's communication and creation.

The semiotic square

After the signifier/signified hinge, a second semiotic tool can be used to make a more profound analysis of a brand's identities: the semiotic square (see Figure 4.8). When Jean-Marie Floch used it in studying Ferragamo's

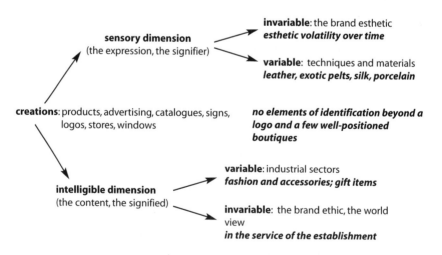

Figure 4.6 Levels of definition of the Taurus universe (effective status in 1997)

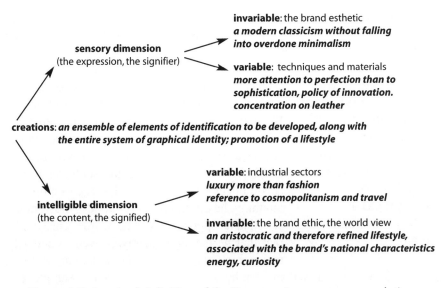

sensory dimension
(the expression, the signifier)

invariable: the brand esthetic
*a modern classicism without falling
into overdone minimalism*

variable: techniques and materials
*more attention to perfection than to
sophistication, policy of innovation.
concentration on leather*

creations: *an ensemble of elements of identification to be developed, along with
the entire system of graphical identity; promotion of a lifestyle*

variable: industrial sectors
*luxury more than fashion
reference to cosmopolitanism and travel*

intelligible dimension
(the content, the signified)

invariable: the brand ethic, the world view
*an aristocratic and therefore refined lifestyle,
associated with the brand's national characteristics
energy, curiosity*

Figure 4.7 Levels of definition of the Taurus universe: recommendations

brand identity in 1992, he was really the pioneer in the use of semiotics applied to luxury brands.[10] The square has since come into wide use by advertisers, specialists in brand management, and trend agencies.

This diagram aims at describing a situation not in terms of static objects, specific events, and the like, but in terms of dynamic relations. To provide an analogy, in describing a boxing match a commentator can concentrate on the actions, the physique, and the personality of each boxer, but can also choose to concentrate on the "flux" of punches exchanged (contacts, acceleration, deceleration), since the dynamics of the bout are what occupy our attention more than the identity or the presumed motivations of the fighters. Even if we know very little about the latter, this approach can still be used to describe the fight. In the same way, the power of the semiotic square lies in its ability to organize an abstract universe coherently, in spite of the fact that it is not recognized as being rational itself. It can point out meanings that are present, from a logical point of view, but latent, not yet active. It can also describe the way in which new meanings will appear.

This approach begins with Saussure's assertion (1916) that any system of meaning is a system of relations and not only a system of signs. These relations are established between "semantic poles" (a thing and its opposite form two poles united by a relation of opposition) to constitute semantic categories and axes of dynamic significance. For example, the category

---

10 Jean-Marie Floch had also used the same technique in defining the layout of a hypermarket in the Lyon area in 1986

"gender" exists only to the extent that "gender" is articulated as a relation between masculine and feminine. Relations are considered as taking precedence over their terms, which are only the intersections of those relations.

/ The power of the semiotic square lies in its ability to organize an abstract universe coherently, in spite of the fact that it is not recognized as being rational itself. /

Putting the accent on the dynamics of meaning effects is a help in finding the latent meanings of a discourse. Take the sentence "I am not a traitor." If a man utters it to an interrogator who demands that he betray his accomplices, he is making a strong assertion, a courageous refusal. But if, later, the man utters the same sentence to his accomplices whereas no one has accused him of anything, he might give his comrades the impression that its opposite may well be true. The simple fact that he mentions betrayal (even to deny it) makes him suspect. What he is denying will be taken into account more than what he is saying. In this extreme example, the relation of opposition in itself imposes another meaning, independently of the logical sense of the utterance.

For similar reasons, no advertiser would ever dare use the slogan "We are not crooks," as a certain US president once did. But there are other, more subtle meaning effects than those shown in these examples, and the control of latent meanings is a primordial issue in the management of a brand. And the semiotic square, developed by Greimas (1979), Courtes (1979), and Floch (1983), has proven its usefulness.

The most significant example of a square, one that is the starting point for numerous analyses, is the one relating to the axiology of consumption (Figure 4.8). This square dealing with consumption values is still much used because it gets at the primary mechanisms of all planned human action.

The two principal typologies presented on the square (utilitarian values/existential values) are taken from narrative semiotics, which distinguishes, in a narration, life values (existential, utopian, or mythic) and practical (or utilitarian) values. In any story – and especially in mythic and folkloric narratives, which are the starting point of this discipline – the life values that give meaning to the hero's quest can be identified. These are generally values of an existential nature, corresponding to a vision of the world, a moral system, and so on. They are sufficiently universal and profound to motivate the hero's actions: good, beauty, glory, sacrifice, love, freedom, and the like. These values are the initial justification of the narrative.

The practical values, on the other hand, are secondary and instrumental. They represent the means necessary to the hero for attaining his underlying objective, expressed in terms of existential values. An example is the hero's search for a sword made of a magical alloy (a practical value) with which to kill the dragon and free his people (a life value).

It should be noted that this type of analysis was posited for structured stories, ones that are self-contained in a certain way. To apply the semiotic square to the analysis of brands, we must accept the presupposition that a brand can represent a micro-universe of meaning. Once this semantic axis, consisting of two opposites (practical – or convenience – and utopian), which applies ideally to the mechanisms of consumption, is in place, the semiotic square can be used to develop all its nuances.

/ This square dealing with consumption values is still much used because it gets at the primary mechanisms of all planned human action. /

Each of the contrary terms can be seen in relation to another term, differentiated by the absence of the characteristics of the first. The practical corresponds to the non-practical, that is, the diversionary, the playful, the esthetic. The utopian corresponds to the non-utopian: the critical, the utilitarian, the practical. On the left-hand side of the square, vertically, are two propositions where the term "critical" or "non-utopian" implies what is practical and utilitarian.

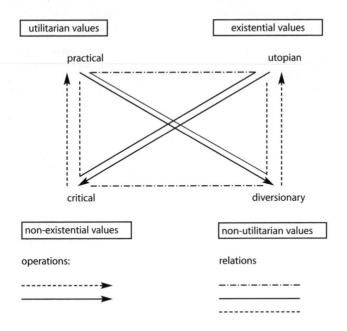

Figure 4.8 Semiotic square of consumption values

Source: Jean-Marie Floch, *International Journal of Marketing* 4, 1998, North-Holland.

Placing the accent on mechanisms of meaning is by no means superfluous where brands are concerned, because the problem here is that of defining the communication on which they base a large part of their relations with consumers. We present below a few examples of use of the square in the study of the identity, the creation, or the communication of a few brands.

The first study concerned Salvatore Ferragamo (1992) (see Figure 4.9). It was conducted by Jean-Marie Floch and François Schwebel, who were then working with Creative Business, at a time when Ferragamo was developing its ambition to become a global brand.

The figure gives a very general and structured picture of the evolution of the brand's positioning. It gave rise to a plan of action for products and communication. The choice made was to stress the right side of the square – the non-practical dimension of the brand. Note than the launch of the first Ferragamo perfume, with its heavy advertising, was meant to contribute to strengthening that mythic and esthetic dimension.

Creator Salvatore had succeeded in imposing the brand by playing on all four corners of the square. In the early 1990s, the brand realized it had slid towards the utilitarian values on the left side of the square.

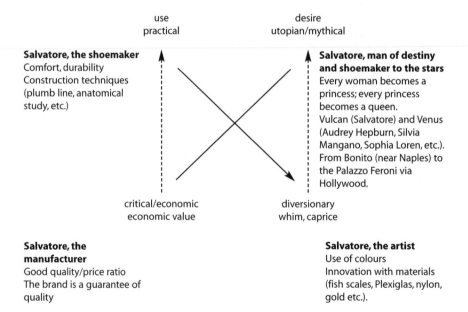

use practical	desire utopian/mythical

Salvatore, the shoemaker
Comfort, durability
Construction techniques
(plumb line, anatomical
study, etc.)

**Salvatore, man of destiny
and shoemaker to the stars**
Every woman becomes a
princess; every princess
becomes a queen.
Vulcan (Salvatore) and Venus
(Audrey Hepburn, Silvia
Mangano, Sophia Loren, etc.).
From Bonito (near Naples) to
the Palazzo Feroni via
Hollywood.

critical/economic economic value	diversionary whim, caprice

**Salvatore, the
manufacturer**
Good quality/price ratio
The brand is a guarantee of
quality

Salvatore, the artist
Use of colours
Innovation with materials
(fish scales, Plexiglas, nylon,
gold etc.).

At this point in time, the brand has lost its evocative power. It is known for shoes that fit well and have a good quality/price ratio.

Figure 4.9 Analysis of Ferragamo's positioning in 1992

We won't deny ourselves the enjoyment of presenting two quick sketches by Jean-Marie Floch. The first concerns a study he conducted to define a packaging system for eggs. The square was developed, still using the practical/existential semantic axis (see Figure 4.10).

The second study concerned an analysis of the communication for Calvin Klein perfumes, at the time of the launch of CK One (see Figure 4.11). It was presented by Jean-Marie Floch to the students of the Luxury MBA at the ESSEC Business School. The most significant semantic axis proved to be culture/nature, where the four Calvin Klein perfumes existing at the time were in natural concurrence.

Jean-Marie Floch's thesis was that CK One could already be anticipated with the launch of Eternity, which is its semantic opposite. His argument is based on the analysis, using the square, of the advertising for the brand's four perfumes:

- Eternity: photo of Christie Turlington smiling and holding a young child in her arms. "Kennedy family" atmosphere. Open, natural people. Several generations. A fecund woman and an active father.

- Obsession: photo of a prone Kate Moss, naked on a divan. The complement of CK One. Closed, contrasted spaces. Sculptural bodies and the brutality of desire.

- Escape: photo of a couple embracing on a deserted beach among the rocks, with a surfboard next to them. The least clearly defined. Baroque white background that encroaches on the rest of the photo.

- CK One: photo of a group of teenagers of both sexes. Attitudes of intense discussion. More homogeneous white background. A single generation. Lack of distinction between the sexes. Tension and discontinuity.

These examples illustrate, if that were necessary, the power and versatility of an instrument that can also be applied, depending on the semantic axis chosen, to a brand's strategic positioning in relation to luxury, to fashion, and to its competitors.

The existential/practical semantic axis has been used extensively, but it is far from providing answers to all the questions relative to brand identity. Another axis introduced by Jean-Marie Floch proved highly useful in the case of Loewe and Bally. This axis could be called "authenticity/ superficiality," that of perpetuating signs as opposed to producing meaning (see Figure 4.12).

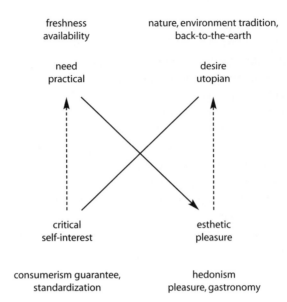

freshness
availability

nature, environment tradition,
back-to-the-earth

need
practical

desire
utopian

critical
self-interest

esthetic
pleasure

consumerism guarantee,
standardization

hedonism
pleasure, gastronomy

Figure 4.10 Main values related to egg consumption

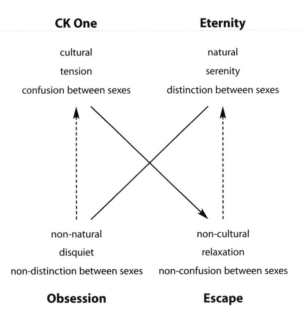

CK One   **Eternity**

cultural

natural

tension

serenity

confusion between sexes

distinction between sexes

non-natural

non-cultural

disquiet

relaxation

non-distinction between sexes

non-confusion between sexes

Obsession   **Escape**

Figure 4.11 Analysis of communication for Calvin Klein perfumes
with the introduction of CK One

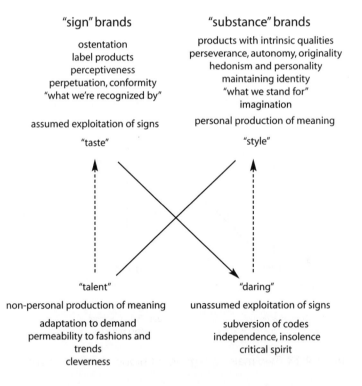

"sign" brands

ostentation
label products
perceptiveness
perpetuation, conformity
"what we're recognized by"

assumed exploitation of signs

"taste"

"substance" brands

products with intrinsic qualities
perseverance, autonomy, originality
hedonism and personality
maintaining identity
"what we stand for"
imagination

personal production of meaning

"style"

"talent"

non-personal production of meaning

adaptation to demand
permeability to fashions and
trends
cleverness

"daring"

unassumed exploitation of signs

subversion of codes
independence, insolence
critical spirit

Figure 4.12 Two major categories of brands

Jean-Marie Floch proposed a classification of luxury brands into two major categories: those that produce their own meaning (the "substance" brands) and those that exploit signs (the "sign" brands). As Figure 4.13 shows, the semiotic square quickly breaks down this basic distinction and provides a very detailed analysis of the respective positionings of all the luxury brands. Since then, many brands who desire to be seen as authentic have sought to position themselves on the upper right corner of the square.

The same formalization can also be used to position the brands in a sector, and thus to find a brand's place in relation to its competitors. However, note that any classification of this type involves a good deal of subjectivity, that brands evolve over time, and that they are all present, with varying intensity, at the four corners of the square. The classification of a few brands presented below is solely the authors' opinion; it appeared to us to be valid at the time of the study.

Late in 1999, one of the authors was in the position of relaunching the Swiss brand Bally, famous around the world since the middle of the

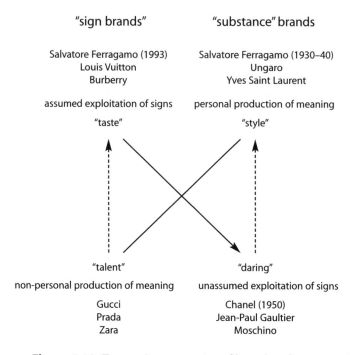

"sign brands"   "substance" brands

Salvatore Ferragamo (1993)   Salvatore Ferragamo (1930–40)
        Louis Vuitton   Ungaro
         Burberry   Yves Saint Laurent

assumed exploitation of signs   personal production of meaning

         "taste"   "style"

         "talent"   "daring"

non-personal production of meaning   unassumed exploitation of signs

           Gucci   Chanel (1950)
           Prada   Jean-Paul Gaultier
            Zara   Moschino

Figure 4.13 Two major categories of brands: a few examples

nineteenth century for its shoes. The brand, very "tired," needed a profound restructuring and a drastic repositioning. The choice was made to take a position on the upper right corner of the square and to promote Bally as a luxury brand in the field of shoes, accessories, and clothing, representative of values that connote Switzerland and modernity. Beginning with the phrase "a Swiss lifestyle luxury brand," all the Swiss values of creativity, security, solidity, and respect for nature were mobilized to inspire the creative and communicative activities. A Northern European brand esthetic of the "classical" type was imposed, leading to the development, among others, of a logo that was square in shape, red, with two white dots superimposed to represent a letter "B" (Plate 38).

At the same time, the airline Swissair was going bankrupt. A company called Crossair, under another form, became Swiss and took over the former airline's international activities. The directorial team did an extraordinary job, both rapid and in depth, with the identity of the new brand. It communicated its conclusions very effectively, in particular through a small brochure entitled *A short story about civilized aviation*, from which the following information is taken:

Our mission:

- to create the most respected airline in the world thanks to an uncompromising commitment to quality, innovation, attention to the consumer, and design;
- to become one of most admired companies in the world through our improvement of the lifestyles of men and women;
- to be Swiss.

Swiss values:

- quality,
- prestige,
- attention to the customer,
- service,
- efficiency,
- reliability,
- security,
- cleanliness,
- attention to detail,
- elegance,
- modernity,
- luxury,
- design,
- coherence,
- solidly Swiss.

This effort resulted in the definition of a new logo and an entire graphic identity, centered around a square with a red background, with the word "Swiss," and emblazoned with a white cross (see Plates 39 and 43).

Two Swiss brands in a phase of repositioning, both with the desire to express Swiss values in their respective sectors, both coming up with the idea of two squares with red backgrounds and white letters. Coincidence, perhaps ...

These considerations prompt us to submit for the reader's consideration a short classification of "national spirits" Jean-Marie Floch prepared using his "sign/meaning" square (see Figure 4.14). The diagram might seem amusing; yet it corresponds to statistical typologies of consumers in the countries mentioned.

In conclusion, the semiotic square has made it possible to formalize guidance concerning general positioning during the concrete projects we have had experience with. It complemented and put into perspective the concrete guidance stemming from the "hinge" studies. The semiotic square, by its nature, cannot offer exhaustive analyses. It nevertheless contributes to giving in-depth perceptions of domains that are too often neglected by the traditional instruments of marketing and strategy.

Semiotic mapping

Andrea Semprini takes the original semiotic square of consumption values introduced by Jean-Marie Floch and turns it into a more malleable and more legible tool for marketers.[11] The principal semantic axis is transformed into the ordinate axis of a two-dimensional graph (Figure 4.15). All the nuances of value, from the most practical to the most utopian, can be located on this scale. The coordinate axis ("critical/diversionary") intersects the preceding one to form a semiotic "mapping."

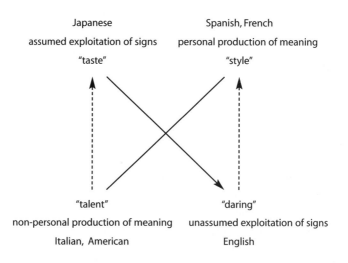

Figure 4.14 National spirits

---

11 Andrea Semprini, *Le marketing de la marque*, Paris: Éditions Liaisons, 1992.

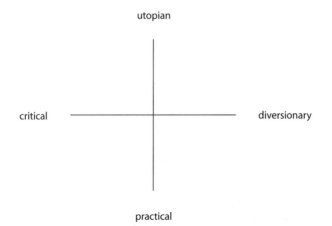

Figure 4.15 Semiotic mapping of consumer values

Source: Andrea Semprini.

The advantage over the square is that a spatial continuity is created on which each positioning is relative to all the others. The author rightly insists on the fact that the mapping, like the "practical/utopian" square, presents consumption values, not attitudes and behaviors. These individual behaviors (passion, enthusiasm, indifference, rejection, and so on) will correspond to the strategies each consumer puts into practice to pursue the consumption values.

Semprini analyzes the four quadrants delimited by the two axes in detail (see Figure 4.16). The northwest quadrant is called "mission": the convergence of critical and utopian values leads directly to the will to surpass the present, project toward the future, and seek innovation. It is the combination of duty and a constant striving towards different worlds. Benetton in the late 1980s (at the time of the launch of the "United Colors" campaign), with its billboards showing young people of all races, characterized this positioning. The brand was offering an ideal world based on new types of social relations. The Body Shop, with its commitment to natural products, is another example of a brand located in this quadrant.

The northeast quadrant is called "project." It conserves the willful dimension of the first quadrant, but the collective commitment is replaced by an individual quest for emotion. There is a strong propensity to embark on personal projects in the desire to find solutions to existential problems. Brands like Swatch and Ungaro are positioned there.

The southeast quadrant is called "euphoria." The convergence of diversionary and practical values is propitious for brands such as Oasis mission   utopian   project

commitments	escape
calling into question	adventure
visionary	dream
collective myths	metamorphosis
new social relations	transgression
surpassing	

critical ———————————————————————————————————— diversionary

useful	distraction
essential	entertainment
restrained	decoration
basic	emotion
economical	gadget
necessary	surprise
functional	provocation
technical	humor
advantages	

information   euphoria

practical

Figure 4.16 Semiotic mapping of consumer values:
specificities of the four quadrants

Source: Andrea Semprini.

or Gillette, whose discourse is positive, reassuring, and relatively pragmatic. These are the brands that focus on the intrinsic attributes of their
products: serenity, good feelings, happiness for all. That, for example, is
Calvin Klein's Eternity perfume. A variant of this quadrant is made up of
brands that entertain using surprise, humor, and provocation, like
Moschino.

The southwest quadrant is the most immediately understandable. At the
crossroads of the practical and the critical, the values presented are
resolutely linked to the quality aspects of the products offered. The essential, the advantageous, the strictly necessary, the rational, and the useful are
uppermost. This is the "information" quadrant, where mass-retail brands
like Wal-mart and Kmart are positioned.

Semprini also uses his mapping to analyze the brands' discourse
concerning time, space, the passions, relationships, and so on. The instrument proves to be just as powerful as the square, versatile, and more flexible to use. It introduces an infinity of combinations, focuses, and
differentiations of consumption values which make it possible to compre-
hend a significant part of the complexity of brand identity management.
Figure 4.17 presents an attempt at positioning several brands.

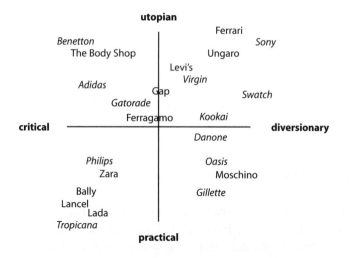

Figure 4.17 Semiotic mapping of consumer values:
a few examples of brand positioning

Source: Andrea Semprini (italics added by the authors).

The narrative schema

The last tool we would like to present is also semiotic in nature, but has less analytical power than the signifier/signified hinge and the semiotic square. It nevertheless constitutes a useful method of structuring a brand's discourse. It is the narrative schema. This schema was originally developed by Vladimir Propp (1928) for analyzing Russian fairy tales. Propp's conclusions greatly influenced the work of Greimas and structural semantics. Propp's initial schema was used by Jean-Marie Floch in his work on brands.

Floch did not use such a tool by chance, since one object of semantics is to categorize the invariant elements of any form of discourse. If a brand can be understood as a complex ensemble of projects or actions that are under-taken within the framework of a system of values, then we are in fact deal-ing with discourse, with narrative, with stories, to which the semiotic methods used by the discipline of narratology can be applied.

In narratological terms, the four "episodes" that make the logical sequence of any story are contract, skills (or competence), performance or action, and sanction. In the first stage, the protagonist accepts a contract (challenge, promise, leaving to seek adventure); he or she then acquires competences (the classic initiatory stage); in the third, the protagonist successfully carries out the action or program with the aid of the competences acquired, and within the framework of the system of values (contract) that defines his or her action. Finally, the protagonist is rewarded (or punished): the sanction is the measurement of performance in terms of the initial contract.

Applied to a brand, the schema becomes as shown in Figure 4.18. In the case of Taurus (Figure 4.19), the schema was used to synthesize numerous elements that had been developed using the hinge and semiotic square techniques. We see that the narrative schema is more a synthetic instrument than an analytic one.

From the semiologist to the manager

Of the five instruments presented, the last four are taken directly from the discipline of semiotics. We have pointed out that such tools, to be applied to managing brand identities, require that we accept the following – quite reasonable – hypothesis: brands are systems of meaning. Some people might object that many brands seem to do exactly the opposite – producing essentially nonsense instead of sense, and insignificance instead of significance! But we're only playing on words a little. A semiologist would object that all meaning, even the most aberrant, is still an analyzable process.

Nevertheless, from a manager's perspective, the tools we have described have a decisive advantage in that they elucidate and control the brand's discourse. And paying careful attention to this discourse and to the meanings it intends to produce, for us, is an elementary part of a responsible manager's professionalism – and also of a responsible consumer's vigilance, since

FIGURE 4.18			
The narrative schema applied to brands			
Contract	*Competence*	*Performance*	*Sanction*
The brand ethic	The company's business areas	The company's activities	The brand's perception: its image
The company's philosophy	Human resources	Products offered to target customers	
	Distribution network		Level of notoriety,
Its world view	Financial resources		desirability and purchase of the
"What it stands for"	Quality of management (vision, coherence, clarity, determination, etc.)		brand's products as opposed to its competitors'

FIGURE 4.19			
The narrative schema applied to Taurus			
Contract	*Competence*	*Performance*	*Sanction*
Promote a new conception of luxury: • by proposing a lifestyle based on generosity, freedom, and the ability to appreciate what is refined and original • by cultivating your own originality rather than following fashion trends • by staying away from ostentatious products	**A modern European spirit, capable of combining vitality and refinement, energy and subtlety:** • being capable of offering a modern and dynamic lifestyle • being in control of all the technical, logistical, and esthetic aspects of the luxury world	**Taurus creates products that engender emotions based on estheticism and sensuality:** • the products are precious yet not outrageously expensive • the perfect gift: exceptional, surprising, that is a pleasure for both the giver and the recipient • the brand offers an universe that responds to the aspirations of people who love life, movement, travel, sensuality, exclusiveness.	**Perception of the brand and economic results:** • a true luxury house, dynamic, innovative, original, and international

consumers are the primary recipients of the brand's messages. We will return to these questions.

The minimum of respect due each of the participants – brand, managers, consumers – is that the brand "make sense." That seems to go without saying. But it's also a much simpler means of being competitive! Amid the media bombardment we are subjected to in our contemporary civilization, having something interesting to say is a first condition for effective communication. In fact, semiotics and advertising have had a privileged relationship from the start. After all, what is advertising's task, if not the intentional production of meaning using signs?

All the semiotic tools that have been presented must be used with an awareness of their limits. Clearly, we can't ask semiotics to do what it is incapable of doing:

▪ It is never able to create.

▪ It cannot invent a style or a bestseller.

■ It does not attempt to substitute itself for the creativity of designers and publicists.

■ It is never exhaustive in its approach.

■ It cannot deal with problems of management.

/ What is advertising's task, if not the intentional production of meaning using signs? /

On the other hand, it does deal with the mechanisms of the creation of meaning, and therefore can:

■ point up the brand's fundamental invariants, if they exist

■ provide a framework within which everything that "speaks" about the brand, and therefore all its manifestations, must be situated: it determines the domain of the possible and that of the plausible

■ manage the coherence of the different signals sent out by the brand

■ manage the brand's consistency with its past and present

■ facilitate the strategic choices directors of brands must make.

We might even go as far as to insert the position of semiotician into the standard organizational chart of a brand. That is what we suggest in Figure 4.20.

Semiotics is at its most effective when it is coupled with a good, in-depth trend survey of society or the chosen consumer segments, and with good basic sales sense. In cases where semiotic analysis doesn't initially show solid results in identifying the brand's ethical invariants, other elements taken from market studies must be brought in. Semiology is then used to rework these elements and draw practical recommendations.

/ Semiotics is at its most effective when it is coupled with a good, in-depth trend survey on the society or the chosen consumer segments, and with good basic sales sense. /

Later we will discuss the notions of a brand's coherence and relevance. We can say here that semiotics aids in the management of coherence, but is only marginally helpful in managing relevance. Even so, it is one of the rare tools that can get away from the subjective considerations of the different players and objectively pose the question of the brand's identity. This is in no way a guarantee of creativity, but in the context of the collectivity any company represents, that objectivity already represents considerable progress.

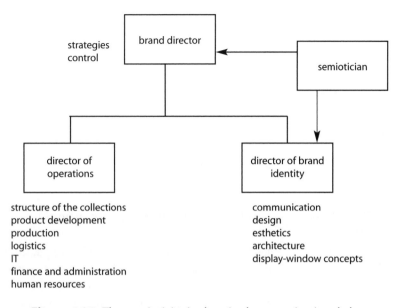

strategies
control

Figure 4.20 The semiotician's place in the organizational chart

Brand identity and consumer identity

What is involved in the passage from identity to image? As we have stressed, identity is emissive in nature, while perception – the culmination of communication with the consumer – is receptive in nature. The two notions are independent. Between what I want to say about myself and what I get across to my recipient, a lot of shifting, pollution, interference, omission, and unconscious revelation goes on. These unavoidable alterations represent the dynamic aspect of any process of communication.

The message of the brand's identity, consequently, undergoes changing interpretations as a function of who is on the receiving end. And a brand's discourse is aimed at winning consumers' approval. Its relevance depends strongly on the lifestyle, customs, values, and tastes of those consumers. Like any speaker, any issuer of discourse, the brand must take into account the identity of its recipients. And since a brand hopes not only to be heard but to be adopted by the consumer, to become one of the signs of his or her identity, the issue takes on crucial importance. Between the brand and individuals' identities, there is necessarily a cultural identity, structured by the cultural codes of a given social group. The brands, in communicating their identities through their various manifestations, will generate what we could call social and individual representations.

This has two important consequences for brand management. First, it must be accepted that perceptions of the brand will always be multiple, and that their diversity can only increase as brand awareness increases. Second, human society changes, and so does the identity of the individuals and the cultures that make it up. To continue to "speak" to them, the brand must also renew itself, change its own identity, without losing its fundamental substance. Be able to change without getting lost in the process: that is the challenge we all face each day as social beings, and it's one that brands also face.

/ Like any speaker, any issuer of discourse, the brand must take into account the identity of its recipients. /

Single identity/multiple perceptions

J.-P. Codol and P. Tap give the following definition of an individual's identity: "Identity is a structured, differentiated system, anchored both in a past temporality (roots, permanence), in a coordination of current behavior, and in a legitimated perspective (projects, ideals, values, and style)."[12] This definition applies closely to a brand's identity; the vocabulary is largely the same.

Psychoanalysis, anthropology, and psychosociology have all studied the notion of the individual's identity, bringing out the intrinsic duality on which it is founded: on the one hand, personal judgment; on the other, comparison with others – in other terms, the purely individual dimension versus social existence. Psychoanalysis (Erik H. Erikson) holds that identity is constructed both by interiorization of cultural and social models and by the imagination of the body and its impulses. Cultural anthropology places the accent on the collective dimension of identity. It sees each culture as tending to produce personality models.

In more semiological terms, these approaches have in common the fact that they temper the idea of universal communication: I can't really say the same thing to everyone, at least not if I hope to be understood by everyone in the same way. The perception of a brand's identity (values, signs) is conditioned by the values, judgments, and models developed personally and in a specific environment by each individual.

Of course, we can't take the position that each individual's subjectivity is irreducible either. Human society appears to be "layered" by many determinisms – depending on culture, region, age, income level, and so on – that can in part be elucidated. But no matter how refined the analysis, the perception of a given message by the individual members of a given group cannot be unique. Therefore this duality inherent in identity must be dealt with.

---

12 *Revue internationale de psychologie sociale*, no. 2, 1988, p. 169.

The generation of multiple perceptions from a single brand identity is an absolutely normal phenomenon. All brands face this reality, above all when it comes to geographical extension. In terms of communication and creation, there are two extremes in dealing with it.

First there is monolithic management, which deals with a standardized consumer. This is the case of the luxury brands, which produce a single communication campaign and collection for the entire world. Even in this case, there is still an implicit segmentation. The brand aims at an urban public who have a high income level and are fond of traveling. It relies on these strong determinisms to eclipse geographical specificities.

Then there is a more flexible form of management which adapts products or advertising campaigns to local cultures. L'Oréal is probably the best example of how cosmetic products and their relative communication can be adapted to different cultural markets. Another example that could be cited is certain liquors (such as cognac) for which modes of consumption vary greatly from one country to another. The automotive industry is another.

Such a range of individual and cultural identities makes all segmentations possible. Certain groups have realized this and take multiple actions in this direction (segmentation by brand, or intrabrand). The criteria are geographical, demographic, economic, and sometimes psychosocial. "Mood segmentation" – which breaks potential markets down according to consumers' moods – has recently appeared.

/ The generation of multiple perceptions from a single brand identity is an absolutely normal phenomenon. All brands face this reality, above all when it comes to geographical extension. /

Ms Consumer is walking down Fifth Avenue. She feels successful and seductive, or wants to; she buys an ensemble at Christian Dior. Or she's a little depressed, feels like a victim, not at ease with herself; Prada offers her the refuge she needs. She's at the top of her form physically and mentally, exuberant, in love with life; Loewe can provide her with the products that reflect Spanish energy and *joie de vivre*. A few days later, feeling a little guilty about all the money she spent, she feels she needs to find a bargain, a product she'll use every day, in good taste and at a reasonable price; she goes to Max Mara on West Broadway and, to soothe her shopping-tortured feet, buys a good pair of Ferragamo shoes.

Consumers have become multifaceted, very difficult to catch in the net. What's interesting in this example is that all these "images" are aimed at the same consumer, who will choose one or the other according to her mood. The choice of Christian Dior, for example, will appear daring to some and frankly unreasonable to others. We are looking at the difference between brand identity and what is called "brand image." The same identity crystallizes into a multitude of perceptions depending on place, social milieu, personality, or mood.

There's nothing to be gained by fighting this diversity. On the contrary, it represents a form of wealth. It constitutes a portfolio of images, each of which enables different reactions to innovations and the risks they entail for a company. So perceptions are multiple. But they are not unstructured and accidental. Semiology, by analyzing the mechanisms by which meaning is produced, is fully aware of the polysemy of its subjects. But this multiplicity of perceptions does not contradict the need to guarantee, upstream, the coherence of the message.

The more coherent the identity, the more it lends itself to a wealth of interpretations. Messages that are vague, on the other hand, either through structural weakness or because of a desire to "cover all the bases," to be an aggregate of all trends, melt away under the light of interpretation. Samuel Johnson, the great eighteenth-century English lexicographer, had exactly this in mind in the quotation we've used as epigraph for this chapter. An identity that borrows from too many categories runs the risk of collapsing under the weight of its referents.

/ The more coherent the identity, the more it lends itself to a wealth of interpretations. Messages that are vague, on the other hand, either through structural weakness or because of a desire to "cover all the bases," to be an aggregate of all trends, melt away under the light of interpretation. /

The need to evolve

Coherence of identity does not mean authoritarianism. A brand's identity must evolve. How many brands have disappeared because they haven't responded to that need? The evolution of mores and sexual liberation were responsible for the initial success of Paco Rabanne, with his metal dresses; that same liberalization of lifestyles took the polish off his image, and very quickly made him more marginal than original.

A brand's decline is an inevitable phenomenon if nothing is done to counteract it. The reasons, both internal and external, are numerous. First of all come errors in the brand's management – loss of relevance in a market, inefficient operations, incoherent strategies, inappropriate investments, and so on. Then there is the competition, ever stronger and more battle-hardened. There is also what we call the "entropy" of brands. Any brand, through the wide use of its products and the repeated broadcasting of its advertising, engenders a certain demystification. It loses some of its mystery, and thereby part of its attraction. In the contemporary context of the race toward novelty, this wearing effect of success is more rapid than ever.

Finally, there is the evolution of the fundamental trends of our civilization: needs, fashions, technology, tastes ... We often cite the example of the history of the color blue, brilliantly told by Michel Pastoureau.[13] In Greco-Roman times, blue did not play a role in social, religious, or artistic life. It was hardly used by the Barbarians. It was not until the thirteenth century and the windows of the cathedral of Chartres that blue took on more importance in liturgical life.

This is because a new theology of light had developed. Light was seen as an emanation of God, the ineffable made visible. The thesis that light and color were identical in nature won out over the idea that colors are only a material artifice. Blue and gold were used to represent that light. Within a few decades, blue became an aristocratic color; it was seen in clothing, artistic creations, religious life. It became the color of the sky, then of the Virgin Mary, finally that of kings. Blue was never to lose that importance. From the uniforms of soldiers, policemen, and postmen in the nineteenth century to the blue jeans of today, blue became the most-worn color in the Western world. It is also, before green, the favorite color of Westerners. The Japanese, on the other hand, prefer first white, then black. Tastes change with time and from country to country.

For all these reasons, a brand identity that is too rigid, defined with too many constraints or in too much detail, hampers the ability to move rapidly with the market. But this does not necessarily imply renewing the brand's ethical and esthetic invariants. In fact, the need for evolution expresses itself differently in these two domains.

The need for change is greater on the esthetic level. More than changing invariants, the need is for keeping an esthetic in step with the tastes of the time. For example, while Loewe's esthetic was defined as "minimalist baroque" in 1996, today it can become "pared-down baroque," since minimalism is disappearing from circulation. While respecting the brand's identity, piloting creative approaches in this way allows the same diversity of offerings to customers.

As for the brand ethic, there is no question of changing the basic values of the brand, but rather of putting a stronger light on those values that seem best in phase with the mood of the markets, and therefore capable of generating the best sales. Evolution does not mean ill-advised transformation of

---

13 Michel Pastoureau, *Bleu: histoire d'une couleur*, Paris: Seuil, 2000.

the invariants, but rather making marginal corrections, variations in focus that will stay on good terms with the markets without altering the brand's substance. Rather than of permanent invariants, we can speak in terms of a stable continuity of the brand esthetic and ethic.

/ A brand identity that is too rigid, defined with too many constraints or in too much detail, hampers the ability to move rapidly with the market./

Finally, we would point out that the need for change is greater for brands whose ethic is based on fashionable values, which by definition are not permanent. In this area, there is "old money" and there are the nouveaux riches: Bentley or Hermès will be able to rely on a brand ethic that focuses on elitist and aristocratic values for some time to come. On the other hand, evolution will very probably be more difficult for Prada or Roberto Cavalli.

The limits of the concept of identity: strategic and operational implications

Throughout this chapter, we've made a point of defending the notion of brand identity and providing tools for getting a grasp of it. This is because we are convinced of its usefulness. Though still not a widespread concept, it is of primordial importance for intelligent brand management. While necessary, this concept is not sufficient. Using a concrete example, we will now try to illustrate the areas where it can come into play directly, in order to determine its advantages and its limits.

Operational implications

Once formalized, the brand identity represents a framework which will serve to manage all, or nearly all, of the manifestations of the brand's existence. Figure 4.21 is taken from a real case – that of a brand of moderately priced jewelry which launched a review of its brand identity in 1998. It shows all the operational projects that came out of that study.

A brand identity study serves first to verify the brand's strategic positioning in relation to its competitors and its target markets, and then to provide a common language and guidelines for verification of all the brand's manifestations:

- products, choices made by creative departments

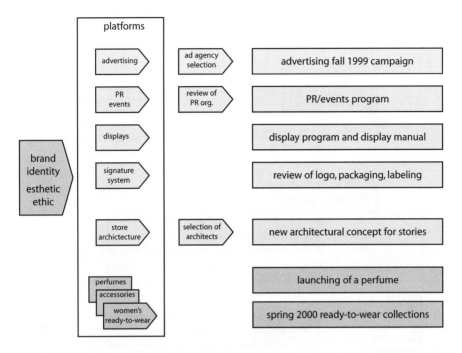

Figure 4.21 Brand identity project: operational implications (actual example)

- advertising campaigns, the choice of media and models

- events, relations with the press

- the architectural concept of the stores and offices

- display-window concepts

- signage, labels, stationery – the signature system in general

- salespersons' uniforms, and so on.

In short, it is a federating framework to aid in eliminating, at the outset, all elements that are incompatible with the identity.

The place of the brand identity in company strategies

Figure 4.22 is taken from the Taurus project. It shows the relative place of the brand's identity within a more complete project of strategic redefinition. It clearly shows the need to launch the brand-identity study – on which the other considerations will depend – before any other project.

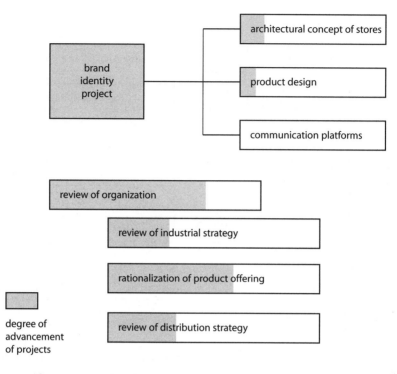

Figure 4.22 The place of the brand identity study in relation to other projects (example)

As can be seen, other projects (organization, products to be offered, and so on) begin in parallel with the identity project, but with a slight time delay. This diagram was used, among other purposes, as a set of indicators of the advancement of these projects.

Still, the brand identity as such cannot be used to act directly on the choices the business makes in terms of structure of the product offering, determination of prices and margins, choice of target customers, or organizational, industrial, and retailing choices. These choices, which also have an impact on the brand's perception, must of course take it into consideration, but the identity study alone is not sufficient to guarantee that the best decisions will be made.

The company's strategic approach defines the scope and the limits of the brand's identity. The overall strategy of a company can be broken down into "specialized" strategies (products, customers, retailing, communication, production, logistics, and organization). We can see that while the brand's identity plays a central role in any strategy of communication, it is also affected in turn by decisions made by other functions. There is no activity, in a company, that does not affect or reflect, in one way or another, the brand's identity.

Figure 4.23 shows the degree of influence the logic of the brand identity should exert in the overall strategy of the company. For companies that share our approach to management of identity, the implications in terms of organization are numerous. We will return to them.

Limitations of the concept of identity

Another limitation of the concept of identity has to do with the paradox inherent in the definition of "identity" itself. Merriam-Webster's *Collegiate Dictionary,* which we cited at the start of this chapter, mentions identity as being not only the distinguishing character or personality of an individual, but also "sameness of essential or generic character."

/ While the brand's identity plays a central role in any strategy of communication, it is also affected in turn by decisions made by other functions. /

Sameness and generic. Identical and unique. The individual and the multitude.

Is identity, then, the state of being both unique and like another? It swings back and forth between the tendencies of the mass market towards uniformity, and radical uniqueness, and probably exists only in terms of this dialectical tension.

These considerations take us back, indirectly, to the difficulty of defining and formalizing an identity that is completely independent of the way in which it is perceived – or, more exactly, of the perception of the brand's director of the way in which the brand is seen by the target market segments. To try to define a brand's identity in a closed circle, independently of considerations related to trends and to the dominant perceptions of the brand in the most significant markets, is a dangerous oversimplification.

Figure 4.24, taken from a study we did as consultants for a brand of jewelry, illustrates this need for taking the competitive context – in the broad sense – of the markets into account beyond the pure semiotic approach.

As we saw in Chapter 3 (the section on "Perfecting markets"), one of the conditions of existence of a brand is the differentiation of its identity. This implies that a brand exists in relation to other brands from which it is different. Pepsi would not exist without Coca-Cola, Coca-Cola would probably not be as important without Pepsi. The right balance must be found

		influence of brand identity
Products	– categories	
	– structure of offering	
	– prices	
	– esthetic	
	– functionality	
	– quality	
Customers	– targets	
Distribution	– networks	
	– esthetic	
	– service	
Communication	– advertising	
	– PR and events	
Production		
Logistics		
Organization	– structure	
	– personnel	
	– culture	
Finance & admin		

■ determining influence ▨ partial influence ▢ minimal influence

Figure 4.23 Place of brand identity in company strategies

between the general conditions of the market and the degrees of flexibility of the ethical and esthetic constants.

Providing the return on investments shareholders demand, satisfying the expectations of existing customers, but also the expectations expressed by customers of the competitors of reference, all without losing the brand's soul: such are the dilemmas brand directors face every day. Ours is an anthropomorphic approach, applying the principles of identity to systems like brands, whose objectives are essentially economic. It opens up an area for more detailed research into the nature of the interfaces between brand identity and cultures and consumers' identities, and into the mechanisms that trigger the act of purchase.

/ To try to define a brand's identity in a closed circle is a dangerous oversimplification./

The goal of brand management being to lead consumers to buy the brand's products, consumers must position themselves in a positive way in relation to values and an esthetic they can perceive. Are these values that

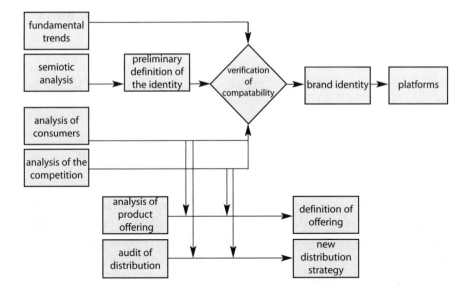

Figure 4.24 Phases of brand identity definition project (actual example)

are aspired to, or ones already acquired? Is a purchase an act of affirmation, of compensation, of protest? The projection of an image of the self that is desired, or actual? We leave this field of research to other disciplines and other books.

Meanwhile, the notion of brand identity is gaining ground, and is being used more and more in the industry. Suzy Menkes (Fashion Editor of the *Herald Tribune*) had this to say about the debut of the winter 2002 collections: "Brand identities are being eroded. Just as a calmer Gucci and a sexed-up Prada no longer seem to spar on well-defined territory, even Armani is now trying to be all things to all people."[14] Or, in the March 12, 2002 edition ("Special report on fashion"), this title: "Houses: a question of identity."

The responsibilities of the company

We mentioned this theme in Chapter 3, when we looked at brands as factors for progress. But we feel that now that we are dealing with the concept of the brand's identity, and therefore with crucial choices for the future of the company, it is indispensable to remind directors of their responsibilities.

---

14 Suzy Menkes, *Herald Tribune*, March 5, 2002.

What to present? What dream can I present? What possible world can I offer?

This is the question the brand director or the CEO must ask when reflecting on the identity of the brand, examining the degree of liberty left by the semiotician.

How to present it? How can I make people dream about the possible world I present?

This is the question the CEO considers with the director of communication. The problems have to do with execution. Needless to say, economic considerations are uppermost. All the resources of experience and intuition will be mobilized to present the facets of the brand's identity that are most differentiating, most in phase with the mood of the moment, the ones that will make the brand the most competitive.

But that is not enough. In order for brands to become a factor of progress, beyond their simply contributing to the perfecting of commercial transactions, they must be able to activate in people (consumers and employees) the qualities that are necessary for progress: innovation, curiosity, a sense of action and of risk, a desire for conquest, the will to surpass oneself, solidarity, a love of hard work, confidence in one's own abilities, and so on. Contrary to what one might think, many brands contribute to putting people in a position where progress can be generated. All brands that procure, in one way or another, material or psychological comfort for their clients fall into this category. The same reasoning could be applied to brands that use seduction (the spirit of conquest), even though the field seems more crowded and it is therefore more difficult to differentiate oneself in it.

When a brand has the power to influence a great number of people, it must be careful what it presents for people to dream about – and how it presents it. The CEO of BMW knows something about this. In February 2002 he withdrew an ad showing a nude couple on a bed, with one of the partners' heads covered by a magazine showing the latest BMW. Unfortunately this need for responsibility is not felt strongly enough today by directors of brands, creative directors, and directors of communication.

We have already discussed the topic of provocation in Chapter 2, but it is very possible, with talent and taste, to promote values like seduction, sensuality, eroticism, and sensual pleasure without crossing the line into the vulgar or the shocking. That was not the choice made by the Sisley brand

– whose advertisement in February 2002 showed a young girl stretched out on a bed, looking at us as she touches herself (see Plates 18 to 21). For a brand director to engage in this kind of advertising is to show a lack of respect for potential customers and the rest of the population. Not everyone shares or even knows about Sisley's approach to managing brand identity as interpreted by photographer Terry Richardson, who decided to position the brand in the domain of "pulp provocation."

We do not feel that the systematic use of gratuitous provocation and vulgarity is a factor for progress. We therefore suggest that two questions should govern the activities of brand directors, beyond the usual economic considerations:

/ When a brand has the power to influence a great number of people, it must be careful what it presents for people to dream about – and how it presents it. /

- Does my brand encourage in consumers qualities or sentiments that can, directly or indirectly, lead them to be factors for progress themselves?

- In all the brand's manifestations (products, advertising, events, and so on), is there a fundamental respect for the dignity of the audience?

To us, these two questions are fundamental. They will reappear several times in our arguments. If brand managers can answer these questions in the affirmative, then they will have found, at the same time, what to present to consumers and how to present it – the two decisional areas which, for us, characterize their responsibilities. If not, then consumers will step in and save us. We shall see in Chapters 8 and 9 how they can contribute to restoring order in the world of brands, and accelerate a movement towards responsibility whose beginnings are already being felt.

5 | The brand life cycle and the global dimension

I remember that Fausto Coppi had a friend called the White Lady.
(Georges Perec)

In a book called *Je me souviens* (*I Remember*),[1] Georges Perec paints the portrait of a generation through the archeology of its collective memory. He lists memories that appear useless, yet engrave themselves on our memories without our knowing quite why, and finally become part of us: the name of an athlete injured in a game that has remained famous, a detail of a short news item that caused a scandal – and, of course, reminiscences of brands and slogans that have disappeared today.

Perec's book shows how much brands are a part of our most intimate history. It reminds us how they take on life, and sometimes die, but also that their history is not quite one with that of the company that brought them into existence. Brands, having become part of our imagination, sometimes survive there long after the company has disappeared.

A brand's history comprises phases of strong expansion alternating with phases of relative stagnation, and even more or less rapid decline. That situation is not really different from what happens with a product or a company, for which the term "life cycle" is commonly used. In fact, this concept can easily be extended to the universe of brands. The life of a brand can be represented on a graph with two dimensions. The time axis is the coordinate; on the ordinate axis is an estimate of the brand's "strength," based on a given convention. (See Figure 5.1.) In the resulting curve, we find the same phases of launch, development, maturity, decline, relaunch, and disappearance that characterize the life cycle of a product. At each of

---

1 Georges Perec, *Je me souviens*, Paris: Hachette, 1998.

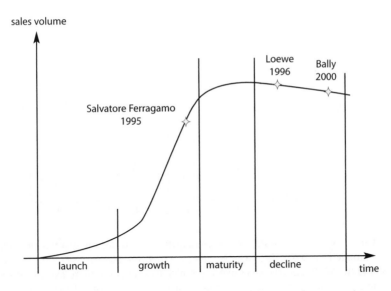

Figure 5.1 Life cycle of brands: the different phases and examples of positioning

these stages, needless to say, the problems faced by the brand's director are posed in specific terms.

The fashion and luxury sector is particularly concerned with the problem of relaunching, which becomes a real one for a majority of brands that are in the phases of maturity or decline. The most spectacular example of relaunching is, of course, that of Gucci in the years 1995 and 1996 following the beginning of a decline in 1992. The crisis that followed or was reinforced by September 2001 affected the brand's results for 2002, and given its already intensive and extensive brand development, is probably the signal of the beginning of its second maturity (see Figure 5.2).

/ A brand's history comprises phases of strong expansion alternating with phases of relative stagnation, and even more or less rapid decline. /

The phenomenon of relaunching corresponds to the creation of a new life cycle, in fact a second life for the brand. A relaunch this spectacular is relatively rare, and corresponds to what we call, later in this chapter, the "great leap." This implies a drastic repositioning of the brand, its identity, and in this case its target consumers. It's like giving the brand a new lease of life, by means of new values, compatible with the earlier values. Still, September 11, 2001 is taking its toll on Gucci's performance in terms of sales, and its effects may also be hiding a certain "loss of momentum" by

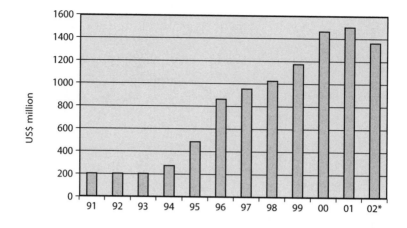

* As the Gucci group financial statements were given in euros for the first time for 2002, we have applied the 9.6 % decrease between the reported 2001 sales (1700.1 million euros) and the 2002 reported sales of 1536.8 million euros , in order to extrapolate an estimate of the 2002 sales in US$ from the reported 2001 sales of US$1514 million.

Figure 5.2 Sales of Gucci products

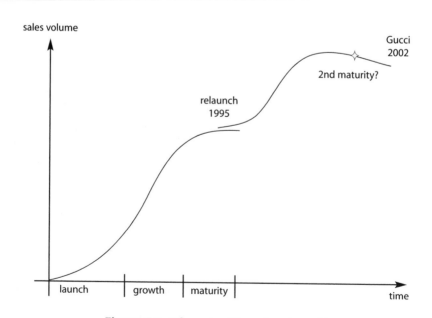

Figure 5.3 Life cycle of brands: relaunching

the brand, which may have reached new limits in its existing business development model.

Continuing in the luxury-industries sector, we will cite a few examples of brands at different stages of their life cycle. Bulgari has undergone a strong growth phase since 1993, even if the rate of growth began to diminish in 2001. As we note in this chapter, the current economic outlook, together with the relative weakness of the US dollar with respect to the euro, are imposing a kind of "forced maturity" on all European players in the luxury industry.

Hermès, a brand that is over a century old, has had relatively constant growth since the early 1990s and seems little affected by the different economic slumps, as if the attraction of authentic luxury were continuing its evolution independently of economic crises. Yet there was, as for Bulgari, a certain slowdown in the growth rate in 2001 and 2002.

Ferragamo, on the other hand, is in its maturity phase. The discontinuity of the year 2000 corresponds to consolidation of the sales of the Japanese retailing subsidiary after its purchase. The curve corresponding to comparative yearly business volume is in fact very close to the theoretical profile of the life cycle. Decline may be lying in wait for the brand if new competitive dimensions are not put into practice to recover the growth rate of the 1990s.

The ambiguities of this last example are a good illustration of the fact that business volume does not provide a very consistent measurement of the strength of a brand. Such an ideal concept is in fact very difficult to quantify. However, as we shall see, approximations are still possible.

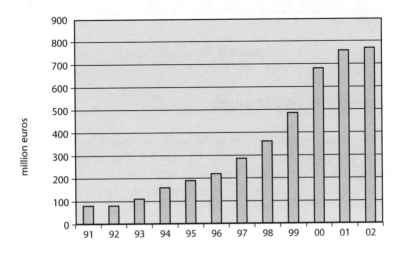

Figure 5.4 Bulgari sales

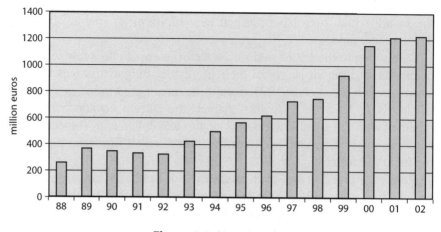

Figure 5.5 Hermès sales

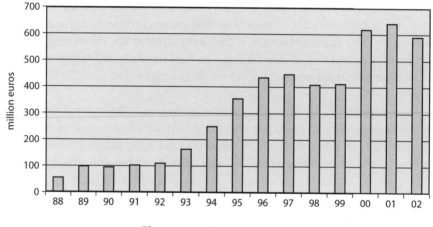

Figure 5.6 Ferragamo sales

Measuring a brand's strength

Business volume constitutes the most easily accessible measurement, but its consistency has to be ensured, by taking sales at retail value, and converting all sales to distributors and license royalties into retail value. If business volume is used as the measurement, the brand's life cycle will correspond to the arithmetic sum of the life cycles of all its products. But such an estimate doesn't quantify such notions as name recognition or desirability. Also, it only partially represents the result of the brand's economic operations, because it doesn't show profits and financial flows.

This approach can be completed without difficulty using other indicators that are superimposed on business volume. Obviously profits and cash flows should attain their maximum at the start of maturity and reach their lowest ebb after a few years of decline. As for stock prices, they can be seen as a measurement of the brand's strength as investors see it – in terms of its ability to generate financial flows in the future.

The birth of a brand

How are brands born? We are talking here of strong brands, ones destined to make their mark on their time. One thing is sure: brand reputation can't be planned. This is true of brands as it is of individuals. Certain measures and resources can aid their ascent, but success is never guaranteed.

In hindsight, it's clear that at the origin of a strong brand there is always an ambitious project, supported by the faith of a talented individual. This will often be the founder of the company. Confidence in his or her own vision and ability to make it a reality are determining advantages. Boldness, vision, and determination are indispensable qualities.

Innovation is the second essential factor. Creative genius consists in reading the mood of the times and offering products that respond to it in novel ways, be it at the level of style, technology, or in the identification of a new need. In the category of stylistic innovation we find all the great names of haute couture and accessories: Coco Chanel, Christian Dior, Yves Saint Laurent, Salvatore Ferragamo, Giorgio Armani, and so on. These creators were able, at a given point in time, to express new ideas that captured the interest of large numbers of people – enough, in any case, to justify the launching of a durable economic activity. In the area of technological innovation there are

/ Creative genius consists in reading the mood of the times and offering products that respond to it in novel ways, be it at the level of style, technology, or in the identification of a new need. /

all the great pioneers of the automobile – Ford, Ransom Olds, Bugatti, Panhard, Renault – and of course Thomas Edison, William Hewlett and Dave Packard, Bill Gates and the like belong here. Walt Disney also belongs here, in a special subcategory of products that had never existed before, at least in the same form.

The innovation we are speaking of is rarely synonymous with invention, because it is indissociable from the conditions of distribution of the product – its production on a mass scale, for example. It often operates through appropriation or extrapolation of techniques already worked out on the theoretical level, to which it gives concrete industrial reality. It is true, for example, that Bill Gates is not an "inventor" of software;[2] but it is also true that this visionary businessman had understood, before most people, the potential of the microcomputer, and was able to turn it to his profit.

Consequently, the dimensions of innovation are multiple. They can be in the development of a specific production tool that makes the mass production of a new product possible. Innovation can also consist in revolutionizing the production or distribution of an existing product, the way in which business is conducted, or the associated services. Benetton, aside from the fact that the company knitted in white yarn and dyed to suit demand, was born of an innovative system of distribution; Zara, out of logistical organization and an exceptional capacity to read the needs of the markets. These assets make it possible for the brand to supply sufficient products to the places where they are required in ten days. Ray Kroc founded McDonald's in 1955 and invented fast food. Prada began to make a name for itself thanks to the use of nylon in the manufacture of its bags.

Communication has also become an important innovative dimension. Take Lise Charmel, a brand of lingerie, which suddenly became famous in Spain in spring 2002 after a billboard campaign people noticed. In the fashion milieu, illustrious personalities like Louis Vuitton, Carl-Franz Bally, Enrique Loewe, and Guccio Gucci were not creators in the stylistic or technological sense of the term, but artisans who developed their industrial and commercial vision beginning in the mid-nineteenth century.

At what exact point does a product become a brand? The question is somewhat rhetorical, but a few commonly-used indices can be mentioned:

- when the brand's creator dies and it continues to prosper

- when advertising is no longer needed to sell the products

- when a sales volume of over US$50 million is reached

- when new categories of products can be developed successfully

- when more than 50 percent of the general public in a given country are familiar with the existence of the brand

- when a brand is present in Europe, the United States, and Asia.

---

2   The basic code of the MS DOS operating system, which was to lead to the development of Microsoft's Windows system, was purchased in 1980 from an independent developer (Tim Allen). Microsoft's strategy has always focused on mobilization of collective resources rather than individual genius.

We feel, in fact, that all economic activity has within it the seeds of brands that will develop if conditions are favorable. How many brands started with the activities of small-scale artisans or merchants? Many brands that are not international and have low name recognition continue to prosper.

Growth of a brand

In a growth phase, a brand will implement a strategy of expansion, both quantitative and qualitative. Most brands that are successful today are in this phase of development, characterized by growth rates in two figures.[3]

On the quantitative level, the brand will try to locate on new geographical markets, while extending its presence in existing markets. The logic of volume is more evident in this phase: more has to be sold in order to absorb fixed costs

/ All economic activity has within it the seeds of brands that will develop if conditions are favorable. /

more easily. But since communication is generally managed in terms of a percentage of sales, the greater the sales, the more the brand can communicate.

On the qualitative level, the brand will optimize its production and distribution tools; possibly improve its product; use its growing reputation to move into new areas. Such extensions through launching new categories of products are of course a growth factor, but they also increase the brand's reputation by making it more accessible, thanks to multiple and/or wider distribution channels. They plant the seeds of future legitimacy in new sectors. The budget for communication and strengthening the brand's identity then serves as an umbrella for several categories of products and more easily becomes profitable.

So, the axes of development are multiple. This explains why this phase can last several decades. Five major axes can be identified: sectoral growth, geographical expansion, introduction of new categories of products, optimization of internal processes, and repositioning the brand. All of them, except for the first, are ways in which the brand can take market shares away from its most significant competitors.

Sectoral growth

The most recent case of sudden sectoral expansion is the explosion of the market for cellular telephones. In this context, Nokia and Ericsson

---

3 Especially if purely accidental factors are eliminated, such as the terrorist attacks in September 2001 and the Gulf War in 1991.

experienced respective growth rates of 252 percent and 120 percent between 1996 and 2000. But this single axis cannot ensure stable growth on a market that is volatile or is rapidly reaching saturation. This is what happened to Ericsson (Figure 5.7), whose sales have dropped by 34 percent since the peak in 2000, while Nokia (Figure 5.8) reached its peak in 2001 and is down by 3.8 percent in 2002. Again the curves are very close to the theoretical life-cycle model.

Geographical expansion

As soon as a product has met with success in a country, it is logical to think that it should sell well in other countries. Attempts to put this into practice are varied and take on a great diversity of forms. In a certain number of cases, the same product, with the same communication strategy, can succeed. That is the worldwide strategy of Coca-Cola or Pepsi-Cola, for example. What we have said about "impossible universality" regarding brand communication nevertheless still remains valid, even in the cases of these products, which rely on target populations that are federated by transnational values (youth, dynamism, a relaxed attitude towards adults). As regards advertising, for certain big advertisers, the central marketing

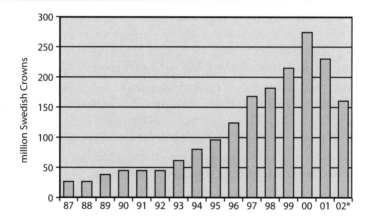

* As Ericsson sales were restated in 2002 to take into account changes in accounting principles, we have applied the 30% decrease between the newly reported 2001 sales (210.8 million Swedish Crowns) and the 2002 reported sales of 145.8 million Swedish Crowns, in order to extrapolate an estimate of the 2002 sales if the accounting treatment had not been changed.

Figure 5.7 Ericsson sales

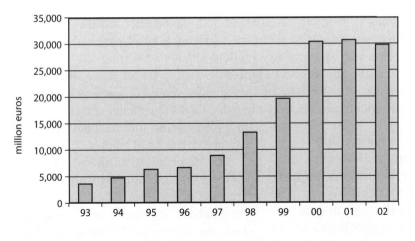

Figure 5.8 Nokia sales

teams send out a complete, modularized kit – for example, several advertising spots corresponding to the same strategy but with different approaches. Each national team can choose the particular campaign that will be most applicable to its environment.

This is also what is done with all fashion and perfume brands where a large percentage of sales is to consumers who are not in their country of residence. The advertising will generally be identical. In certain cases, however, it may have to be modified slightly, for example for the Persian Gulf countries. In other cases, such as the cosmetics industry for instance, the product will be identical, but the communication will vary depending on the country. This is what happens when, from one place to another, the product does not serve quite the same function. In the United States a Yamaha 125 cc motorcycle is a leisure product; in Taiwan it's a means of transportation. In these two cases, the advertising will be different.

There are also cases where the product is different while the communication remains more or less identical. Take, for example, a shampoo for which the same ads – using a universally-known actress – are broadcast everywhere in the world, but whose formula might be adapted locally in certain places. In countries where the water is hard, a certain type of formula will have to be developed. In others where the water is softer, this will not be necessary. In certain countries, the standard bottle is 8 or 12 ounces; in others, it will only be 100 or 125 ml. Another example is the Sara Lee brownie. In the United States, it's sold as a refrigerated chocolate cake product. In France, it's marketed as a dry cookie-type product. But the name is the same, the advertising is similar, and the taste is not really very different.

Finally, there are cases where both the product and the communication differ. An example is detergents, which must be adapted to different laundry practices in each country (national habits of sorting the wash, washing machines with vertical or horizontal axes, types of water, different heating systems); the diversity of formulations required is a strong argument for different brands. The only thing that might remain the same is the guarantee provided by the international company (for example Henkel or Unilever).

/ Leaving aside organizational dysfunctions related to a poor understanding of local specificities, a brand, or its product, can sometimes prove to be simply unexportable. /

This diversity of situations is a good illustration of the multiple difficulties that can be involved in exporting a brand. Cases of failed geographical expansion are legion. Leaving aside organizational dysfunctions related to a poor understanding of local specificities, a brand, or its product, can sometimes prove to be simply unexportable.

There are products that have a cult following in a given country, but whose potential outside the national borders is limited. Pastis 51 and Suze, typically French products that are heavily consumed in France, are difficult to export. Italy's Martini is used as a before-dinner drink in the United States, but it will never be an international product consumed habitually and at high volume.

Another type of brand that is very strong in its own country, but difficult to export, is department stores. A good example is Marks & Spencer's recent failure in Continental Europe. As Frenchmen, we might wonder why the Galeries Lafayette stores have not succeeded in locating elsewhere – in New York, Singapore, Bangkok, or Berlin. The explanation is simple. The success of the Galeries Lafayette in France is linked to a certain French lifestyle, represented by a group of French brands that are known and liked by French consumers. In Berlin or New York, those French consumers are not present, and brands thought of as representing French chic are not necessarily available to the store. If they are very strong brands, they already have a presence in the target market, often through exclusivity agreements with other local department stores or with their own boutiques. The challenge is that of creating a French lifestyle abroad, without French customers and without the leading French brands. It's hard to build a strong case for the existence of such a store. The only cases of successful exportation of department stores are the presence of Japanese stores (Sogo and Daimaru, for example) in Southeast Asia, but they benefit locally from the support of numerous

Japanese residents and tourists. The French Le Printemps store in Tokyo, unable to stock any of the major French brands, reinvented a "French style" aimed at very young girls. It offers new brands, unknown in Japan and sometimes even in France, or created especially for the store.

Zara is a special case. The company's growth during the 1990s happened without advertising, based on the opening of new single-brand stores outside Spain, which relied on its skill in reading trends and its rapid logistical reactivity. In 20 years, Amancio Ortega created the Inditex group, the owner of the Zara brand, which has 1636 stores around the world, with sales of US$3.97 billion in 2002 (the group is more or less doubling its sales every three years).

In conclusion, while geographical expansion would seem to be the most natural dimension of development, it is also complex, and requires time and heavy investment. In addition, the results are often unpredictable – as the French chain Séphora, which at the end of 2001 closed the stores it had opened in Japan and Germany in 2000 and 2001, has just learned. For these reasons, the process of development on the international level makes for a more wide-open game, but a more difficult one.

New categories of products

It's natural to want to amortize communication efforts across a larger number of products. That is why the development of new categories has always been a favorite area for brands. One of the keys to success is a correct reading of the lines of relatedness between the original product and the area of diversification.

/ One of the keys to success is a correct reading of the lines of relatedness between the original product and the area of diversification. /

The *Michelin Guide* (1900) and road maps (1910) are an interesting historical example of this type of diversification. The promotion of automobile tourism, for a tire manufacturer, showed a concern for innovation, but also fitted perfectly into the context of an industry that was in its infancy. At the time, the automobile remained a leisure item for the privileged classes rather than a generalized means of transportation.

If diversification seems natural in the fashion and luxury milieu, it's because couturiers became aware very early on of the importance of their labels. The famous No. 5 fragrance, launched by Coco Chanel in 1921 and now the world's largest-selling perfume, is still one of the great successes. During the past decade, this trend has reached feverish proportions, with launches of new products that are sometimes quite removed from the legitimacy of the original products.

The couture brands, without venturing too far from their original matrix, first moved into secondary lines: Rive Gauche for Yves Saint Laurent, Ungaro's Emanuel, and Balmain's Ivoire, Versus by Versace, "Emporio Armani," D&G for Dolce & Gabbana, and so on. Among American brands, we could cite Donna Karan's DKNY. Then, during the 1990s, they developed lines of accessories (luggage, shoes, silk articles, eyewear, and so on), a sector with higher margins and rates of growth, and also an effective vector of communication.

Ungaro, after being taken over by the Ferragamo family, launched a line of accessories. Louis Vuitton began offering shoes. Loewe did, too – only to discover that you don't become a shoemaker overnight, and that to succeed with a new category of products, you have to be able to get across to the consumer a message of seriousness, competitiveness not only in terms of product quality, wealth of the offering, service at the point of sale, but above all coherence with the brand's values. In an inverse movement, accessories brands (Ferragamo, Gucci, Bally, Prada, Loewe, and others) diversified into ready-to-wear. They developed (generally through licensing) lines of eyewear, perfumes, and often watches. Bulgari, which began as a jeweler, then developed accessories and perfumes – successfully, as we all know. Jewelry and watchmaking took on importance in the mid-1990s. It now looks as if "intimate feminine apparel" will be the new frontier: Christian Dior and Burberry, for example, are developing their activity in this area strongly.

Finally, the hospitality business is attracting luxury brands. In 1987 Maruccia Mandelli (Krizia) opened its K Club hotel in Barbados. The Ferragamo family began investing in it in the mid-1990s, but without associating the brand with it. Armani, in the wake of the launch of its Armani Casa products and stores, invested in hotels in Sardinia. Bulgari has associated its brand most openly with the industry, in association with Marriott International Luxury Group to create Bulgari Hotel & Resorts. Bulgari is in charge of decoration and Marriott handles management. There is also Versace, which opened the Palazzo Versace in Brisbane in 2000, and intends to develop in this sector. After all, creating a living space bearing the brand's values should be an effective way – if well done and compatible with the brand's values – of tending towards the coveted status of "lifestyle brand."

Other types of company have also taken an interest in the potential offered by diversification. Marlboro launched a line of clothing in keeping with the mythology of the wide open spaces of the West on which it has based its advertising for decades. Coca-Cola has opened single-brand stores to sell a whole series of gift and souvenir items, from T-shirts to coffee mugs, and including such items as trays decorated with advertisements from the 1930s. Disney, Warner Brothers, and even soccer clubs (Manchester United, Juventus of Turin, Real Madrid) have successfully developed this diversification towards "gift and souvenir" products. Automotive and motorcycle brands offer clothing and accessories more or less associated with the use of their basic products. It's no surprise any more to find Ferrari and Porsche watches.

For certain brands, these incursions can be perceived as more or less anecdotal. Such is clearly the case with "brand restaurants," which have met with varying degrees of success (Lustucru, Eurosport, Nescafé in Paris). And one may also wonder what future there is in Harley-Davidson fragrances? Others, on the other hand, have succeeded over the years in developing new territories of legitimacy that have made them stronger. Time is the essential factor here.

In his determination to reduce the number of brands in his group, Edwin Artz, the former CEO of Procter & Gamble, would urge his people to "Find the way, the unique selling proposition or the reason for being, which will enable you to sell several products under the same brand."

The second key to the success of a strategy of product diversification is the brand's degree of conceptualization. The more the values expressed by the brand are conceptual in nature, the easier it becomes to "helicopter." This has led to the current vogue for the notion of "lifestyle brand," the natural culmination of the principle of diversification. The concept is a strong one. It aims at all objects and services people use every day – what they wear, eat, drink, and smoke, but also their sedentary or traveling environment – furniture, bedding, wallpaper, decorator items, draperies, floor tiles, paint, tableware, luggage, and so on. The lifestyle is carried through to the hotel people stay in. Having a single umbrella brand is a way of guaranteeing the profitability of all the investments made on the promotion of this all-encompassing identity.

/ The more the values expressed by the brand are conceptual in nature, the easier it becomes to "helicopter." /

For brands whose identity was originally founded on a lifestyle, product diversification is often easy. Such is the case of Ralph Lauren, which promotes the traditional New England "WASP" lifestyle. All the products are very well presented in the stores, in particular the flagship in New York, on Madison Avenue, where the lifestyle offered is easily perceptible. It carries not only all tableware and entertainment products, but also, for example, paint for apartments.

Other brands, whose identity is strongly linked to a product or to specific signs, have more difficulty or are more prudent. Missoni, which established its identity on a specific type of fabric and a specific chromatic palette, does not venture far from the domain of clothing and a few accessories. Besides, the most original initiatives are not necessarily crowned with success. It happens that at best, they result in a temporary gain in notoriety for the brand, but without paying back the investment they represented. Consumers are always there to remind us that the further products depart from the domain of established legitimacy, the more difficult it is to score a quick success.

Diversification, then, is an area that can be profitable if a general principle – intelligent relatedness – is adhered to. But that is not at all obvious. When the new "Tambour" watch was launched in May 2002, did any fashion writers or customers remember the watch launched (and then withdrawn) by Louis Vuitton in the early 1990s? What is the significance and the future of the Louis Vuitton nail polish launched a few months ago? Is it a prelude to the development of a complete line of cosmetics, or just a diversion?

It's important to take every precaution, to be skilled in piloting the evolution of the brand or the characteristics of the products over time, and above all, to treat time and the limits of evolution of the brand's identity with respect.

We offer for your perusal a few examples of advertising for the Pirelli brand, which has moved into shoes, watches, and clothing in recent years (see Plate 54).

Optimization of internal processes

This is an area of development that is too often neglected because it is too difficult to deal with. It's easier to design and open new points of sale than to reduce the development time of a product. Yet optimizing internal processes is what often succeeds in taking market share away from one's most direct competitors.

In the fashion sector, receiving the products from the new collections promptly means increased sales, and above all significant increases in margin. The reduction of the development time for new products (in the sense of "time to market," that is, the time that elapses between the initial concept and the availability of the product for sale) can be the decisive competitive weapon in numerous sectors: automotive, food products, telecommunications, clothing, accessories.

An effective reading of market signals, product design oriented towards surpassing the competition and satisfying the target customers, production that adheres to quality standards, and flawless logistics that supply distribution networks at the proper time, all have a positive impact on brand performance.

Brand repositioning

In fact, the term that should be used is "adjustment." By repositioning, we generally mean the "great leap," which consists, for a brand, in exchanging its existing clientele for another one with which its strategists are more comfortable. This operation is fraught with risk and is obviously not undertaken in that form in the case of a brand in its growth phase. As we will see, it is a radical remedy, more appropriate in phases of decline.

/ The reduction of the development time for new products can be the decisive competitive weapon in numerous sectors/

In our case, therefore, the action is more subtle. It aims at making the brand more attractive, without the intention of alienating the existing customers. On the contrary, the brand can try to entertain them a little, while taking advantage of the circumstances to try to draw new ones in.

When Marc Jacobs was recruited by Louis Vuitton in 1997 to develop a ready-to-wear collection, many people were skeptical. The first show got a cool reception from the press and the brand's hardcore fans. They had trouble seeing the connection with the "art of travel" or the "conservative spirit" that had come to be associated with the brand's identity. However fashion, which had seemed incompatible with the brand at first, proved to be an unexpected source of dynamism. The fashion shows and the opening of the "global stores" in Paris, London, and Tokyo extended its media coverage, and the choices made for the collections accomplished the tour de force of rejuvenating the brand's identity without alienating the existing customers. The sales volume of the luggage and leather branch of LVMH – where Louis Vuitton represents the majority – increased from US$1.837 billion in 1998 to US$4.194 billion in 2002.

This success is the result of a profound understanding of the brand's identity and of the way it is perceived. Louis Vuitton was able to find, in its historical identity, the elements of a "fashion discourse." The values of tradition associated with the luggage connote not so much conservatism as excellence and distinction – the nostalgic evocation of a time when travel was still an adventure and the privilege of a small circle of privileged individuals. "Nostalgic exoticism" is in vogue today in the fashion magazines, but style counts less than fantasy. The brand has made extensive use of this imaginative capital. In a time of mass-marketization and homogenization of leisure, where the trend is toward the search for originality and refinement, such distinctive signs have an undeniable seductive power. Louis Vuitton itself perpetuates this tradition by publishing books that are appropriate to its brand territory. In 1994, the collection *Voyager avec ...* (*Travels with ...*) offers authors' travel accounts. The *Carnets de Voyage* (*Travel Notebooks*) present the world's great cities in the form of colorful illustrations. The *Louis Vuitton City Guide – European Cities*, just launched, has the ambition of becoming a guide for high-end tourists.

What is called the "turbo effect" of fashion is also at work in the case of Coach, an American luggage brand with hand-crafted origins founded in 1941. The designer Reed Krakoff was recruited from Tommy Hilfiger in 1996 to give Coach – known until then for its sturdy leather bags – a fashion aspect, and to "invent the classics of tomorrow," in the words of its CEO, Lew Frankfurt. The brand has also introduced new categories of products (shoes, eyewear, watches) and the talent brought to bear has spelled success.

The latest example is the success the team led by Rose Marie Bravo at Burberry has been experiencing for four years now. Superb ad campaigns blending modernity and British tradition (see Plate 35), a product offering with appropriate prices, the systematic use of the brand's famous tartan – all these strategic choices have paid off. Growth rates are in three figures. Burberry's results positioned the brand ideally for the float launched in 2002.

/ The turbo effect works because it is based on an intelligent transposition of the brand's identity values – its invariants – to the stylistic grammar of fashion. /

In the three examples we've mentioned, the turbo effect works because it is based on an intelligent transposition of the brand's identity values – its invariants – to the stylistic grammar of fashion. Far from being an obstacle, the "traditional" connotations of Louis Vuitton or Burberry become in themselves the sign of a certain world of imagination that can be reinvented, extended to other products, adapted to the taste of the times. These successful adjustments show an accurate assessment of the brand's identity and of how it is perceived by the markets. Such strategies, when they meet with success, lead to substantial increases in growth rates.

Conclusion

There are lessons to be learned from all these experiences of growth.

- The less the values expressed by the brand's identity are conceptualized, the more difficult it is to "helicopter."

- Time alone lends legitimacy to brands that penetrate new product sectors, but only to the extent that these new products fit within the brand's pre-existing ethic and esthetic (or cause it to evolve while respecting a certain continuity) and where the brand shows tenacity, authenticity, and determination with its new offering.

- It is wise to approach any drastic change in brand identity with great circumspection when one is in a growth phase. When the "great leap" is made, one never knows whether the new clientele will more than compensate for the one that may be alienated. It's a risky exercise that is best applied to brands in decline.

- All growth areas have their limits. Maturity lies in wait for brands as it does for men and women.

A brand's maturity

This is the time of optimum cash flow – but also the time to wake up. Generally, the rate of growth has been in the single figures for several years; decline is approaching. In ordinary language, we would say that a "new lease of life" needs to be found, and that is what brand managers of mass-consumption products work at. They first try ceaselessly to improve the technical performance of their product, but they also introduce novelty in the form of extensions such as, say, a lavender and a lemon-lime version for a fabric softener or a room deodorizer. This diversity of course entails additional production and storage costs, and above all a business volume that is averaged downward by the lower-selling products. This sometimes makes it necessary to rework the different existing sizes to make sure that the diversity of packagings is compensated for by the performance of each of the new varieties.

The period of maturity, then, is a period of broadening and diversification of the product offering. One product may move into specialization in one application while another is launched to cover another application – but care must be taken to avoid excess. When Pampers, for example, launched its disposable diaper differentiated for girls and boys, it seemed like a very creative idea, but what did mothers think of it? Did the innovation seem as obvious to them? In any case, the experiment was quickly abandoned.

For luxury or fashion brands, managing maturity is even more delicate. This is because the possibilities of introducing extensions or complementary products are limited. Of course, a new and slightly different clientele can always be aimed at. Fendi did that by launching a line of ready-to-wear and accessories targeting young people, under the brand name Fendissimo; Charles Jourdan did the same, with its CJ Bis line of shoes, in a slightly lower price range. But the difficulty then, if the experiment works, is to find ways to bring the new clientele back towards the principal brand.

/ The period of maturity, then, is a period of broadening and diversification of the product offering. One product may move into specialization in one application while another is launched to cover another application – but care must be taken to avoid excess. /

Chanel has been facing this phenomenon of maturity for several years. The brand reacted by broadening its product offering and launching – with much effort and impressive results – first a leather goods line, then a line of watches, and finally a line of luxury jewelry. But, one is tempted to ask, what can come next? Products for men, maybe? But would the brand's essentially feminine positioning allow that?

In this maturity phase, the same possible growth vectors exist as in the preceding phase. The sole difference lies in the fact that certain brands are capable of anticipating their maturity and their decline while still experiencing strong development, while others can only resign themselves to their fate.

Decline, relaunching, and death of a brand

Decline is announced by a progressive loss of market share and decreasing sales volumes. At this point, there are only three possible developments: continuing decline over a more or less long period, then, in the end, the death of the brand or its relaunch.

Continuing decline

That is possible as long as financial resources permit. Such is the relatively common case of brands that have been trying for several years to curb a decline that is not yet under control. Examples are numerous. Bally's business volume has been decreasing since the early 1990s. Twelve top management teams and two shareholders have strenuously attempted various solutions to contain the decrease in sales. Losses have been accumulating. We can see that the "turbo effect" of fashion doesn't work for everyone. Dunhill, Kodak, Bata, and Lu are all brands that have been attempting for many years to engineer an upturn, so far without visible results.

The curve of Eastman Kodak's business volume since the early 1960s (see Figure 5.9), again close to the theoretical curve of brand life cycles, is typical of a brand in decline. In this particular case, the reasons have to do essentially with technological evolution and choices.

The death of a brand

Death comes from a lack of financial resources, erosion of demand, or as a result of a management decision. Management can condemn a brand at the time of its acquisition. When the Spanish department-store chain Corte Ingles bought out its competitor Galerias Preciados from Venezuelan financiers, it kept the best sales outlets and got rid of the others, but put all the stores under the single Corte Ingles name. Overnight, the Galerias Preciados name disappeared – as also happened in France with the Nouvelles Galeries after their purchase by Galeries Lafayette. The stronger, more evocative name won out.

This is a frequent scenario in acquisitions of companies, but the launch of a new product can also prove to be the death knell of a product of inferior quality. When Gillette launched its Mach 3 razor with three pivoting

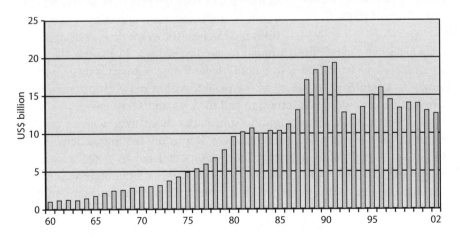

Figure 5.9 Kodak sales

flexible blades, it spelled the end of its former "top of the line" products, Gillette Contour and Trac II. Of course Gillette will have to continue manufacturing and distributing "Contour" blades for the many owners of this type of razor, but little by little they'll be won over by the new product and move to it.

To limit the economic effects of this "planned cannibalizing," at the time of the launch of a new product that might be in direct competition with another company product, it has to be ensured that the newcomer will have a greater percentage gross margin than its predecessor. Johnson Wax France has launched a new floor-care product, Solplus. It produces markedly better results straight out of the bottle than the old product, Klir, and in addition it can be used diluted for a quick application that brings back the shine on a tile floor. Klir no longer has much in the way of competitive advantages. Either the company can maintain it as an entry-level product, or else – which is after all the desired objective – Solplus will have a strong enough commercial success that Klir has no choice but to disappear.

Many companies have sacrificed brands on the altar of their expansion or their survival. We've already mentioned the process of drastic reduction Procter & Gamble has undertaken. The brand La Roche Aux Fées, created in 1926 in France, disappeared in 1988 when the owner company merged with Chambourcy. The latter, created in 1948, was closed out in 1996 by Nestlé.

/ Many companies have sacrificed brands on the altar of their expansion or their survival. These decisions, motivated by economic interests, are not without risks. /

These decisions, motivated by economic interests, are not without risks. In particular in the case of prestige products, whose added value is high and very apparent – automobiles or watches, for example – to disappoint loyal customers can expose a brand to harsh penalties. In France, the failure of the move from Simca to Talbot by the Peugeot group is an example. Simca represented a brand in its own right, with a network of energetic, efficient dealers who were proud to sell the cars and serve customers who were devoted to the Simca brand. Simca was more than a name on the hoods of cars; it was a federated universe. Replacing the Simca name with Talbot on models after a certain date was bound not to make everyone happy. In particular, what of customers who had just bought new Simcas, and were happy to drive the cars and project themselves into the brand's values? The least that might have been done – and wasn't – would have been to let buyers have the dealer exchange the brand names on the hood, steering wheel, and trunk lid, in the guarantee booklet and manuals of their model, and so on. Should that have been done for all owners of Simcas, even ten-year-old models? Probably; and again, it probably wouldn't have been enough.

The directors of Peugeot thought it would be enough to repaint the dealerships and launch billboard campaigns for consumers to accept the transition. But consumers don't react rationally. They subscribe to the values of a brand and make them their own. For example, each time a driver is in a line of cars behind a car the same model as his own, or the same make, he or she experiences a slight feeling of satisfaction. How will drivers react when they lose this type of reference point?

While companies sometimes sacrifice their brand, it happens, conversely, that its notoriety survives indefinitely. Makes like Panhard or Hispano-Suiza are still alive in the imagination of several generations, although the plants that produced the cars have long since disappeared. Such resilience, in the case of most prestigious brands, can also lead to their resurrection (as, for example, with Westinghouse). There is the case of the famous Orient Express, now a registered brand, the property of the American group of the same name; or Solex motorbikes, now produced under license since 2000 following an agreement between the brand's owner, Magneti Marelli, and the manufacturer Impex Hungaria. These examples show how the concept of the brand is also associated with ideal values, different from the economic realities faced by companies in their day-to-day operation.

The service sector is not exempt from resounding disappearances. The case of Arthur Andersen will be mentioned at the end of this chapter. In November 2002 the bank UBS announced the disappearance of the prestigious financial names Warburg and Paine Webber. Their activities will be continued under the parent company's name, UBS.

Relaunching

The last means for a brand to achieve growth is what we call the "great leap." Up to now, few brands have succeeded in making it. It generally means a repositioning of the brand that implies a programmed change of clientele. It applies to companies in decline that have already undergone heavy restructuring and improvement of their internal processes without managing to reverse the trend.

The decline of a brand is always visible in an erosion of its relevance to consumers. The brand and its products are no longer interesting; or rather, they are less interesting than the competitors'. The evolution of the brand's identity which results from a successful relaunching plan is a synthesis of the brand's response to this problem.

One of the most stunning cases of relaunching is surely Gucci. The business volume of Gucci N.V. went from US$199 million in 1992 to US$2.544 billion in 2002. The Gucci products division, which was the only one existing in 1992, made it possible to purchase other brands, and itself achieved a peak of sales in 2000 of US$1.494 billion. After the preparatory work done by Maurizio Gucci and Dawn Mello, the team of Tom Ford, Creative Director, and Domenico de Sole, CEO, conducted the largest operation of creation of wealth in a minimum amount of time starting with a brand in the fashion sector.

This is an exceptional case that can probably never happen again. The brand of today bears little resemblance to what it was when Tom Ford took over as Creative Director in 1992. His action transformed Gucci's identity. The brand's traditional values – quality craftsmanship, the Italian jet set of the Cinecittà years – as they were perceived before his arrival were replaced by the universe of the Hollywood "swingles." Seduction is now central in all the brand's discourse, and it can be said that the new designer has truly made it his own. The clientele, entirely renewed, has more than compensated for the one that was disappearing in the late 1980s.

Puma is another example of a successful relaunch. After seven years of losses, the organization called on Jochen Zeitz to lead it. During the initial years, his action concentrated on a return to profitability by improving internal processes (in particular rationalization of the production facilities). In 1998 the brand repositioned itself from the playing field to the street. Marketing expenditure doubled. Sales followed suit, doubling between 1998 and 2001, while Nike's results were stagnating and Adidas's grew by only 20 percent. "We want to make Puma the most desirable brand for young people, representative of their lifestyle," said Jochen Zeitz to the French daily *Le Monde* in February 2001.

/ Brand relaunches are always difficult exercises. Growth has natural limits, and it seems doubtful that a successful brand can be relaunched indefinitely. /

Consolidated sales went from €279 million in 1997 to €910 million in 2002 (a growth of 52 percent in 2002 alone) and the share price went from €18.61 Euros on December 31, 1997 to €65.03 on December 31, 2002.

Brand relaunches are always difficult exercises. Growth has natural limits, and it seems doubtful that a successful brand can be relaunched indefinitely. Gucci understands that and is now developing as a multibrand group. In the past two years, it has acquired Balenciaga, Sergio Rossi, Bottega Veneta, Boucheron, Alexander McQueen, Stella McCartney, and Yves Saint Laurent.

Global brands, local brands

The opposition between the local and global dimensions of brands is most visible in the urban milieu. Brands which naturally follow their markets contribute to this breakdown of cities into heterogeneous segments. The global brands occupy the most prestigious shopping streets; minor and local brands are in the adjacent streets, the periphery, and the malls.

Conditions and advantages of a global strategy

We have seen the advantages of geographic extension as a principal area of growth: amortization of the costs of managing the brand's identity (creation, research, and communication), growth of reputation, implementation of volume strategies (economies of scale) which are still prevalent in many industries. The degree of possible globalization depends on the degree of universality inherent in the brand's offerings, but also on its ability to offer its products or services everywhere at competitive prices.

The chances of globalization of a brand as a function of the potential for universalization of its identity could be diagrammed as shown in Figure 5.10.

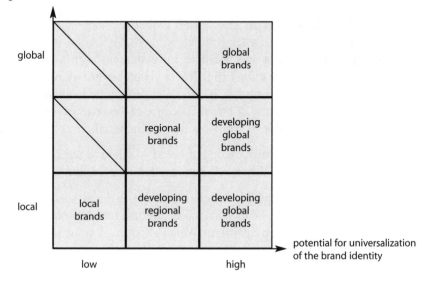

Figure 5.10 Strategies of geographical extension, as a function of the potential for universalization of the brand identity

We can see that, except for certain constraints that prevent the export of a product, the essential ingredient of successful globalization remains the potential for universalization of the brand's identity. There's no point in hoping to locate abroad successfully if the values expressed by your brand don't interest the Japanese, the French, or the Chinese.

/ The essential ingredient of successful globalization remains the potential for universalization of the brand's identity. /

That doesn't mean you have to produce Model T Fords for the whole world. As we've seen, perceptions of a brand in different markets generally form a heterogeneous ensemble. An intelligent global approach will try to fit into local markets while maintaining, as much as possible, the invariants that make up the brand's identity.

A truly global product is rarer than it might seem. Aside from the financial services, aeronautics, consumer electronics, perfumery, and perhaps fashion sectors, there are few where global strategies are conducted, where products and communication are both identical on all markets. The major global brands aim at least for regional integration around the three major zones: the United States, Europe–Middle East–Africa, and Asia.

Possibilities for local strategy

What are the types of activity that cannot globalize?

- Activities linked to a specific place: a restaurant with a view of the Golden Gate Bridge or the Eiffel Tower, a hotel overlooking the Monte Cervino or Mount Rushmore. In this category can be included all products, like cement, that won't travel because of the costs of transport and the nearly universal availability of the raw materials.

- Basic products like milk, rice, and bread – although the recent vogue for "organic" and quality foods has resulted in a few timid initiatives.

- Brands with local appeal, which are tied to a local specificity very often related to taste – dark-tobacco cigarettes, for example (Gauloises in France, Ducados in Spain), or Welch's Concord grape juice.

Between brands with local appeal and the "major globals," there is an entire range of aspirants at various stages of their evolution towards the status of global brand. All brands begin as local ones. If you can't be competitive in your own territory, what will you be able to do in the rest of the world? This argument is surely the best proof that there is such a thing as local strategies for success.

Once competitiveness has been achieved on the local market, provided the brand doesn't fall into the categories we have mentioned where export is impossible, global development then requires only the presence of entrepreneurs and capital ready to mobilize based on projected returns, depending on the risks inherent in the project. The difficulty lies in evaluating the potential for universality of the brand's identity.

/ All brands begin as local ones. If you can't be competitive in your own territory, what will you be able to do in the rest of the world? /

Local cultural specificities are often the guarantee of clear differentiation from competitors in the sector, and a determining factor of success. Exoticism works in all directions. Any culture with a strong identity is a candidate for offering products with universal appeal. And directors of local or regional brands have a more profound knowledge of the sensibilities of local consumers. The success of Korean films, television, and songs in the past few years is a good illustration of how a successful regional strategy can be put in place without giving up the specificities of a local culture.

For ten years or so, the musical genre hip-hop, which originated in African-American ghettos, has dominated Korean pop. It was introduced by Koreans born in the United States. The graft was accompanied by adaptation of the themes. The favorite themes of American hip-hop (as sung by Eminem or Puff Daddy, for example) are not to be found in its Korean equivalent. Sex, guns, money, and drugs are absent; themes like questioning the authority of parents or teachers and revolt against the strictures of traditional Korean society are substituted. As a result the music finds regional echoes with young people in Southeast Asia, who lean towards rebellion, but not to the point where they identify with American "gangsta rap." Today, in Korea, sales of music by such local groups represent 70 percent of total sales.

The same phenomenon is at work for television and film. The shows broadcast are relatively conservative and borrow from Confucian values. Families made up of three generations are shown living under the same roof. The Chinese market is the principal importer, because of cultural similarities and the quality of the productions. At the box office, the Korean film industry achieved audience ratings of 50 percent in 2000.

One result of this affirmation of a cultural specificity is that Seoul is becoming a fashionable destination for regional tourism. That effect was greatly increased by the 2002 Soccer World Cup held in Korea and Japan, with the surprise of the Korean team reaching the semi-finals.

The vulnerability of global brands

Any strategy of globalization represents both a strength and a weakness for a brand, in a paradox Naomi Klein does a good job of pointing out. The more brands are globalized, the more vulnerable they are to consumer actions. As their internationalization progresses, the worldwide giants prove to be increasingly sensitive to whatever can affect the way in which their identity is perceived. The combination of immediate global dissemination of information, and a rigid production and logistical apparatus that handles considerable volumes of business, makes them particularly vulnerable to consumers' reactions.

The example of Coca-Cola "Classic," which was reintroduced less than three months after the launch of the new formula, and the discovery of traces of benzene that threatened Perrier are well known. The sweatshop scandal that threatened producers of sporting goods like Nike and Adidas is well documented in *No Logo*. And very recently, the implosion of Arthur Andersen is a good illustration of the vulnerability of global brands.

Among the "Big Five," Arthur Andersen was the auditing firm that was best integrated internationally, in both the coordination of its human resources and its methodological expertise, deployed in 80 countries. In an extremely fragmented sector, it had succeeded in creating a model company and an authentically global brand. But that very strength is what might well result in its disintegration. The scandal of the bankruptcy of the American energy giant Enron, for which Arthur Andersen was auditor, landed the American directors in court in late 2001, accused of having destroyed sensitive documents. The result was an immediate disaffection among the firm's clientele, which was not limited to the United States.

As this is being written, most local branches have negotiated mergers with competitors to avoid professional fallout. The Arthur Andersen brand identity has been marred to the very core of its being: the confidence of consumers, its ability to maintain the same professional standards of independence and professionalism. If the brand survives in some regional offices, it will be insignificant compared with what it once was.

6 | The brand audit

> The influence of theoretical principles upon real life is produced more through criticism than through doctrime, for as criticism is an application of abstract truth to real events, therefore it not only brings truth of this description nearer to life, but also accustoms the understanding more to such truths by the constant repetition of their application.
>
> (Clausewitz, *On War*)[1]

We have looked in turn at the characteristics of brand identities and the dynamics of their life cycle. This has led to our focusing on various aspects of the relationship between the brand and the consumer, and on the need for managers to take it into account. Now can we assemble all these considerations into a synthetic and coherent methodology, one that can increase the probabilities of performance and that can be applied to any brand, regardless of business sector?

Such a "universal formula" remains to be constructed, and of course there will always be counter-examples which will limit its scope. Nevertheless there do exist generalist approaches, used more and more frequently by brand managers, with notable success. In this chapter we concentrate on describing, in its broad outlines, a method of this type, aimed at ferreting out examples of faulty brand management that can prevent the brand from leveraging all the possible factors of success. It is drawn from experience both of us have gained when in the position, at several points in our respective careers, of needing to verify a brand's expressed and potential strength. This required – often in an emergency situation – undertaking an audit of the brand in order to bring out the characteristics of a brand management that is adapted to the particular circumstances.

---

1 Clausewitz, *On War*, ch. 5, trans. Graham (1873).

The pragmatic aspect of this approach must be underlined. Faced with the obligation of getting results, its theoretical value counts for less than its concrete usefulness. Our point of view remains that of practitioners, not theoreticians. In any case, there is no miracle method. As we have had occasion to say elsewhere, formalization makes for a clearer picture and a more rational approach to the factors at stake. It is a major advantage for a manager. But it is no substitute for creativity, both individual and collective; that is, in the final analysis, the real foundation of any brand's strength.

/ Any specific methodology must focus on the coherence, effectiveness, and relevance of the communication of the brand's identity. /

Our basic idea is that any specific methodology must focus on the coherence, effectiveness, and relevance of the communication of the brand's identity. To structure our approach, we will introduce an initial tool: the chain of communication.

The chain of communication

This simplified representation is aimed at showing the path the brand's message takes, from its source (its identity) to its logical culmination (the act of purchase). The principle is simple: the brand expresses its identity through varied manifestations – its products, its communication, the behavior of the people who work in the company's name, both inside and outside the company. These manifestations are perceived variably by the various market segments, and the perceptions created in consumers result in a certain number of acts of purchase which, once consolidated, make up the sales volume.

The diagram (Figure 6.1) comprises four states and three transitions from one state to another. Throughout the process, numerous and complex phenomena take place. To highlight them, we will discuss the seven constituent links in the chain of communication one after the other.

For the brand manager, each transition from one state to another calls for controls that can only be made after the fact, once the transition has been made. That is why our practical presentation of the chain differs slightly from its theoretical description. We examine, one after the other, the brand's identity; its manifestations; the need for consistency and coherence (which guarantees the transition from the identity to the manifestations);

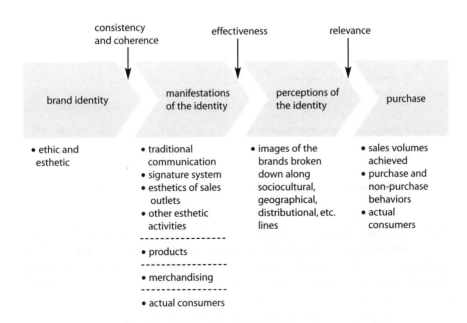

Figure 6.1 The chain of communication: the three critical transitions

consumers' perceptions of the brand's identity; the need for effectiveness (which guarantees the transition from the brand's manifestations to its perceptions); the act of purchase; and finally, the need for relevance (which guarantees the transition from perception to purchase).

The brand's identity

We have already defined brand identity. Note that in practice, any company that has made a serious study of a brand's identity has a whole series of documents in its possession with which to examine it to varying degrees, from the most superficial to the most detailed and in-depth. These documents are not limited to a simple description of the brand's ethical and esthetic invariants, such as can be obtained using the tools we have described previously – the hinge, the semiotic square, or the narrative schema. Those are points of departure for collective reflection. Generally, the project of defining an identity closely involves the principal directors, and then moves on to a broad-ranging internal discussion. All the results are then added to, and enrich, the basic data.

To give an example, Figure 6.2 is a document Taurus used to disseminate its brand identity internally. Beyond the content specific to the brand,

A brand with a history...not a traditional brand

A luxury house...not a fashion brand

A luminous, classical esthetic..not baroque and somber

A brand rooted in its country of origin..not folkloric

A mark associated with refinement...............................not meaningless sophistication

Rare products....................................but not inaccessible and outrageously expensive

Figure 6.2 Taurus: brand identity: what it is and what it isn't

note the format used here. The most technical and semiological concepts have been converted into simple, concrete recommendations. The result is a document that is much more accessible, one that can be distributed broadly, throughout the company, because it's important that everyone agree on the final assessment. This dimension of internal federation is an essential condition for the emergence of a brand identity.

The manifestations of the identity

The ethics and esthetics of the brand's identity form the original framework within which all the creators and communicators working on the brand, whether dedicated to products, advertising, or any other aspect, must create, innovate, invent, and develop. It is on this framework, therefore, that the manifestations of the brand's identity will be based.

We have seen how the brand identity affects all aspects of a company's strategy, to varying degrees. Staying within this perspective, we can classify the manifestations of brand identity into four distinct categories.

First category: the general esthetic

This covers the activities that should normally be under the direct control of the person in charge of the brand's identity and don't have to do with the products:

- Traditional communication: advertising, press relations, organization of events.

- The signature system (or the brand's graphical identity): logo, store signs, product labeling and packaging, letterheads, and so on.

- The "esthetic" activities related to points of sale: the architectural concept of the stores and showrooms, display windows, interior displays, uniforms worn by sales personnel, methods and style of sale.

- Other "esthetic" activities: architecture of the offices, tone and style used in all interfaces with the exterior (receptionists, hostesses, managers, directors, the president's sartorial style, etc.).

When CEO Lou Gerstner arrived at IBM, his decision to wear sky-blue shirts was a real revolution in a company where the norm had long been white shirts. This minimal change had a major impact on the perception of the brand by all the players in the market, and above all the employees.

For all these manifestations of an esthetic nature – in the broad sense of the term – there should be "briefs" prepared by the person in charge of managing brand identity, which makes the transition easier. These documents are written for the creative people, in their language. Figures 6.3 and 6.4 gives a few examples taken from the Taurus case, which stemmed directly from the work done on defining identity.

Second category: products

This category concerns all the esthetic and tangible aspects of the products: colors, materials, shapes, cut, style, quality, durability, performance, and so on. The product remains the most important medium for communicating the brand's identity. It's clear that style, applied to products, is an essential

---

1. Illustrate a lifestyle

2. Suggest the characteristics of that lifestyle by stressing individual values:
    - freedom, autonomy, personal projects (but not rebellion, anticonformism, adolescence)
    - breaking with the daily routine, intense emotions
    - generosity, frankness
    - refinement, assumed sensuality
    - combining values of energy and refinement, urban life and the outdoors

3. Snapshots or visuals that suggest movement and dynamism in a classical context
    Invent a neoclassicism that comprises modernity, innovation, and surprise, without losing sight of the best of tradition

4. Bring out the link between technological innovation and refinement in the product

5. Suggest the richness and coherence of the brand universe without giving the impression of a "panoply of signs" or a label brand

Figure 6.3 Taurus: advertising brief

1. Place less importance on the store and more on the product offering. Use verticality, the expression of energy and vitality.

2. As for the products, take particular care with combinations of materials to suggest refinement, a taste for the rare and the beautiful. Use of glass, wood, and steel.

3. Define traffic patterns and store fittings that encourage handling and touching the products.

4. Design furnishings that transmit identity:
    • lamp
    • armchair, table
    • lectern for presentation of historic products
    • framing for documents related to the history of the brands (old advertisements, posters, photos with celebrities etc.).

5. Stress light and transparence. No closed display windows. The store interior has to be visible from the street.

Figure 6.4 Taurus: preliminary brief for a new store architectural concept

component of identity. And everyone knows that the worst thing that can happen to a brand is for it to disappoint its customers where the quality or performance of its product are concerned! The perception of the brand's identity is immediately affected.

/ The product remains the most important medium for communicating the brand's identity. /

This means that both expectations and their implementation must be managed. For example, Volvo products must clearly express the brand's fundamental value, safety; Hermès products, the ultimate in quality and refinement; Audi, a combination of design and performance.

Product design, development, and production are also dealt with in initial briefs. Figure 6.5 is an example using Taurus. Again, note the positioning of this type of document: vague generalities ("elegance," "conviviality") are eliminated, but the concrete recommendations do not go so far as to hamper the work of the designers. For example, no particular color or shape is imposed. An accurate perception of the brand's invariants allows a strict framework to be drawn, within which the designer's creativity is free to express itself.

/ An accurate perception of the brand's invariants allows a strict framework to be drawn, within which the designer's creativity is free to express itself. /

Such creative briefs endure beyond seasonal changes. They don't replace the more detailed documents – drawn up in collaboration with the designers – that affect development for each season.

1. Assertion of luxury status: work more on design than on fashion effect. Focus on accessories and gift items.

2. Design details that identify products (buckles, buttons, stitching, chains).

3. Extend the logo through a whole series of products. Invent a "logomania" fabric.

4. Define several chromatic ranges inspired by nature in light shades for application to scarves and neckties.

5. Extend iconic products into ranges of colors, materials and a "logomania" fabric.

6. Redefine standards of quality for gilding to improve the quality. Make customers aware of finish.

7. Seek to innovate with leather in general, stressing tactile qualities (suppleness, softness etc.) and visual ones (pleats, waves, etc.) and creating new associations of materials.

8. Evoke active, even athletic lifestyles.

9. Intensify eforts to find new materials to promote a more modern image.

Figure 6.5 Taurus: brief for product development

Third category: merchandising

This category essentially covers defining the structure of the product offering, defining prices, and defining the stocking policy and the inventory of the sales outlets. The fundamental decision is to define what product the brand will offer, where, to which customers, at what price, and at what time. This is a question of basic strategy and of merchandising in its literal sense (what the "merchants" decide).

These decisions have predominant importance for the brand's positioning, and therefore for the way in which its identity will be perceived. Mercedes-Benz's decision to develop the Class A or the Smart Car had a considerable impact on the German brand's identity.

Fourth category: the consumer

This is a particular category of manifestations as it is the only one of the four which is not under direct management control. However it is not the least important. The people seen wearing or using the brand's products – and we should extend it to all the people who are talking about the brand – are part of the issuance processes building the market perceptions of the brand.

In any strategy worthy of the name, an attempt is made to define the ideal consumers to whom the brand aims to sell its products – not only because creation, communication, and distribution are entirely oriented towards these target customers, but also because the product's being worn, driven, or used by a certain type of person contributes strongly to the perception of the brand's identity. Lacoste saw the way this works when its shirts and sweat-suits suddenly became wildly popular among inner-city youth.

This reality remains valid even if the "mood marketing" we mentioned earlier is used. If the market is segmented by mood, you have to know what moods you are aiming at. The target consumer can be seen as a "potential manifestation of the brand" until its real manifestation – the actual customer – is revealed via the audits and regular controls all companies conduct.

The consistency and coherence transition

This transition corresponds to the first critical point where the brand's success is at stake. Any activity that influences the perception of the brand's identity – any manifestation of the brand – must contribute to strengthening that identity, and therefore be consistent with it. If this first condition is fulfilled, all these manifestations should be consistent with each other. Nevertheless, the transition from identity represents such a creative leap, and the activities are so diverse, that it becomes necessary to ensure that consistency.

/ Any activity that influences the perception of the brand's identity – any manifestation of the brand – must contribute to strengthening that identity, and therefore be consistent with it. /

High-quality champagnes – Dom Pérignon or Krüg, for example – are not distributed in supermarkets, even though this distribution channel sells the highest volume of this type of product. They are found only in specialized stores – wine stores and gourmet groceries. Customers who buy these products would be shocked to find them on the shelves at Wal-Mart. This example illustrates the necessary consistency between price, quality, and positioning of the product and its sales outlets.

At this stage, before having conducted the necessary studies on actual customers, the target customer is used (as the potential manifestation of identity) to verify the consistency of this profile with the rest of the manifestations. It is also important to make sure that all the components of the strategy are compatible and in phase with the brand's identity. It would make no sense to take Hermès as a competitor of reference if you produce your leather bags in Asia or distribute them in supermarkets. Yet such is the fate that awaited Louis Vuitton and Hermès in Japan, in spite of their

efforts. Since 2001 the French Carrefour chain has been offering their products in its Japanese stores. It acquires them from Japanese wholesalers, or
else probably through parallel-market buyers like one sees in Europe near
brand stores, asking passers-by to buy their products instead.

This controversy is a major one when you realize that in Europe,
luxury brands have requested and won from the courts the opportunity to
choose their retailers in order to prevent their products from appearing on
supermarket shelves. The case is worth watching.

Perceptions of identity

Above all, we must not expect potential customers, once in contact with the
manifestations of the brand, to become conscious of its identity in the same
terms that led to its development. Few consumers carry analysis beyond the
concrete aspects of the product, or the emotions (and the causes of these
emotions) aroused by such and such a purchase experience.

As we've already said, we must not expect a monolithic perception of
the brand. Perceptions vary depending on
culture, on each customer's personality, on the   / Few consumers carry
competitors present, on the duration of the   analysis beyond the
brand's presence, and so on. The difficulty is   concrete aspects of
in evaluating the compatibility of these   the product, or the
differences with the brand's development   emotions (and the
strategies.   causes of these
There are several approaches to the analysis   emotions) aroused by
of consumer behavior, and it is possible to focus   such and such a
on this notion of perception more clearly. One   purchase experience. /
possibility is to use a model called the "hierar-
chy of effects," which suggests how, based on the reception of messages, the
consumer first becomes conscious of the existence of a brand, then defines an
attitude towards it, then changes that attitude into a preference, and finally
moves from preference to actual purchase. We will return to this question in
Chapter 7.

The effectiveness transition

This transition corresponds to a second critical point in the development of
a brand. Do all of the manifestations of the brand reach the consumers they
target? And do these consumers perceive them in a way that corresponds,

in a broad way at least, to the brand's identity? These are the two types of effectiveness that are expected of any communication effort. To use a ballistic metaphor, we might use the terms precision (in aiming at the target) and impact (the effects caused by the round).

After it has been verified that effectiveness with target consumers is satisfactory, the actual coherence of the brand's manifestations can also be tested authentically through their perception.

The act of purchase

This time the actual consumer is analyzed in order to get the best possible understanding of the mechanisms that led her or him to make a purchase. Of course, the market is always partly shrouded in mystery, and everybody is quick to come up with explanations of a success after the fact. Still, understanding past successes is essential in explaining the functioning – and the dysfunctions – of the chain of communication.

/ Communication can be completely successful – can succeed in being fully perceived and understood by the consumer – and not set off a sufficient number of acts of purchase. /

Differences between the target consumer and the actual consumer need to be analyzed, if they exist.

Survey techniques can also be used to isolate a crucial aspect of the chain of communication: non-purchase by the target clients. This information is often more useful than what is known about actual purchasers, because it can be used to isolate major dysfunctions in the chain of communication.

The relevance transition

Communication can be completely successful – can succeed in being fully perceived and understood by the consumer – and not set off a sufficient number of acts of purchase. The chain of communication can function in a fluid way up to the stage of perception. The message can faithfully reflect the brand's identity and make the product highly desirable – but the consumer's intentions to purchase never become concrete.[2]

---

2 In the interest of simplification, we have left out an intermediate transition in the chain of communication, between perception and the act of purchase: desirability. We deal with the concepts of desirability and accessibility as one.

This can be because distribution is insufficient, or because poor logistics result in repeated out-of-stock situations, or because prices are out of the affordable range. Another situation, much more difficult to manage, can be encountered: the brand has less relevance than its competitors. Its identity gets across well to the consumers, but it is based on values that interest them less than others.

Obstacles to the full realization of the brand's potential fall into several categories:

- merchandising problems: the structure of the offering, in terms of number of groups of products at the sales outlets, price, and margin policies

- problems of operational execution, which stem from difficulties at the level of production, logistics, or organization

- finally, problems related to the brand's identity being out of phase with the mood of the market – or, at least, having become less desirable than that of its closest competitors.

The brand audit

The methodology we recommend takes three areas into consideration:

- The chain of communication, which we have just described. By underlining the difficulties inherent in the transition from one phase to another, from brand identity to the act of purchase, it presupposes the analysis of the consistency, coherence, effectiveness, and relevance of the communication.

- The competitive context in which the chain of communication operates. The brand is obviously in competition, not only with its competitors of reference (the ones that were used as an aid in seeking differentiation of the brand's identity), but also with the "noise pollution" of all the brands that are constantly vying for the consumer's attention. As diagrammed in Figure 6.6, this media bombardment contributes to creating a perception of the brand in the consumer, even if it is sometimes fragile and elusive.

  We have insisted on the comparative and competitive dimension of the concept of brand: there can be no identity without differentiation. It follows that there can be no identity without the elements of comparison provided by the competitors of reference. Bally, for example, in its re-launching effort, defined Louis Vuitton, Gucci, Ferragamo, and Prada as its competitors of reference.

/ The brand is obviously in competition, not only with its competitors of reference (the ones that were used as an aid in seeking differentiation of the brand's identity), but also with the "noise pollution" of all the brands that are constantly vying for the consumer's attention. /

■ Finally, the consumer. All communication is built on hypotheses of perception and reaction on the part of consumers. In the context of an audit, these hypotheses need to be verified.

The methodology of the brand audit, as presented in the diagram below, is built around three phases:

■ First, the "snapshot" of the current state of the chain of communication, through the four states that make it up. This is the longest and most costly stage of the audit.

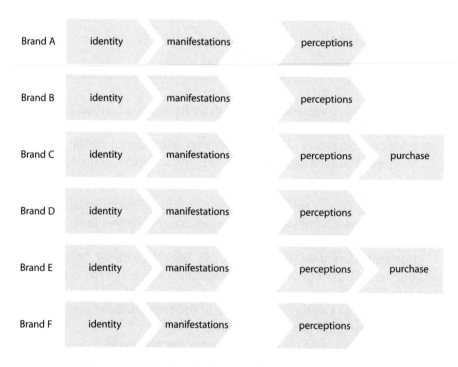

Figure 6.6 Chains of communication: the competition for consumers' attention

It calls on market research techniques and requires the absorption of a large quantity of data, which are not always easily accessible. It includes three types of analysis, focused respectively on the company, the consumers, and the competitors.

■ Second, the verification of what we have called the transitions from one state to another in the chain of communication.

■ Finally, recommendations for change, which are broken down into three functional categories: identity management, merchandising, and operational and organizational processes.

We will look at all the phases and transitions described in the audit methodology (the rectangles and diamonds in Figure 6.7).

Observation of points of sale

All brand audits begin with several days of observation of what is happening at the brand's points of sale, and also at those of its competitors

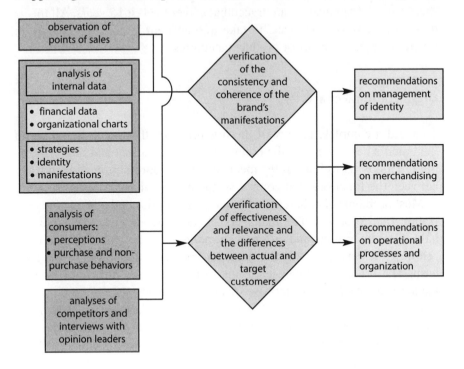

Figure 6.7 Brand audit methodology

of reference. The purpose is to form a personal opinion of the brand's degree of differentiation, of the products, the behavior and type of customers, and finally the environment and atmosphere of the points of sale. This experience is fundamental, and we cannot stress strongly enough the importance of this initial observation, especially before any close contact is made with the personnel of the brand being audited. After all, the points of sale are the place where the brand's destiny is being decided.

Financial and management data

These are the basic data needed to locate the brand in its life cycle and measure its strength for the different product categories, distribution channels, and geographic zones. This study must be conducted in terms of volume and of margin.

The deliverables comprise a formalization of the brand's life cycle: business volume (corrected for retail value), expenditures on communication, number of points of sale, operational margin, operational cash flow, and share value (if applicable) are traced back over the last 15 years. All this is done in a homogeneous way, to take into account brands that operate in several market segments or product categories.

Organizational charts

To avoid a complete review of the organization, the focus should be on the brand's nerve centers: the communication, creation, and merchandising functions, as well as all the mechanisms of coordination and arbitrage between the functions that control all the brand's manifestations.

Most problems of coherence of brand identity arise at the level of organization (and process). The managers of the different functions involved have different training and different specialties. The merchandiser wants to sell now; however, the identity manager cultivates the brand for the long term. The production manager wants to reduce costs; the brand identity manager always looks to improve quality, and so on.

It frequently happens that the product design function is dissociated from the traditional communication function, and that the latter is dissociated from the function of development of the architectural concept of the points of sale. Yet all three come under the heading of "esthetic" management of the brand. The ultimate director of the brand's identity, above all in the luxury sectors or for retail stores, is often the CEO, because he or she is the only one who can settle all conflicts.

The techniques used are simple interviews with the managers concerned and study of the documents supplied by Human Resources. The deliverables are:

/ It frequently happens that the product design function is dissociated from the traditional communication function, and that the latter is dissociated from the function of development of the architectural concept of the points of sale. /

- organizational charts of the first two levels of the structure

- complete organizational charts of the creation, communication, and merchandising functions

- a description of the mechanisms of coordination between the managers of the brand's different manifestations.

Strategies and brand identity

The aim here is to compare the version of the brand's identity as it is known and used by the managers with the official version, if such a version exists. Very often, different vocabularies are found from one company to another, and even within the same company ("brand image," "image characteristics," "brand philosophy," "brand essence," "genetic code," and so on). Often there is a confusion between the notion of image and that of identity.

The brand auditor, if he or she has access to no existing formalization of the identity, will have to synthesize the opinions of the principal managers. The audit can reveal an identity that is vague, confused, and poorly defined. If the need to launch a more in-depth study of a semiotic nature is felt, it cannot be done in the context of the audit. It will take the form of a recommendation.

/ The degree of formalization of the brand's identity in terms of ethic and esthetic is always an indication of the quality of the management of its communication. /

The degree of formalization of the brand's identity in terms of ethic and esthetic is always an indication of the quality of the management of its communication.

Since the brand's identity is a "subset" of overall strategy, care should be taken to also study the documents that formalize the company's strategies, in terms of target consumers, communication, structure of the product offering, distribution, production, and culture, to ascertain whether there is a strong coherence between them and the brand's identity.

The techniques used are the classic interviews with the principal managers and the study of the existing documents. The deliverables are:

- The brand's identity in terms of ethic and of esthetic, in its official form (if the brand has produced such a document), or failing that, in the form of a synthesis compiled by the auditor. At this stage, it is ascertained whether the identity as expressed has the necessary competitive characteristics, such as differentiation from the competitors of reference, and constancy or continuity of a brand ethic and esthetic over time.

- A synthesis of the expression of the brand's identity as understood by the managers. Particular attention will be paid to analyzing the degree of homogeneity of the managers' comprehension of the identity, and any areas where they are out of phase with each other or with the official version.

- The company's strategies. Possible incompatibilities will be pointed up between strategies and identity. For example, is the presence of Chanel perfumes in department stores like JC Penney compatible with the brand's luxury positioning?

Manifestations of the brand's identity

The aim is to take a "snapshot" of all these manifestations so as to then be able to focus on the consistency of these manifestations with the identity, and on the coherence of the manifestations among themselves. Depending on the type of industry, the following material will be gathered for the four categories of manifestations we have identified.

For the first category (the general esthetic), under the direct control of the person in charge of management of the identity:

- All the briefs (if they exist). Evaluate the level of detail, the coherence of the creative directions, and the degree of consistency with the identity. These briefs are especially important because they are the official relay between the identity and its manifestations. Generally, they are not sufficiently formalized.

- All the audiovisual material relative to traditional communication – for example, the six or eight latest advertising campaigns, the media plans, videocassettes of events (product launches, galas, fashion shows, and so on).

- A sampling of all the elements of the signature system.

- If applicable, the plans for the architectural concept and photographs (interior and exterior) of the points of sale.

- Photographs of the most recent window-display concepts.

- The training manuals for the sales personnel and the internal merchandising rules.

For the second category (products):

- All the products (or photographs of them) offered over the past two years. The best sellers and worst sellers should be identified by geographical region, by distribution channel, and so on. This is one of most significant processes, and also one of the easiest to carry out.

For the third category (merchandising):

- Programs for product launches, and plans for the structure of the product offering with lists of consumer prices.

For the fourth category (the consumer):

- The definition of the target consumers, which should be part of the strategies.

Observations of the behavior and appearance of all the persons who interface between the company and the outside world (from the receptionist up to the CEO, and including the sales personnel) should be organized. Deliverables are:

- Formalization (if non-existent) of all the briefs for the first category of manifestations.

- Formalization of the structure of the product offering (development plan for automotive industry, launch plans for detergents, collection plans for accessories and ready-to-wear), viewed as the initiating document of the brand's merchandising.

■ An assemblage of the brand's entire "iconographic corpus" and all the material collected.

■ A synthesis of the degree of familiarity with the constituent elements of identity on the part of the various people in charge of the brand's manifestations, and of their strategies.

Verification of consistency and coherence

The work on consistency and coherence begins with the hypothesis that the more the manifestations tend to send a "compact" message, the greater its chances are of being perceived. Using the documents and conclusions assembled during the preceding activities, each of the manifestations is compared with its objectives, or directly with the documents that express the brand's identity. Generally, the most flagrant "inconsistencies" (manifestations that blatantly contradict the values or the esthetic the brand wants to promote) quickly come to light.

This verification is coupled with an evaluation of the coherence of the manifestations among themselves. Of course, if the verifications point up a high degree of consistency with the brand identity, the coherence of the manifestations among themselves should be automatic. However the evaluation of the consistency of the manifestations with the identity is an area where personal opinions and intuitions can take precedence. So it's a good idea to maintain the coherence criterion as an additional control.

All the material assembled under the "deliverables" category for the brand's manifestations is studied to measure the coherence of all these elements among themselves. The communicative content of each object, each advertisement, and each store is a specific experience in itself. This experience carries within it numerous messages which generate emotions of varying intensity. The delicate process of evaluating coherence is of the same nature as evaluation of consistency with identity, but in a much broader field.

/ At the optimal stage, each manifestation is both a relevant and an effective expression of the brand identity, and at the same time reinforces the impact of the other manifestations. /

Absence of incoherence is the easiest stage to measure; it is a positive aspect in itself. At the optimal stage, each manifestation is both a relevant and an effective expression of the brand identity, and at the same time reinforces the impact of the other manifestations.

The volume of work an analysis of this type requires can be staggering. Therefore it's better to give priority to working on the manifestations that have the greatest impact: products, traditional communication, and points of sale, if applicable.

The scale of importance of the brand's manifestations can vary from one industry to another, but it has been shown that the experience of the product, coupled with that of the point of sale, remains essential to transmitting the brand's identity. Then come street communication (display windows, billboards, and so on) and the social experience – consumer word of mouth ("That's a great tie. Where did you find it?"). The accent should be placed on the products, product merchandising and esthetics, the esthetics of the points of sale, and the target consumers. Deliverables are:

- Diagnosis of the consistency of its manifestations with the brand's identity, and their coherence among themselves. Description of the causes of inconsistencies and lack of coherence. Classification of these problems or lacks according to the nature of the recommendations they prompt (identity, merchandising, organization, and process).

Analysis of consumers

Two parallel analyses must be conducted if the target customer and the actual customer are too different. The differences will be analyzed closely. What is studied above all are actual customers' reasons for purchase, and the reasons target customers fail to purchase. In the interest of simplicity, we will use the hypothesis here that the target customer is also the actual customer.

Traditional quantitative and qualitative techniques should suffice to cover simultaneously the aspects of perception and of purchase or non-purchase behavior. Each respondent falls into one or the other category. An attempt will be made to get the best possible picture of the following aspects:

- the consumer's familiarity with the brand and his or her consciousness of its different manifestations: products, characteristics, benefits related to products, esthetics, materials, price, points of sale, service, accessibility, advertising, and so on

- the consumer's perception of the brand's identity in terms of originality, esthetics, significance, and so on

- his or her idea of the brand's ideal customer

■ whether or not the consumer wants or doesn't want the products, and the reasons motivating this desire or absence of desire

■ the reasons for the purchase or non-purchase

■ the frequency and amount of the consumer's purchases over the two last years

■ who he or she thinks are the competitors of reference

■ the competing brands the consumer buys and the reasons for these purchases

■ his/her recommendations for making the brand more competitive.

Deliverables comprise a synthesis of all the differences noted between the brand's objectives and actual results:

■ differences between the desired identity and its perception

■ differences between the various perceptions of identified segments

■ differences between target and actual consumers

■ differences between the competitors of reference chosen by the brand and those perceived by customers

■ pointing up of the brand's degree of familiarity and the attractiveness of the products, compared with the competitors of reference, and any problems of product accessibility.

Analysis of competitors and interviews with opinion leaders

An analysis of the competitors of reference is done in part at the start of the audit, through observation of the different sales outlets. What was learned needs to be complemented by studying the other manifestations of the brand's competitors: advertising, press clippings, financial data if accessible. If the competitors perceived as most significant by target consumers (and purchasers) seem to be different from the competitors of reference defined in the brand identity, the brands designated by the consumers will also have to be studied.

Interviews with leaders of opinion, who generally come from the world of the press or economics, serve as a kind of "safety net" to confirm the impressions and facts collected during the audit.

Deliverables are:

- pointing up the strategic and operational differences with the competitors, and above all, of the degrees of differentiation of the brand's identities.

Verification of effectiveness

Using all the material assembled concerning the differences between the planned and the real, the mechanisms that led to these differences are dissected in order to identify the source of the difficulties. Since problems of coherence have already been dealt with, the only remaining ones should be those related to:

- The effectiveness of the resources chosen for communication. This applies more particularly to traditional communication methods.

- Cultural differences between segments. The different perceptive realities can be characterized by the differences still existing between best sellers and worst sellers as a function of geographic region. At Bally, in October 1999, this exercise – conducted on the five best-selling shoes in the Japan, Hong Kong, United States, and Switzerland regions – showed that these regions had only 20 percent of these products in common. In studying the different perceptions of the brand, care needs to be taken to evaluate their relative importance and degree of compatibility.

- The identity itself. Often it can be perceived in a vague way because of a lack of a clear definition at the outset. Or more frequently, the brand proves not to be sufficiently differentiated from its most significant competitors. What difference do consumers see between a Pilot ball pen and a Pentel, both of modern design and manufactured in Japan? Or between one brand of rice and another?

The deliverables are:

- Continuing with our ballistic metaphor, a synthesis will be made of the responses to the following questions:
  Have the shells fired at the different segments reached their targets? Has the target customer been hit? This is the measure of the effectiveness of the resources used.

Have the messages contained in the shell been received? This is the degree of awareness of the brand's existence.

How have the messages been received? This is the perception of identity.

- A list of the causes of disruptions of the transmission of identity. This takes the form of a list of the causes behind all the differences and all the problems summed up in the deliverables.

Verification of relevance

The market itself is in fact what verifies the brand's relevance. An analysis of the brand's desirability in comparison with its close competitors is used as measurement. If my brand interests people less than others, it's because what I offer them in terms of brand experience (visits to the store, use of the product, contact with its advertisements, and so on) doesn't do as good a job of reaching their sensitive spots and generates less emotion.

Being in phase with the mood of the moment without betraying the constants of the identity requires talent, intuition, and processes that are difficult to rationalize. It is at this level that creativity and intuition for the market make the difference.

/ Being in phase with the mood of the moment without betraying the constants of the identity requires talent, intuition, and processes that are difficult to rationalize. It is at this level that creativity and intuition for the market make the difference. /

Thanks to their experience and their intuition, the product marketing teams at Renault thought that, if their Espace model was a success, there would be room for a much smaller car that would have the characteristics of a small family monospace. Who could have predicted that this model alone would account for almost half of the sales of the Mégane line since its launch? It would have been difficult, too, to predict the success of the Swatch watch. It was not an obvious move, on the face of it, to launch a plastic watch with a band that was also plastic and a case that was esthetically very simple, and make it a worldwide success. The relevance of the concept was in having sensed that the market was waiting for such a product. As for the ST Dupont brand, its business volume is lower than that of competitors like Mont Blanc and Cartier. Is it because of its strong positioning in cigarette lighters, which symbolize an activity contemporary society strongly condemns? Or is it related to a somewhat vague and poorly differentiated brand identity?

All these examples illustrate the difficulty, for the auditor, of getting a handle on the notion of relevance. It is in this area that semiotic tools can be of great help. The semiotic square, which we presented earlier (see page 116), can be used to classify brands into two major categories:

- "Substance" brands (which produce their own meaning), which ride our society's groundswell trends. This was the case with Chanel at the time of the appearance of the women's liberation movement; it's the case with Volvo, with the trend towards automotive safety.

- "Sign" brands, interested in more short-term trends. This is true of Zara, for whom reactivity is the core competency, and for Louis Vuitton, the majority of whose sales volume is with its "monogram" fabric.

But the relevance transition, as we have seen, can also be hampered by numerous obstacles related to merchandising or operational execution. Therefore, all the problems related to accessibility of the products are studied, pointing up the operational difficulties that prevent the brand from realizing the sales potential its degree of attractiveness should generate. These difficulties generally come out in the internal interviews, and above all in customers' comments. They can be of various types:

- A distribution network that is not dense enough, or points of sale that are poorly located, compared with the competition.

- Inadequate deliveries. This is a recurring problem in the fashion sector, where too often the products presented in the advertising material arrive in stores a month after the advertising appears.

- Lack of certain sizes, colors, or models, or insufficient quantities to meet demand.

While discovering these problems is relatively easy, a complete diagnosis of their causes is not always simple to make. The real causes are often related to the processes of monitoring the markets, design, and development of the products themselves.

Deliverables are:

- diagnosis of attractiveness, summarizing the principal differences noted in comparison with competitors

■ diagnosis of product accessibility, with the problems noted classified by type and importance.

Recommendations

These are suggestions for solving all the problems encountered during the audit, summarized in the deliverables for each phase. The company's priorities, feasibility, and the time needed for implementation of the recommended solutions will be taken into consideration. These will be classified according to type:

■ recommendations relating to the brand's identity, for improving its coherence, its relevance, the effectiveness and the consistency of its communication

■ recommendations having to do with merchandising, to improve the product offering in the broad sense

■ recommendations concerning organization and operational processes.

The limits of the audit

The methodology we have just described can give a considerable tactical advantage to management teams or brand managers. It constitutes a "dictionary" of all the aspects to be taken into account. It requires analysis of all processes, from creation through purchase, and identifies the weaknesses: lack of coherence, a difficult transition from one state to another, shortcuts, or glaring omissions in a key point in the chain of communication.

All this is true provided that the essential thing is not forgotten: sometimes, creativity or the power of seduction are better than a systematic approach and procedures that are too rigid. The audit remains an introspective and analytical tool, not a creative operation. It has to be appreciated for what it is. It often allows proper assessment of the problems, but solving them will depend on individual talents. It's one thing to identify recommendations, and another to put them into practice.

Still it makes sense, in painting or in music, to carefully analyze your predecessors' academism and construct rules from it – so that you can then break them, using your own creativity. Personal expression always increases in relevance and maturity from such an exercise. Similarly, on the battlefield, the most thorough strategic reflection must not smother the crucial dimension of opportunistic improvisation; in fact, it feeds on it. That is the sense of the passage from Clausewitz we use as an epigraph to this chapter. The great theoretician of the Napoleonic wars, the founder of modern military strategy, never forgot what he had learned on the ground.

> / The most thorough strategic reflection must not smother the crucial dimension of opportunistic improvisation; in fact, it feeds on it. /

For these reasons, a relevant audit must make clear, both to the client and to the auditor him or herself, its own strengths and limitations. Nothing is worse than to lose your lucidity in the face of the mass of data collected, and to imagine that all the solutions will naturally flow from the assessments made from them. Nevertheless a problem whose outlines are clearly drawn is always better than a latent problem; it's also better to methodically study the reasons for a success or a failure than to sit pat on the "mystery of creativity." And if each stroke of genius is accompanied by systematic organization of the actions to be undertaken, the results can only be better.

We might describe this little extra dose of rationality that leaves nothing to chance as being like the double zero on European roulette wheels, which guarantees that the casino will have slightly higher gains than the players. Therefore it's a very necessary, if never sufficient, tool, all the more so because in its strictly analytical dimension, it is not immune to criticism. Its main weakness is that there is no real methodology for studying problems related to the brand's relevance in detail.

Major market or societal trends can miss being identified during the study of the development of the company's strategy, and also not appear in the analysis of consumers: because consumers have longer vacations, they travel more and hotels in certain tourist areas are full. Because they are better fed and their average weight is increasing, more of them want to lose weight and turn to diet food products. Because they spend more time on leisure, they buy more monospace, Jeep, and SUV-type vehicles. The success of the cell telephone can be explained, in retrospect, by the desire to stay in contact with one's "tribe" at all times and the need for greater mobility. Yet nobody was predicting, just a few years ago, that there would end up being more cell phones than fixed phones in the developed countries. Clearly, certain external elements determine the success of a product or category of products, but they are not always easy to identify.

For certain simple cases, however, anticipation is fairly easy. We mentioned cell phones. It's already possible to predict that their dissemination will cause a reduction in calls made from telephone booths. Booths should partly disappear, or in any case become less profitable or less well maintained.

This type of concern is not new. In the books on strategy, one always starts with "analysis of the environment" to evaluate the potential of a market. Are the general conditions of the environment favorable to the development of a certain market or product? But there are sometimes sudden changes that are difficult to predict. Again continuing the ballistic metaphor, marketing strategists today talk about "windows of opportunity" – which implies, as for the launch of a rocket, that favorable conditions are very circumscribed in time.

Some 20 years ago S. C. Johnson, which specialized in the production of household cleaning products, considered the perspectives over the very long term for furniture polish and products for the care of tile floors. The assessment was simple: the percentage of working women was increasing, so women would have less time to devote to the upkeep of their houses. Household income was on the rise, and people would invest more in leisure. Eventually, sales of household care products could run into problems. Johnson launched an energetic diversification campaign. A "leisure" division was created, and bought companies that made tents for camping, canoes, fittings for boats, and scuba-diving systems. These activities did develop, but much more slowly than household-care products. S. C. Johnson would certainly have been more inspired had it stuck to its core business, and instead of canoes, bought companies that made competitive and innovative household products.

In conclusion, the audit is a tool for rapid verification that complements necessary studies, more costly and of longer duration, of the evolutions of the market as a whole.

Criteria of good brand management

As this new millennium begins, what brands are succeeding? September 11, 2001 and the invasion of Iraq have not helped a world economy already on the verge of recession and threatened by the deleterious process of deflation. Yet several brands seem better equipped to survive the downturn: Ralph Lauren, Tod's, Hermès, Burberry, Armani, Hugo Boss, BMW, and a few others.

Do they have something in common that explains their success? They are all in a growth phase or in early maturity. They all know the importance of their brand, and sell substantial quantities of recognizable products with constant quality. Beyond these shared points, each one has its own history, its own way of running its business and staying competitive. But that applies to many other successful brands that have proved more vulnerable to the current economic downturn.

/ Successful brands all know the importance of their brand, and sell substantial quantities of recognizable products with constant quality. /

A recognizable product is the central element for successful brands, but it is only the tip of the iceberg, the final crystallization of complex processes. The major brands are characterized by:

- a product that is recognizable, popular, and the basis of its own brand awareness

- an identity that is well differentiated, relevant, and well managed

- effective organization and processes

- a culture of innovation, attentiveness to the markets, and rapid reaction to change.

The product

We have already stressed the fundamental importance of the product. It is the most visible and most tangible component of a brand. It is the instrument of both revenue generation and communication about the brand itself. Let's look at the various functions of the product.

Expertise

The product is the foundation of the brand's legitimacy in a specific sector. It is proof of expertise in a business area (the client is rarely aware of licensing or franchise agreements and is only marginally interested in them) and guarantees the "substance and authenticity" offered by the brand.

The product is the principal dimension of creation and innovation

It is on the product that the bulk of research and creativity efforts are concentrated. It is also where they are most visible. Stylistic and technological research go hand in hand. Audi is perhaps one of the brands that have succeeded best in concentrating their efforts in both areas, with visible success.

The product is its own best advertising

We have stressed the fact that the product itself is the most effective manifestation of the brand's identity. It is advertising in its most direct, evident, multisensory form, generating immediate impressions. It is also the foundation of brand awareness. The more it is sold, the better it is known, especially if the product is identifiable from across the street. This explains the use of logos, materials, colors, metal accessories, and other style codes that are aimed at facilitating its identification.

/ Canceling groups of products that sell well, on the grounds that they no longer correspond to a style or to a new brand identity, shows a lack of respect for the market. /

The search for new elements of recognition must be continuous, even for already-established brands. Prada, which already had its use of black nylon and its triangular metal plaque as elements of recognition, then launched the little red rectangle to set off its Prada Sport line.

The product must be managed with full awareness of its impact on communication. Never kill a bestseller. *Restyle* it. Canceling groups of products that sell well, on the grounds that they no longer correspond to a style or to a new brand identity, shows a lack of respect for the market. Certain brands have tried it and regretted it. It amounts to a massive "layoff" of one's own customers! Yet those same customers could have become spokespeople for the brand's change had it been carried out progressively and intelligently. The automotive industry has been successful at this. The Volkswagen New Beetle and the new Mini Cooper (BMW group) are good recent examples (see Plates 55 and 56).

The product is the key to the brand's relationship with the consumer

The product is the source of repeat purchases, of the confidence or the disillusionment that is created between the consumer and the brand. The product spends a lot of time with its owner (more, in any case, than the second's distracted attention a page of advertising in a magazine gets). An "affective" tie develops. Brands of cars, motorcycles (see the example of the Ducati advertisement, Plate 34), perfume, shoes, and coffee know this well.

Except in certain extreme cases, bad advertising rarely deters a faithful customer, whereas poor quality in a product always will.

The product is the basis of economic results

The product will have the same rank as the brand's identity, at the center of all processes and all reflection.

Identity

All brands that succeed have an identity that is well differentiated; in the public eye, and thus visible; and relevant, because they sell. In short, they are the result of an identity that is well managed.

A differentiated identity

The benefits the product brings to customers are not only tangible in nature. It also carries with it a panoply of images, emotions, and representations. The brand's ethic and esthetic must define a vision of a specific world, yet its seasonal products must offer, in the shorter term, originality and innovation within the framework of that vision. What Burberry, Puma, and Coach have done in recent years are good examples of this ability to innovate and differentiate while preserving an identity.

A perceived identity

Successful brands know how to talk. Consumers listen, and they understand. This is proof of the effectiveness of their communication in the broad sense. The more coordinated and effective the manifestations of brand identity are, the stronger their impact will be. This is why there is a constant effort at coordination of all the functions that contribute to the brand's manifestations. It's why fashion and luxury brands have a growing preoccupation with controlling their distribution. It represents one of the essential manifestations of their identity.

/ The more coordinated and effective the manifestations of brand identity are, the stronger their impact will be. /

Gucci's success lies in the fact that Tom Ford not only controls all esthetic aspects of his brand, but is also a great retailer and merchandiser. This lets him strongly coordinate all aspects of the product and most of the brand manifestations.

A relevant identity

Successful brands sell because they interest the people who buy the products. This critical transition, as we have seen previously, is the most difficult one to plan. It requires sales genius and intuition about where the market is going. Faced with the mysteries of the market, the only constructive, rational attitude that can be taken is to watch it very closely, being prepared to react as quickly as possible to significant signals. That requires systems for ongoing observation of markets, and operational processes oriented towards rapid response.

A well-managed identity

This means first of all that the company's strategies are in phase with the brand's identity. Next comes a corporate culture with strong awareness of the concept of identity and all its operational implications. Finally, it means remaining constantly aware that identity management works on two different time scales: the middle term, when dealing with the invariable components of the brand ethic and esthetic; the short term for everything to do with the manifestations of the brand identity.

To sum up, managers of brands that want success will be as aware of the concept of identity as a major component of the company's strategies as they are of the product itself. The brand will have a relevant identity which will be communicated (in the broad sense of the term, that of entering the chain of communication) effectively and coherently. Managers will be constantly attentive to consumers and closely observe their competitors of reference.

Organization and operational processes

We too often forget that behind a product and a brand, there is a physical performance. When Coca-Cola decided to sell its Minute Maid fruit juices in Europe, it met with real difficulty and had to associate with Danone. Coca-Cola's trucks are not refrigerated and can't distribute fresh fruit juices.

Two imperatives will govern the structure of the organization and the operational processes: putting the company in a position to react as quickly as possible to market signals, and coordinating the manifestations of identity as well as possible so as to maximize communicative impact.

Logistics

Today the effectiveness, reliability, and reactivity of the logistical chain have become a decisive competitive playing field in nearly all industrial sectors. The right products, delivered at the right time, and available in the right places, are the ones that sell well and whose presence and quality the consumer appreciates.

This is the case for consumer products. The principal points of sale need to get deliveries almost every day, and the major retail chains bill their suppliers for delivery delays and inventory shortfalls. But it's also the rule for luxury products – in particular fashion products. All the stores in a chain have to receive shipments on time, and each generally has specific orders. A week's delay in shipping corresponds to an average loss of 2 percent of seasonal sales.

/ Today the effectiveness, reliability, and reactivity of the logistical chain have become a decisive competitive playing field in nearly all industrial sectors. /

It's still frequent to run across a supermarket shelf that's out of stock for a brand of shampoo – while three cases of 48 units of product are sitting in a storeroom, hidden behind pallets of mineral water.

Logistics is only one of the elements that make it possible to respond rapidly to signals from the market. The essential yardstick here is time to market, which we have already mentioned – the time between the product concept (a two-dimensional sketch for a pair of shoes, for example) and the product's being made available to consumers. Short development times make it possible to "stick to" the market and react more quickly to the competition's innovations. The luxury industry has seasonal development times of 9 to 12 months. Zara has reduced that period to ten days between the initial sketches and the presence of the product in the store for apparel items.

Organization

For a brand to succeed, the organization of the company has to be up to the challenge. The company culture, and in particular the coordination of its different functions, will play a determining role. In a context of increased competition, the cultural attitude of the company must be closely in tune with market conditions. A company that thinks it has the key to consumers' expectations and can sell them whatever it offers will have a tendency to feel it doesn't need to meet all their requirements. We believe it is essential to develop a culture of respect for the market and its mysteries.

The second element comprises all the mechanisms of integration or coordination of the functions that oversee the brand's manifestations: committees, regular meetings, specific reporting. Nothing is more efficient than a common manager. As we saw with the example of Gucci, uniting the design and merchandising functions under a single manager makes for optimum reconciliation of the relevance of the offering – in terms of the brand's ethic and esthetic – with business volume and margins. The difficulty lies in finding, for a given job, the individual who will be able to use both hemispheres of his/her brain! This rare animal is sensitive both to the rationality of figures and the esthetic of the products, and is also curious and understands human behavior.

In organizations that are not structured like consumer products companies and have no product managers assigned to each brand in their portfolio, we recommend the creation of the position of brand identity manager. The brand identity manager will have control over all the functions corresponding to the esthetic aspects of the company's activity. His or her skills will extend to all of the brand's manifestations as we described them earlier, from the design of the products to the uniforms worn by the receptionists, and including the store display windows and traditional communication.

Finally, there are other elements – the computer systems, for example – that are also essential factors in competitiveness. They operate in tandem with logistics and the real-time circulation of data needed for rapid reaction.

Innovation, attentiveness and reactivity to the market

The product is not the only dimension through which innovation is expressed. As we have already noted, there are many possible axes: advertising, events, distribution, human resources management, and so on. Management of human resources holds one of the keys to innovation. For there to be innovation, people must first be empowered to innovate. This means venturing into new territory and not being afraid of making mistakes. In a word, people need to be encouraged to take risks. This requires developing a corporate culture where certain types of risks, and thus of errors, are permissible. This means defining those errors that are not admissible.

/ For there to be innovation, people must first be empowered to innovate. /

At Bally, in 2000, at a point when risk-taking was being encouraged in each person's field of endeavor, a list was sent out giving the outlines of a typology:

An environment that encourages initiative and new ideas can't be created if transparence, curiosity, the right to ask questions, and a certain tolerance towards certain kinds of errors are not encouraged.

However, there will be no tolerance whatsoever of:

■ making the same error twice,

- a lack of effort and refusal of the principle of continuous improvement,
- dissimulation and non-communication
- lack of interest and refusal to accept responsibilities,
- imbalance between professional ability and the responsibilities inherent in the job.

In the same way, if we are convinced of the need to be attentive to the market, we must develop a culture of respect for consumers, systems for listening to them, a process of transmission of data to the decision makers concerned, and a whole series of rapid-reaction procedures.

A simple recapitulative diagram

We have examined the four elements on which the success of a brand is based:

- a recognizable product

- a well-managed identity

- an innovative organization

- effective operational processes that allow rapid reaction to the signals coming from the market.

We can recapitulate these four points on a progressive diagram that includes all these different variables (see Figure 6.8). This simple diagram provides a graphic illustration of the essential points where a brand's success is built. It also lets us reposition the different transitions in the chain of communication.

To conclude this chapter, we must insist again on the pragmatic nature of our approach. We have tried, in these pages, to bring together in a synthetic form and as clearly as possible a set of reflections and suggestions aimed more particularly at brand managers, a "toolbox" in which we hope they will find inspiration for their work. If the formal structure of our argumentation calls on various disciplines, in particular semiotics, it's because in our experience its application in the field has produced good results. But it's not a good idea to get caught up in the method and see it, to use Clausewitz's expression, as an expression of "immutable truths."

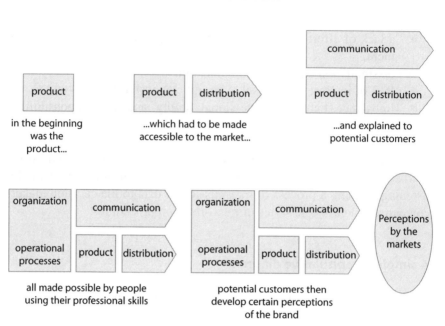

Figure 6.8a Synthetic flow chart of factors of brand success

Just as a semiological study of brand identity translates into very pragmatic recommendations, the methodological recommendations we have made in these pages, as we have just seen, lead to "common-sense" suggestions. But our presentation, we feel, has the advantage of painting an overall picture of brand management, in order to make sure that no

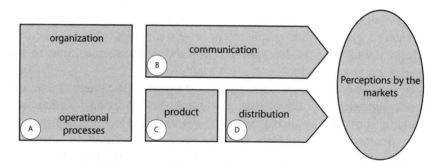

1. Recognizable products (C)
2. Well-managed identity (B, C, and D)
3. Innovative organization (A)
4. Processes that are rapidly reactive (A)

Figure 6.8b Synthetic flow chart of factors of brand success

Transitions in the chain of communication

Figure 6.8c Synthetic flow chart of factors of brand success

aspect has been neglected. Having said that, it is still our fundamental conviction that the important events and decisions affecting a brand are made "on the ground." That is why we militate resolutely for responsive and "humble" attentiveness to the market, where, we are convinced, too-rigid formalisms will always fall short, and opportunistic ingenuity and creativity are always needed.

In the next chapters, we will return to that dimension. We will take a close look at the great unknown quantity of the equation that decides a brand's fate: the consumer. Consumers, we feel, are full-fledged players in the life of a brand, and their role as "check and balance" is necessary to its full realization.

PART III

The Role of the Consumer

We have presented the consumer as the individual towards whom all a brand's specialists aim their efforts, but also as an unpredictable element, capable of enthusiasm, strong rejection, or simply indifference. In that they make the choice whether or not to buy a product, consumers are first and foremost a target for brands. But by that very fact, they become players. By deciding to support one brand rather than another, they justify a given sales approach, and quite often reject strategies that are out of touch with the market – not to mention the absence of any coherent strategy. We go even further and say that consumers have become the censors of the values brands express, and by extension, the potential moralizing force of economic life.

Consumers are at the center of the system. As autonomous individuals who determine their own behavior, they decide whether or not to buy a product. Through this act of purchase, they grant or withhold their support for the entire marketing proposal presented for their scrutiny. The symbolic and economic force of that act, when it is expressed in a significant way by a large number of potential purchasers, is often enough to eliminate certain products from the market – consumer products of insufficient quality, with a poor quality/price ratio, or ones that stand for values they do not share.

These individual decisions are not always determining. Opinions can diverge and statistics can fail to make a clear call. We saw this earlier, with the provocative advertisings by Benetton. While 36 percent of the population stayed away from the stores to show disapproval, that didn't keep the ads from continuing, with 21 percent of consumers rushing to the stores. It remains to be seen whether the interest of some has the same force as the indignation of others. In the final analysis, who has the better chance of influencing the brand?

In fact, a "vote" of this kind will depend on two parameters: an individual and qualitative parameter, which expresses the intensity of the acceptance or rejection felt individually, and a collective or quantitative parameter, which expresses the degree to which that acceptance or rejection is shared within a given population. The debate will be between more or less broad groups of persons who are motivated to varying degrees. They will use this combination of mass effect and tenacity to make their voices heard, and sometimes sway the logic of purchase statistics.

Beyond the act of purchase, consumers can use this qualitative criterion, by making their voices heard as concerned citizens, and all the resources a democracy provides are available for doing it. Consumers can, for example, demand accountability and behave as citizens or shareholders. They can write to the CEO or to the consumer service department of the company and inquire about its practices. Generally, such letters don't go unread. The companies know well enough what is at stake, answer the great majority of complaint letters, and – above all – keep track of them.

Consumers can act at the level of the media. They can write to reporters to try to find a responsive voice. And if someone in the press picks up the ball, the company may well respond by changing its behavior. In fact, to the extent that such actions reach a certain critical mass – our collective parameter – they take on structure and turn into mobilization. This can take the form of massive letter campaigns aimed at companies and the press, petitions, lobbying, demonstrations, or boycotts. Through the snowball effect or the media coverage they get, such structured actions can effectively change the "mathematics" of opposition and support.

The role of the consumer is all the more strong in our postmodern society, characterized by the disappearance of ideologies. Theoretical justifications no longer exist. There are no more credible systems to explain the world, but only aggregations of partial visions – legitimate within their limits – which constitute the only points of reference for our daily lives.

In this context, civil society – the sum of and the compromise between individual actions and values – appears as an ever more important power base when it comes to social and political decisions. And consumers, at both the qualitative and the collective level of their means of expression, can constitute a major influence on the strategy of the major brands. To quote Yves Boisvert, "The values of eclecticism, pluralism, freedom of choice and of information, and freedom of speech are all intrinsic to the brand system and developed through its instrumentality."[1] The individual act of purchase is a sign of acceptance of the values expressed by all the manifestations of the brand's identity.

Postmodernism also means "participationism." Consumers organize to disseminate their ideas. They express themselves as users of products or services, but also as citizens, in terms of social or political goals. For example, they can love or hate nuclear generating plants, and pressure electrical utilities either as citizens or as users, and thus as customers. It is their decision whether to make their individual voices heard, or to join an active, mobilized pressure group.

Since the 1960s, consumer advocacy and lobbying groups have become more numerous and have developed significant power. Boycott campaigns and spectacular actions against major brands in recent years are evidence of this, and Naomi Klein's book documents them. Another recent trend is the emergence of short-lived and very mobile associations. They come into being to organize a boycott or an action against a specific company, then disappear. In this respect, they are the reflection of a postmodern society where commitments, while sincere and total, dissolve rapidly.

All these phenomena concern consumers and their desire to make their voices heard. Let us repeat that we feel that their role is crucial to maintaining balance in the system. Making consumers fully conscious of their power and their responsibilities, but also guaranteeing them the means of exercising them, is a major issue for the years ahead. The third part of this book will try to explain how that is now coming about.

In Chapter 7, we describe the basis of the theory of consumer behavior. This subject alone could fill many books. It is not our purpose here to try to rival the already very complete (and complex) work that has been done, but to quickly give the principal keys to consumer behavior. Attitudes, preferences, perceptions – these terms will be described and narrowed down, as will their role in the process of conviction that leads to the act of purchase. We can tell you now that the research done on the behavior of consumers has produced incontestable results that are very far from what one might have believed intuitively.

Chapter 8 studies consumers' rationality and the nature of their power. Are their purchases prompted by rational motives? We will see that the answer to that is mixed. This approach nevertheless has the great advantage of characterizing the mechanisms of successive approximation that are at

---

1 Yves Boisvert, *Monde postmoderne, analyse du discours sur la postmodernité*, Paris: Éditions L'Harmattan, 1996.

work in our purchase decisions. It points up the risks of manipulation of certain more impressionable groups of consumers. Finally, by underlining the complexity of the parameters involved, it recalls that, except for these specific cases, it is the consumer who remains in charge and renders his or her verdict, just as in a political election.

In Chapter 9, we go back over the history and the issues of consumer advocacy movements, so as to integrate their activities into the totality of the control and regulatory measures that companies are subject to. We speculate about the effectiveness of such actions, which we refer to as "structured," as regards the possibilities of dialogue beyond confrontation and the dangers of co-option of consumer advocacy by special interests.

This third part will clearly establish the nature of the formidable power consumers possess over brands. It argues that this power needs to be fully exercised, consciously, but also responsibly, in order to impel the brands, through the interplay of competition, to fulfill their mission of economic, cultural, and social progress.

Consumers' behavior

Your head turns away: O the new love!
Your head turns back – O the new love!
(Arthur Rimbaud)

The Rimbaud lines we've chosen as epigraph to this chapter are from a poem entitled, somewhat ironically, "To a reason."[1] Though their scope is much more universal, we feel they are something a brand manager should keep in mind. With their startling concision, they cast alarming doubt on the soundness of our motives, whatever they may be, and regardless of the act they may motivate.

What do we choose? How and why do we choose it? That is the question that hangs over all human activity. As far as our present discussion is concerned, it is at the core of the web of economic and social relations that commerce weaves among human beings. It could be called "the mystery of the consumer." In discourse on marketing generally, and brands in particular, this mystery often takes the form of a paradox.

If we believe anti-brand activists, the consumer is necessarily manipulated by fiendishly clever communicators. And yet the very existence of the protest, the success of *No Logo*, and the collapse of certain megabrands are proof that that manipulation has its limits! In the eyes of marketing executive, consumers are volatile, unpredictable creatures whose heads can be turned at the slightest breeze, like a weathervane. They represent the unknown quantity that can cause the best-laid strategies to fail, or turn a creative stroke of genius based on pure instinct into a resounding success. And yet researchers, scientists, consultants, and communication and marketing experts continue to spend more and more human and financial

---

1 Arthur Rimbaud, "À une raison", in *Illuminations*, trans. Louise Varèse.

resources on the attempt to rationalize consumers' motives. They must feel those efforts are worthwhile. They are grappling with the problem of brand relevance we dealt with in the preceding chapters.

How much credence should be given to such research? To what extent can we predict what will "turn the consumer's head"? In this chapter, we propose to sketch a panorama of the theory of the consumer, its usefulness, its limits, and sometimes its dangers.

Towards a formalization of purchasing behaviors

Numerous books on consumer behavior exist. Its study has almost become an autonomous discipline, at the border between psychology, social psychology, sociology, and marketing. The field has its experts, its specific reviews, and a great number of research centers.

Social psychology studies the individual and his or her relations with others and with collectivities in general. The Americans Festinger and Katz, for example, set out to elucidate the mechanisms through which individual attitudes are formed and opinions transformed, under the influence of social pressure or that of the leaders of opinion who serve as its relays. Their work attempts to describe the circumstances under which a change of opinion can come about in an individual, and which individuals are most susceptible to such changes.[2]

The theory known as behaviorism proposed the principle of viewing human behavior within the framework of a deliberately reductionist schema (stimulus and response) in order to construct models. This work led to the popularizing of the hypothetical model of the "black box," where the stimulus is considered as a given piece of information input into the "box"; this piece of information undergoes processing and results, as output, in a reaction. Since only the input and the output are observable, the problem consists of identifying the operative stimulus/response pairs and attempting to reconstruct, through inductive reasoning, some of the "opaque" mechanisms by which information is processed.

This approach has found applications in marketing for some 50 years. Consumers can be seen as being subject to a large number of stimuli (advertising, other forms of product communication, merchandising actions, different price levels). At the end of the circuit, they will decide to buy one product rather than another – or perhaps not to buy anything.

---

2 See e.g. Leon Festinger, *A Theory of Cognitive Dissonance*, Stanford: Stanford University Press, 1957.

The black box theoretically contains all the relations between each of the stimuli viewed separately and the observed behavior they induce.

For example, we can suppose that there is a clear reaction between price and purchasing behavior. Let's imagine two products, P1 and P2. A consumer will buy P1 rather than P2 if the price of P1 is lowered by 10, 20 or 50 percent compared with the price of P2. There must therefore be an identifiable relation between these two variables of relative price and the possibilities of purchase of the respective products. If product P2 then increases its advertising budget or comes up with more effective advertising, these stimuli will also affect the consumer. To what degree do they play a role compared with the preceding ones? The black box approach is aimed at describing the totality of these relations, or impact functions. Researchers have tried, little by little, to define a certain number of binary relationships.

Still, behaviorism is not an exact science. Its conclusions are often descriptive: people buy such and such a car depending on their income, their lifestyle, their relations with friends and family, their personality type. It's much more difficult to reach inductive conclusions (if such and such a person has such and such a personality type and belongs to such and such a socio-demographic segment, I can predict with a low risk of error the model and the color of the automobile that person drives). It's clear that the relationships hidden inside the black box, between an individual's characteristics and his or her observed behavior, are multiple and difficult to describe precisely.

/ Behaviorism is not an exact science. Its conclusions are often descriptive. It's much more difficult to reach inductive conclusions. /

To explain behaviors, researchers distinguish between rational motives and emotional motives. When studying rational relations (for example, the relationship between an income level and the purchase of luxury or bargain brands – which, incidentally, is far from being a simple or linear relationship), statistics or microeconomics are used. To deal with the emotional reasons for a purchase, on the other hand, psychology and sociology tend to be used. The general field of consumer behavior research, then, calls on a highly varied range of disciplines, from social psychology to cognitive psychology, and from sociology to econometrics.

The black box model has extended the study of the relations between initial stimuli and behavior, resulting in a hierarchy of effects. How do we go from a non-purchase situation to an act of purchase? The survey reveals that there are several stages in this evolution, stages we will encounter again throughout this chapter:

- knowledge of a product or a brand

- attitude – positive or negative – towards the brand

- preference for one or another brand

- purchase intention

- the act of purchase itself.

For a long time, behaviorism refused to lift the cover of the black box to try to understand the complex interplay that leads from input (stimulus) to output (response). We have gone beyond that point. Instead of simply observing the transition to the act of purchase based on a given personality profile, researchers attempt to show how one or several consumers move from one level in the hierarchy of effects to another – from the purchase intention to the actual act of purchase, for example. Reactions regarding price or the presence or absence of a given brand on the shelves are also studied, as is the occurrence of spontaneous or impulsive behaviors. It is also observed how, and in what proportions, certain attitudes are transformed into preferences. The field of study is becoming more rigorous and more systematic.

/ Researchers attempt to show how one or several consumers move from one level in the hierarchy of effects to another – from the purchase intention to the actual act of purchase, for example. /

The scope of this research goes beyond the domain of the phenomenon of purchase. It is used more and more in politics. It is becoming frequent to test the tone and the terms of a message or press release, or the impact of a speech, or certain of its points, on the most loyal members of a party, but also on those who have left the party to join other political groups, or on the members of another party. For example, 100 supporters will be brought together in one room and 100 opponents in another to hear a speech or a draft of a speech. They will be asked to react, using an individual voting device, to words or topics in order to measure their acceptance and rejection.

They may also be asked about their voting intentions (as would be done for purchase intentions) by using a projective system. It has been shown to be more effective, instead of asking the respondent if he or she plans to vote for the Democrats or Republicans, to couch the question in these terms: "In your opinion, what kind of person votes Republican or Democrat?" It is then verified whether the profile described by the person being surveyed is close – or far away – from his or her own profile.

In the following paragraphs, we'll return to this ideal pathway that leads up to the act of purchase. We will begin with certain characteristics of the individual – personality, values, the phenomenon of perception – and continue with attitudes, preferences, and purchasing behaviors, and finally the influence of the group on individual decisions. As we shall see, the "box" is far from having given up all its secrets, and the lines from Arthur Rimbaud still hold true.

Personality and values

As we said above, predicting purchase based on the personality of a consumer is a very tricky exercise. This dimension, which takes into account the specificities of individuals – their ways of feeling, thinking, acting, and reacting in concrete situations – might however seem able to explain many behaviors. One might suppose that more aggressive people drive Porsches or Ferraris, or that more reflective individuals are attracted more to purchase economy brands or store brands. But up to now, these personality variables have shown only limited power to predict behavior.

/ Up to now, personality variables have shown only limited power to predict behavior. /

The same is true for socio-demographic criteria: age, geographic location, sex, type of household, income level, and so on. These elements sometimes lead to tautological conclusions – purchasers of baby bottles have one or more babies, buyers of schoolbags have school-age children, and so on. They rarely provide information about the choice of one brand over another.

Values, as described below, prove to be more effective criteria:

- view of human nature
- humanity's relationship with nature
- orientation in terms of time (past, present, or future)
- life attitude (freedom, reactivity, attitude towards norms, action, reflection)
- the type of relation with others (in general ascendant, descendant, or balanced).

Based on these values, researchers have defined lifestyle profiles that produce better results. These lifestyles can identify evolutions. For example, certain groups draw closer to or move away from a given brand. Yet these results must nevertheless be considered as difficult to predict.

The notion of perception

Perception is the process by which a person becomes conscious of an environment and interprets it in terms of his or her own frame of reference. Thus it is the mechanism whereby information – a specific message – is acquired, identified, interpreted, and stored; that is, memorized by a person.

Our view of the world is specific to us. Each of us does not perceive the information we are presented with in the same way, even if it's presented under identical conditions. If we decide to buy a new car, we will be much more receptive to advertising for cars than to other types of advertising. But this new information must enter into our pre-existing frame of reference. For example, there are passionate devotees of Ford or BMW. Each will identify ads for these two brands differently; in addition, they will treat the information differently as a function of their frame of reference. The "Ford fan" won't pay much attention to advertising for BMW; on the other hand, he or she will be more receptive to information about Ford. If this information presents new elements, it will be added to the consumer's overall perception of the brand. If the information contradicts his or her vision of Ford, very often it will be blocked out and not added to the consumer's frame of reference.

An example often given is that of a picture taken in the New York subway, showing a white man threatening a black man with a knife. When this photo was shown to whites, some of them subsequently described it as a picture of a black threatening a white. So there exists an a priori mental structure, a conception of the world that resists being challenged by new information. Often the contradictory elements are filtered, rejected, not retained. The information is not "seen."

/ There exists an a priori mental structure, a conception of the world that resists being challenged by new information. Often the contradictory elements are filtered, rejected, not retained. /

This phenomenon, called cognitive dissonance[3] explains why it is useless to create advertising to try to contradict a preconceived idea. The risk is than no one will even see it; in any case, it will have little chance of being retained and radically changing the general opinion. There is an adage that's well known to communi-

---

3　See Festinger (note 2).

cation specialists: the hardest thing to is to make consumers change an opinion.

Humans don't easily give up their ideas. That's why brands, as we have seen, have difficulty transforming their identity without alienating their existing clientele.

Perception is selective, cumulative, and circumscribed in time. The process can be divided into three stages: attention, classification, and acceptance.

Attention

Attention is a function of the size, color, position, and content of the message. The more complicated a communication becomes, the less chance it has of being perceived. This means that cultural habits of information acquisition are determining factors for the degree of attention. A color page will be more easily spotted than a page in black and white. A recto page will be perceived better than a verso, and so on.

In the 1990s an AIDS prevention campaign was planned by international organizations for several West African countries. The essential communication medium was a handout touting the advantages of condoms. To get around the barrier of illiteracy, the idea was to explain these advantages with a very simple comic strip, a chronological succession of pictures devoid of text. A universal language? In fact what happened, in the Islamic regions, where Arabic writing is common, was that people – even illiterate people – looked at the pictures following the right-to-left direction of Arabic. Read that way, the succession of symbols resulted in a message that was incomprehensible, and the discouraged readers gave up trying to understand it. This counter-example is a good illustration of how the frame of reference affects the communication of content well upstream.

Classification

After the attention stage comes that of classification. The person to whom the message is addressed will "file" the acquired stimulus in a precise category; that will be made easier to the degree that that category is clearly defined. The stimulus will be interpreted as a function of the subject's presuppositions – in other words, the frame of reference – before being integrated into the field of knowledge.

Acceptance

Once the message is decoded, the content has to be accepted. This is facil-
itated if it confirms existing beliefs and attitudes and if the person bearing
the message appears credible. When Claudia Schiffer promotes L'Oréal
products or Inès Sastre Lancôme products, they are credible as specialists
in beauty; a pop singer who declares support for the foreign policy of George Bush, Jr. is perhaps somewhat less credible.

/ For a message to successfully get past the stage of acceptance by a consumer, it must be perceptible within this consumer's frame of reference; be presented clearly and incisively; be repeated often enough; and its content must be in phase with the recipient's a priori judgments and beliefs. /

For a message to successfully get past the stage of acceptance by a consumer, it must be perceptible within this consumer's frame of reference; be presented clearly and incisively; be repeated often enough; and its content must be in phase with the recipient's a priori judgments and beliefs. Its impact can also vary from individual to individual, depending on whether its tone is rational or emotional.

A study was conducted in the United States on the impact of a campaign on the dangers of tobacco. Among non-smokers, the message got through to 80 percent of the population, who perceived it and accepted it. Among heavy smokers, 29 percent of individuals rejected the message or did not even perceive it. These figures nevertheless vary with educational level. Of heavy smokers with no high-school diploma, 44 percent rejected the facts and conclu-
sions on the dangers of tobacco. Only 25 percent of those with a
post-secondary educational level rejected the demonstration.

Now let's take the recent example of the anti-tobacco campaign
launched by the French health ministry in June 2002. To get around the
"barrier to perception," the advertisers hit on the idea of playing on a very
widespread concern: food safety and the issue of traceability. The
campaign was based on a teaser TV spot explaining, without further
details, that traces of toxic substances had been found in a popular
consumer product. Viewers were told to call an emergency telephone
number. Only then did they find out that the product in question was
tobacco and get the anti-smoking message. The effect of surprise generated
near panic in TV viewers. The statistics collected just after the campaign
show an excellent rate of perception for the overall population. That was
the main objective, and the advertisers can congratulate themselves on

having attained it. An immediate shock message, even a very violent one – for example: "If you smoke, you're killing your children" – probably wouldn't have gotten the same results among smokers in terms of perception. Nevertheless the level of acceptance of the campaign, not surprisingly, shows a clear gap between smokers and non-smokers.

To sum up, a message will be perceived if it is simple, clear, powerful, repeated often, and is in keeping with the prior opinions of the people it's aimed at.

As popular wisdom has it, we tend to see what we want to see. People see better messages that concern them directly, or for which they have a passing interest. One thing is certain: the level of perception depends on the personality of each targeted individual, his or her concerns, and the mood he or she is in when exposed to the message.

Attitudes and preferences

An attitude is a predisposition, resulting from learning, which allows a person to react to an object or group of objects in a given way, generally favorably or unfavorably. Attitudes are based on beliefs, on experience or knowledge accumulated over time. For example, attitudes towards a brand will result from an a priori mindset ("All brands of toothpaste are alike") and from actual experience ("Signal is nice and it tastes good").

The result is attitudes that are in part affective (calling emotion into play), and in part cognitive (calling on experience and reasoning). These attitudes will directly affect a consumer's reaction to the image he or she perceives of a product. For example: "This car gets better mileage than its competitors, but I want to buy a company car, and I don't pay for my gas directly. So for me, that's a secondary criterion." Or: "These apricots are more expensive than the ones across the street. They're probably better quality, so I'll buy them."

/ The passage from attitude to preference will depend, for each individual, on the way that individual classifies the brand's different attributes and the value he or she assigns to them. /

We can see that the passage from preference will depend, for each individual, on the way that individual classifies the brand's different attributes and the value he or she assigns to them. For example, it's easier to sell a "Swiss-made" watch than a watch made in Portugal or Hong Kong. That is the result of old perceptions, of learned behaviors, and of personal experiences. It would be too difficult, too time-consuming, and too expensive to try to present the fact that a watch is made in Portugal as a significant advantage. That could change, but the change would necessitate a long-term process.

To sum up, attitudes are based on a set of beliefs or experiences that affect the individual's structuring of the environment. As a frame of reference, this construct facilitates or decreases the perception of different stimuli and messages. The messages perceived can confirm or change an attitude, and eventually give rise to a preference for a given brand or product.

The purchase decision

Consumer behavior differs with the product the consumer is purchasing. Consumers are more attentive to their purchases if the price of the article is higher, if the risk of error is great, if the product is technically complex, and if it carries a strong symbolic content. The degree of attention also tends to increase when the perceived difference between brands is stronger. When buying a pound of rice, the consumer will ask a minimum number of questions and decide quickly; if buying a motorcycle or a pair of shoes, on the other hand, he or she will take more time to evaluate the different alternatives.

/ The degree of attention tends to increase when the perceived difference between brands is stronger. /

Further, depending on the circumstances, the decision-making process will be more of a cognitive or an affective nature. New parents with their first baby have a tendency to buy their baby food in a pharmacy. The process has a strong emotional connotation for them: they want to give their child the best of everything and thus prove their devotion. For the second child, they will have learned more about the market and its differences, and the differences between products and brands, and will hesitate less to buy baby supplies in their usual supermarket.

Faced with the proliferation of brands and the diversity of product offerings, consumers adopt the behaviors they feel are most appropriate. For certain products, they remain loyal to a brand they've been satisfied with (Tide detergent, say, or Skippy peanut butter). For other products, they'll buy one of several brands without distinction or make a product's being on sale a priority. Finally, in other cases, they will stress variety and try different products or brands in turn.

At this stage, we can hazard a classification of purchasing behaviors according to the degree of prior deliberation. There is a technical term that is used here – "resolution." There is "limited" resolution when the consumer does not deliberate, but more or less purchases the first product he or she sees. There is "intensive" resolution when the consumer thoroughly seeks out information before deciding. As has been said, this will depend above all on the nature of the product. Figure 7.1 shows the different possible cases.

The decision to purchase represents a major element in our approach to brands and their relations with consumers. The decision to purchase is the expression of the consumer's fundamental freedom; for the brand, it can mean a death sentence with no hope of appeal. We see this in the extreme cases of organized boycotts, and sometimes more or less spontaneous ones.

/ The decision to purchase is the expression of the consumer's fundamental freedom; for the brand, it can mean a death sentence with no hope of appeal. /

To us, this power consumers have is a very positive force. We advocate the promotion of an attitude of reflection that goes beyond the satisfaction of personal needs. We have said how essential we feel it is that brand managers assume their responsibilities towards consumers. We feel that the reverse is just as true. If consumers become conscious of the weight of their purchase decisions, if they learn to lean towards brands whose values they support and see as factors for social progress, they can exercise a decisive influence on the evolution of society.

On this point, we share both Naomi Klein's assessment and her relative optimism (visible above all in the second part of *No Logo*). Where we part

FIGURE 7.1		
Acts of purchase by type of resolution		
Limited resolution	1	Purchase is automatic and without consequence
Average resolution	2	Purchase of a simple product, without risk or consequences
Strong resolution	3	Purchase of a simple but relatively important product
Intensive resolution	4	Deliberated purchase of a complex product of an essential nature and involving risk

Social
involvement

1. Compulsive, pathological purchase ("shopaholism"). An obsessive and compulsive behavioral disorder.

2. Impulse purchase. Purchaser "falls in love at first sight" with the object. An impulsive, unplanned purchase.

3. A planned, deliberated purchase for the satisfaction of individual material or psychological needs.

4. A planned, deliberated purchase of the products of a brand whose values the customer shares and whose actions in favor of social progress he or she approves of.

Figure 7.2 Purchase acts by degree of consumer involvement

ways with her is that we don't speak in terms of a war to be fought against branding, but rather of a balance to be re-established in the dynamics of commercial exchange. For us, consumers and "brands" (producers, distributors) have an equally legitimate place in our world, our society, and our lives. Rather than setting them against each other, we feel it's more constructive to look for ways in which the interplay of their respective interests and responsibilities can contribute to building a better world. We will come back to that in Chapter 8.

If we simplify them, we can attempt to represent all the complex processes that lead from ignorance of the existence of a product to the act of purchasing it in a diagram (Figure 7.3). To do that, we will locate the cognitive and affective dimensions on two different axes, and then delineate zones where purchase is possible. In the possible-purchase zone, we can then introduce the notion of preference, locating products of different brands within it while maintaining the levels of information and the forms of consumer attitudes. To each square there corresponds a quite different purchase situation and dynamic placement of the brand.

The influence of the group on individual behaviors

Psychosociologists have conducted numerous laboratory experiments to measure the pressures brought to bear on individuals by their social group. Their conclusions are quite enlightening. For example, an observer is asked to compare three lines, of different lengths, to a fourth one on the other side of a blackboard. The exercise is quite simple in principle, since the three lines are clearly differentiated in length. Nevertheless, before the observer is questioned, other subjects – who are in fact confederates in the experiment – are questioned and deliberately give wrong answers. In a great

a) zone of possible purchase delineated by cognitive and affective dimensions

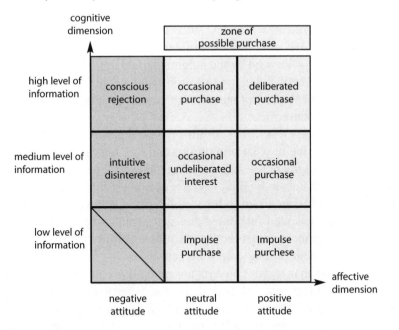

b) zone of possible purchase and preferences

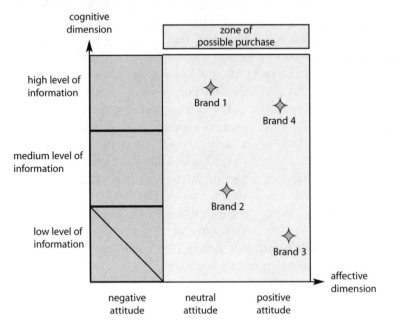

Figure 7.3 Consumers' purchasing behavior

majority of cases, the observer is highly influenced by what he or she has heard, and gives the same answer as the others.

What this experiment, which has since been repeated, shows is that an isolated individual has only partial confidence in his or her own judgment and can be greatly influenced by the judgment of others. This is because we are motivated by a need to belong to a group: to a certain extent, we prefer to be wrong in the company of our "friends" rather than be right if it means departing from a consensus.

During the various repetitions of this type of experiment, psychologists have tried to describe in what proportions and circumstances we refuse to communicate a judgment we feel is correct under the pressure of others. It has been shown that an individual who has a strong, central position within a group is generally not afraid to break solidarity. On the other hand, individuals who are less well integrated and who want to be assimilated into the group have a much greater tendency to show solidarity with the others, even to the detriment of their own judgment.

It is often said that recent converts are much more inflexible regarding the dogmas of their new religion or political party than long-standing members. This is related to the need for integration into a group – as if we feel the need to prove the strength of our new commitment. It will be easier for a member of the Central Committee of the Communist Party, for example, to revise a point of doctrine in the light of new facts. A new member will not have that freedom, and will conform to dogma to avoid being rejected by his or her new fellow members.

We can draw the conclusion that our judgments result in large part from what we think others expect of us. Our opinions are more affective than they are cognitive.

/ Our judgments result in large part from what we think others expect of us. Our opinions are more affective than they are cognitive./

This phenomenon can be verified in the area of apparel. In a school classroom, newcomers will be eager to become part of the group and buy the clothes that seem to be part of the norm: a Gap jacket, say, or New Balance shoes. But the leader of the group or the top student in the class will enjoy greater autonomy as to his or her way of dressing. Often he or she will launch new fashions by going against whatever trend is in force, and then be copied by the others.

These conclusions also have great importance for products that are customarily given as gifts – for example chocolates and neckties. By choosing Maison du Chocolat or Godiva, we rely on the brand reputation as an assurance of good taste and refinement in order to win the recipient's good graces. The gift is the issuance of a social sign. Similarly, when people entertain friends, they generally make a point of serving a high-quality champagne instead of an economy brand. Beyond generosity and the enjoyment of a special occasion, there is also the desire to project a certain image to one's guests.

Conclusion

Individual personality, the need to belong to a group, frames of reference that affect how a message is accepted: the reasons our head "turns" and "turns back" are numerous and far from being fully understood. In fact we feel that elucidating all of them is neither possible nor desirable. We continue to stress the importance of an attitude of humility towards the market. Consumers' freedom of choice will soon chastise those who are arrogant enough to think they have found the miraculous formula.

At a more fundamental level, the consumer's freedom of choice is the sole guarantee of fair exercise of trade and of social progress for all the players concerned. What we should remember is that consumers don't always base their decisions on economic, rational motives that are indifferent to the circumstances. At times, their attitudes and prejudices come into play. Or they take into account the technical or social risks related to the use of a given product. And above all, their behavior is individualistic and differentiated. To them, the diversity of brands means vast and complex perspectives of consumption, which are very often linked to affectivity.

/ The consumer's freedom of choice is the sole guarantee of fair exercise of trade and of social progress for all the players concerned. /

Trying to lift the cover of the black box is far from being a vain endeavor, however. Even the most elementary attitude of attentiveness to the market requires it, in fact. Each brand must analyze its identity and seek out the target consumers it can most easily convince. And, when consumers' judgment – expressed by their decision to purchase – goes against them, they must also be willing to call themselves into question.

Brands cannot act without restriction. Their history, which has constructed their identity, also imposes constraints on them. They are contained within the strictures of their ethical and esthetic invariants and by consumers' attitudes towards them. If they try to abstract themselves from the dominant perceptions, their message will not register. Above all, they can't afford to disappoint consumers. This disappointment applies to "overclaim" about the tangible or intangible qualities of the product, as well as to its social function, or the brand's image as consumers perceive it and judge it.

Finally, a question arises as we look at these different approaches to purchase motivations. It's the same disquiet we feel as we read the lines from Rimbaud we cited: where are the real reasons for the "new love"? Do we really maintain our freedom of choice? Or are we manipulated by the brands?

Manipulation via advertising does exist, of course, but to a lesser degree than the alarmists would have us think. It's not possible to condemn the distressing absence of intelligence and creativity in the marketing milieu, as the brand bashers often do, and at the same time accuse advertising of having Machiavellian power. In fact, nearly all advertising draws on fundamental trends that pre-exist in terms of cultural models – trends that are more or less generalized depending on the consumers at whom the advertising in question is aimed. The phenomenon of cognitive dissonance, which we referred to earlier, considerably limits advertisers' ability to innovate in their discourse.

Advertising does not invent the fashionable themes – freedom, purity, eroticism, violence. It co-opts them, importing them into the domain of mass communication, and only to the extent that these themes can get a favorable hearing from the recipients of that communication. This tendency to "restate" clearly tempers the accusations of manipulation.

/ Brands work at responding to the latent desires of their markets. They tell us what we want to hear. /

Brands work at responding to the latent desires of their markets. They tell us what we want to hear. Therefore the failure of some to take responsibility for certain societal abuses can be criticized. As we have stressed clearly in a preceding chapter, we feel that it is not admissible to encourage consumers to fantasize about just anything. But it's not possible to claim objectively that brands, and all brands, are responsible for these abuses.

8 | Consumers' power

The people had forfeited the confidence of the government and could win it back only by redoubled efforts. Would it not be easier in that case for the government to dissolve the people and elect another?

(Bertolt Brecht)[1]

What if the act of purchase proved to be the revolution of the twenty-first century? In this chapter and the following one, we will describe the emergence of a new type of power consumers wield on the playing field of globalized trade. We have finally come to the development of the third proposition of our thesis: when consumers behave responsibly, they can make brands reinforce actions that generate social, cultural, economic, and even moral progress.

The revolutionaries and militants of the old days, determined to change the world at the initiative of small, highly motivated groups, without excluding recourse to violence, asked the question "What is to be Done?"[2] It's possible that this watchword has been replaced with "What is to be chosen?" – that is, the choice, by the broadest possible group of consumers or citizens, whether or not to give their support to current practices, be they of a political or commercial nature.

This ensemble of individual choices, which is essentially democratic in nature, obviously presupposes the observation of a certain number of basic rules. But when it can be exercised transparently, it proves to be formidably effective. We see this phenomenon as fundamentally positive. It guarantees

---

1 Though he was a participant, just after 1945, in the building of Socialist Germany, playwright Bertolt Brecht was appalled at the Soviet tanks' crushing a worker insurrection in East Berlin in 1953. This quote is taken from a text written on that occasion.

2 This is also the title of one of Lenin's early works.

the brand's positive effects on society. This is why we militate for a responsible consumer, but a responsible consumer is not the remedy for all the ills of our economies. The important thing is therefore to characterize their limits and what is in the balance.

An ethical counterbalance

In the course of this book, we have insisted at length on the responsibilities of brand managers. Our conviction is that there is no long-term corporate leader who does not have his or her own strong system of specific values founded on solidarity, applied at least within the company itself. We like to think that high responsibilities naturally lead to reflection on power and its use, and that high-level directors naturally tend to be people with humanist sensibilities. But it must be recognized that the possibilities of long terms of office are more and more rare, and that the imperatives of the stock market and stock options are not conducive to altruism.

/ Our conviction is that there is no long-term corporate leader who does not have his or her own strong system of specific values founded on solidarity, applied at least within the company itself. /

Let us return to the two fundamental questions we used as criteria for an approach to brand management that would refrain from "encouraging consumers to fantasize about anything and everything":

- Does the brand encourage qualities or sentiments in consumers that can, directly or indirectly, lead them to be themselves factors of progress?

- In all the brand's manifestations (products, advertising, events, and so on), is there a fundamental respect for the dignity of the audience?

We are not so callow as to think that the majority of brand managers can answer these two simple questions in the affirmative. But that is where the consumer comes in. Consumers are the masters of the economic game and can impose their will. The constant introduction and disappearance of products on the supermarket shelves is constant proof of that, and examples abound.

We can return to Coca-Cola, which decided – in 1985, at the initiative of its president, Roberto Goizeta – to create a new formula for its flagship soft drink. What is extremely interesting in this famous case is that, initially, the change was the result of a desire to be attentive to the market. The company had noticed that in blind tests, consumers very clearly preferred Pepsi-Cola to Coca-Cola. Accordingly, the company had developed a new drink, for which the blind tests showed a distinct preference – over both Pepsi-Cola and the traditional Coca-Cola. After much reflection and analysis and many surveys, the decision was made to remove the old Coca-Cola from the supermarket shelves in the United States and

/ Consumers are the masters of the economic game and can impose their will. /

replace it with the New Coke, in an almost identical packaging. The brand's notoriety and a battery of tests proving the excellence of the new formula seemed to guarantee the success of the initiative, which was accompanied by a strategy of massive advertising.

The Coca-Cola company at least had the bitter satisfaction of discovering a brand image it had never dared dream of – that of an untouchable American institution – as it underwent the most resounding failure in a century of existence. Consumers' emotions reached proportions no one could have predicted. Coca-Cola received thousands of indignant letters calling on patriotic pride and saying the American identity was threatened. Hectoliters of New Coke were dumped in front of the company's headquarters by angry consumers. It became clear that people didn't buy Coca-Cola for its taste, but for its name and its permanence in American society. The outcry was such that, less than three months after the highly-publicized launch of the new formula, the company dropped New Coke and returned to Coca-Cola Classic, obviously at enormous cost.[3] Consumer pressure had been too strong.

This same pressure, implicit or explicit, justifies the extremely strict policies of the major brands as regards quality. The innumerable recalls of defective products in the automotive sector bears witness to that. Fear of lawsuits is not the only explanation for this trend, as in the case of policies recommended by certain luxury brands or retail chains (Nordstrom, for example) allowing the return of products customers don't like anymore.

Pressure has been brought to bear in recent years above all in the area of ethics and environmental concerns. *No Logo* features a well-documented account, told from the point of view of the activists, of the actions undertaken against the sweatshops used by companies like Nike and Gap. These actions proved to be quite effective. The introduction of biodegradable packaging and the recent and growing commitment of most major brands to humanitarian causes are examples of the direct influence of consumers. Needless to

---

3 Not long afterward, the company tried to play humorously on the episode when it launched its new Cherry Coke, using the slogan "Outrageous!" This product failed too. It has survived only in the United States, in the limited (for Coca-Cola) market of bars and discos. The lemon-flavored version launched in 2002 seems to be more of a success.

say, this is not because these companies are awakening to their ethical conscience overnight, but it does show they are extremely attentive to the concerns of their clientele. As an organization and as an economic player, a company is both a scale model and a thermometer of our society. It never fails to quickly reflect the transformations taking place there, for better and for worse, and often accelerates them through its culture of reactivity and its dynamism.

/ As an organization and as an economic player, a company is both a scale model and a thermometer of our society. It never fails to quickly reflect the transformations taking place there. /

That is why the influence of consumers is decisive, and why their collective responsibilities are very real. As Western consumers climb up the pyramid of needs, their ethical role stands out more clearly. We may be at a historic crossroads of which a book like *No Logo*, despite its sometimes arguable conclusions, is a symptom. Not only do consumers ignore the least competitive products, and impose their criteria of quality, service, and frankness in communication, but they are beginning to moralize economic life by encouraging actions of social solidarity. At the most immediate level, these actions were long aimed at redressing the illicit maneuvers of certain major brands. Today they are extending more and more to the promotion of major humanitarian causes.

Any capacity for influencing brands requires conviction on the part of the brands' managers – or else the leverage to coerce them – because they are the ones who have direct access to the levers of the brand's identity and its manifestations. The preceding examples point up different forms of consumer power, in reaction to diverse situations:

1. The consumer acts directly, via the act of purchase. This is surely the message managers understand best. In this case, the message received by the brand is extracted from the sum total of all the purchases made by the sum total of all consumers. This is not a relation between two individuals, but the collective rejection of a proposition of the brand in relation to its competitors. It is the judgment of the competitiveness of the product at a given time and in a given place.

2. Consumers also have an arsenal of direct actions at their disposal, such as responses to the surveys and interviews frequently conducted by brands or specialists in communication. Direct letters to a company director or to the customer service and messages sent via the brand's web site are taken more and more seriously by brands that are ahead of the game as regards customer relations.

3. Consumers also act indirectly based on the speculations managers make about their future acts of purchase. The essence of marketing is to predict the future reactions of specific consumer segments. In 1990, traces of benzene were found in Perrier water. The quality of the water was not at issue, but rather a technical problem involving a defective filter. Perrier's reaction (the immediate recall of millions of bottles) was of course an anticipation of the market's reaction, and was appropriate to the seriousness of the problem.

4. Finally, consumers can make use of intermediaries, such as the public authorities or the opinion of other citizens, to reinforce their action.

Here we enter the domain of structured actions, which can take the form of demonstrations, boycotts, press campaigns, specialized publications, industry monitoring, the creation of associations, and so on. We discuss these in the next chapter. For now let's concentrate on the act of purchase, the initial form of exercise of consumer power, the clearest and most direct, and the one whose effects are felt most concretely by the brand.

Virtues of the act of purchase

We are witnessing the rise of the consumer-citizen, who expresses his or her opinion through the vote cast by the act of purchase. In the stand-off between the brand manager and the consumer, we feel that the latter has the upper hand, having the power to buy or not to buy a product.

It is easy and superficial to take aim at McDonald's and criticize its products, the esthetics of its restaurants, the effectiveness of its global strategy, or the fact that it is the symbol of American neo-imperialism. But the real issue remains why consumers go there in droves! No doubt because they can eat a quick meal, in excellent hygienic conditions – which is not the case with the usual fast-food outlet – and cheaply, and also because their children like it and clamor to be taken there. Among McDonald's bashers, a schism often develops between those who have children and those who don't.

The first McDonald's restaurant in Singapore opened in the late 1970s, at the corner of Scotts Road and Orchard Road, the two main shopping streets. All the experts predicted it would fail, because of the gulf between Chinese culinary tastes and American "gastronomy." But it was an immediate success – not because of the food served, but because the place quickly became the meeting place for hip teenagers. The McDonald's restaurant in fact performed a social function that had no equivalent on the island at the time.

The consumer is always the one who turns a commercial operation into a success or a failure. The act of purchase has at least two features in common with the democratic vote. First, it is the expression of an individual choice in the face of a diversified offering. Second, it makes sense only in its collective dimension, through the accumulation of all acts of purchase, out of which trends will develop.

It is interesting to observe a certain convergence between political elections and the policies of brands. It gives the impression that the former are becoming more "mercantile" while the latter are becoming more political. The differences are sometimes slight between the candidate-product, with a slogan aimed at getting voters to pull the right lever, and the product-candidate, which is after a maximum number of vote-purchases in the cash register. The slogans have become almost interchangeable. For politics: "The great society" or "Putting people first." And for brands: "We generate promises" from Duke Energy,[4] or "Changing for the better" for Kmart.

/ It is interesting to observe a certain convergence between political elections and the policies of brands. It gives the impression that the former are becoming more "mercantile" while the latter are becoming more political. /

The comparison with electoral politics has its limits, however. The act of purchase does not take place in a context that is as well defined in time and space as do political elections. The consumer can vote all year round, several times per day, and the results are not presented on the evening news. The voting population remains poorly delineated and it's not really possible to define an absolute majority. To express itself fully, the vote-purchase needs the accumulation of purchases over a longer period. Its effects are also more progressive. A political vote can lead to a sudden change of regime; a change in the management of a company following rejection by the markets is slower to come about and, though frequent, is not automatic. Yet while the form and function of the act of purchase and the political vote are somewhat different, it remains true that they share a certain "civic" nature. In both cases, the individual decision takes into account – or should – all the possible consequences on the future life of society.

Is that really so much different with brands? We will soon look at the phenomenon of more-or-less spontaneous boycotts, collective sanctions that are based on other criteria than consumers' immediate interests. But there are less radical examples. In all countries, there exist categories of automobile purchasers who make a criterion of choice of a certain national solidarity. Whether they are factory workers, managers, government work-

---

4 *Fortune 500*, April 15, 2002.

ers, small-business owners, or CEOs, whether they defend or condemn protectionism and market regulation, they find themselves in a consensus regarding values that clearly go beyond their individual interests.

We feel that it is of crucial importance to be aware of these mechanisms of purchase and the power they wield. Our conviction is that the choice of a product must be made not only on the issue of its qualitative superiority. It must also recognize or reject the brand's over-all politics, as dictated by the conscience of the purchaser – with the awareness that the effectiveness of each individual choice will depend on the number of persons who make the same choice.

The act of purchase is an act of social responsibility.

/ The choice of a product must be made not only on the issue of its qualitative superiority. It must also recognize or reject the brand's overall politics, as dictated by the conscience of the purchaser. /

The limits of consumer power

Even assuming that it is a responsible act, the exercise of consumer power nevertheless has limits. They are principally related to two causes: the fundamentally reactive nature of the power of the consumer, and the existence of that category of consumers we have referred to as "fragile."

The reactive nature of the act of purchase

The act of purchase is the exercise of an indirect power. It is transmitted by the intermediary of a brand's managers. While it has all the advantages of a democratic power, it also has the faults. This power remains passive in nature, and is more a vehicle for sanctions than for innovation. Consumers can be content with making their purchases and hope that the creators, merchandisers, product managers, and brand directors interpret and even anticipate their desires.

Most major brands remain, however, very open to suggestions from consumers. Generally, they keep channels open for contact with their clientele. In certain sectors, such as the software industry, feedback from users is a fundamental resource, and the brands devote significant investments to gathering and processing it. It is common practice among software publishers to distribute their prototypes ("beta versions") free to users who agree

to send in their comments. Nevertheless, it is generally through more structured collective action that consumers can actually propose measures the
companies would never have launched without their input.

"Fragile" consumers

There is too often a tendency to see consumers as defenseless victims who
are forced into buying products they don't really need. Still, it has to be
recognized that certain categories of consumers exist who are weaker and
more impressionable than others. They are not always in a position to exercise their "purchase power" freely and as the result of a conscious and
deliberate choice.

Lower incomes

Analyses show that the wealthiest consumers, as could be expected, are
more indifferent to the price of products than the average consumer. But it's
more surprising to note that these well-heeled consumers are joined in that
indifference by the least wealthy. If we draw a curve of price elasticity as
a function of income, we see that it takes the form of an inverted "U" (see
Figure 8.1). At each end, we find the high and low income groups, and both
are characterized by the same indifference to the criterion of price.

Numerous studies have attempted to explain this behavior on the part of
low-income consumers. One theory is that the reasons are psychological.
In a situation where indebtedness is perma-
nent, and within certain limits, price differences cease to have any meaning. But there
are also more pragmatic explanations. First of
all, the most disadvantaged consumers often
have no automobile. So they make their
purchases near their home, since they don't
have the physical means to travel to where
they can get a bargain. They also have less time to shop. They are also less
curious and less well informed about price differences. Finally, they sometimes prefer small shops where they are known and where the retailer is
willing to extend them credit.

/ The high and low
income groups are
both characterized by
the same indifference
to the criterion
of price. /

A polemic developed about this, a few years ago, with the opening of the
first Crazy Eddie store in France. The store had developed well in the UK.
Crazy Eddie is an appliance and television store which operates on the basis
of total easy and immediate credit. In exchange, the merchandise can be taken

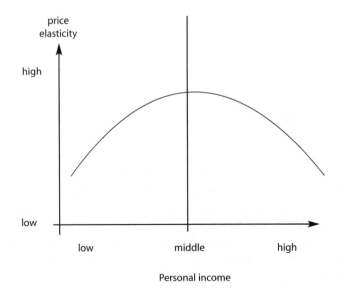

Figure 8.1 Price elasticity as a function of income

back by the store if the payments are not kept up. It's possible to buy a television set at Crazy Eddie with a very low down payment and the commitment to pay 12 monthly installments. If the consumer pays regularly, he or she will become the owner of the television set at the end of a year – and, no doubt, will have paid 50 percent more than its cash value. If a payment is missed, the TV can be taken away with no possible recourse on the buyer's part.

When the store opened in France, the press criticized this system, which encouraged poor people to buy things they could not afford, inciting them to trap themselves in a spiral of indebtedness. Above all, indignation was expressed at the way the company was "getting rich off the poor." Others objected, on the other hand, that Crazy Eddie was providing a specific service to a group of customers who had been systematically refused by traditional credit entities. The system in fact uses mutualization of poor credit – that is, each purchaser pays a higher price because others will be incapable of honoring their commitments.

So was it usury or a needed service? The moral debate surrounding the nature of and the need for such businesses remains unsolved. Only one thing is sure: the French Crazy Eddie store closed its doors for lack of customers. It may be possible to see the differing fortunes of Crazy Eddie in France and in the UK as a confrontation between two societal models. In any event, consumers voted against the existence of the store. They made full use of their power.

Children

Are young consumers easier to influence than others? In any case, it would be a mistake to think that advertising aimed at children is a recent development in our society. As early as 1935, the French review *Vendre* published a feature called "Children, present and future customers." It said, among other things:

> Children are gullible. Any argument works on them. An entertainer would say they are the perfect audience. Simply tell them the reasons why they should have your articles purchased for them. Since their instinct of self-defense is still slumbering, no instinctive reaction will counterbalance your demonstration …
>
> Advertising will be joyous. Your texts will be amusing, your images clear, in gay but not gaudy colors, and will portray only happy, healthy individuals.

So there is nothing new in this area.

The issue of children and advertising leads us to make a distinction between two cases: the one where children make their parents buy products and the one where they buy them for themselves. Everyone has seen, at one time or another, children throwing a tantrum in a supermarket to force their parents to buy them candy. It's well known that children are often the ones who decide what breakfast cereals, cookies, chocolate drink mix, and even cars their parents buy.

/ It's well known that children are often the ones who decide what breakfast cereals, cookies, chocolate drink mix, and even cars their parents buy. /

Advertisers sometimes aim their campaigns primarily at children so that they will lobby for a product with their parents. There was a campaign for the Peugeot 806 with the slogan "The car children recommend to their parents." Though it was not aimed at children alone, the campaign cleverly played on their position as order givers and, using humor (the children were presented as little tyrants), recalled the model's intended use as a family car. To assess not the effectiveness, but the appropriateness of such methods, we must judge above all whether they are used in good faith, with humor and restraint, and if they meet the two criteria we mentioned in the introduction to this chapter ("factors for progress" and "dignity"). If they do, there is no reason to criticize these campaigns aimed at children.

Children are also targeted as direct consumers. In this case, the same rules should apply. The amount of the expenditure compared with the average budget of the targeted age group also constitutes a criterion of good sense as regards tolerance. A study conducted in March 2002 for the French Ministry of Education[5] sums the problem up well. On certain Wednesdays – when many French children are not in school – children between the ages of 6 and 12 are subjected to as many as 192 advertising spots. Such an avalanche, consisting essentially of spots for food products and toys, cannot be without consequences for these children.

Certain countries are more concerned than others by the problem. In the UK, the BBC plans to create two free, no-advertising channels for children. As we will see, Sweden has a rich tradition of defending the rights of consumers. The SVTI network recently launched a weekly 30-minute program in which different brands are presented to children, comparative tests are made to teach them to exercise their freedom of choice, and certain advertising is parodied. The program is an opportunity for young children to be objective about what they see and to become reasonable, informed purchasers. Certainly everyone, from brand managers to the major media and educators, has an interest in young children learning to distance themselves from their habitual environment and develop a critical and selective attitude, early on, in order to fully exercise their power as consumers.

The global teen

This phenomenon is analyzed in detail by Naomi Klein in her book. We feel it is one of the useful contributions of *No Logo*. The adolescent market segment has probably been one of the most sought-after for the past ten years or so, and probably the most globalized. Brands like Nike, Adidas, Tommy Hilfiger, Benetton, Gap, but also Apple, Sony, and above all MTV, have made teenagers their preferential target and built their success on them.

Like children, teenagers have only limited experience of products. They have not purchased 25 pairs of shoes and are much more vulnerable to advertising messages and to the opinions of their social groups than to an objective analysis of the tangible benefits of a product. Global brands, the increasing income levels of their parents, sports, the "youth" trend, and the cult of the human body have all contributed to making this age group the one that is probably the most homogeneous on the planet, in terms of clothing and musical choices. But that doesn't mean that adolescents all think the same and that they forget their own cultural roots. We will come back to this theme in our conclusion.

---

5 Monique Dagnaud, "Les enfants, acteurs courtisés de l'économie marchande," *Le Monde*, May 28, 2002.

The uncontrolled buyer

There is a particular category of consumers who are victims of "shopaholism." This is not a fashionable buzzword, but a real societal problem. Specialists feel that approximately one person in five has a problem controlling his or her purchasing. These problem purchasers are broken down into four major categories:

/ Teenagers are much more vulnerable to advertising messages and to the opinions of their social groups than to an objective analysis of the tangible benefits of a product. /

- Compulsive purchasers, who buy to reduce their anxiety or to console themselves about their physical appearance. They consume clothing as a priority.

- Impulsive purchasers, who buy to obtain immediate, short-lived pleasure. They are, in a way, collectors of objects they don't necessarily need.

- Dependent purchasers, for whom purchasing is a form of physical need they have difficulty doing without.

- Finally, the manic-depressives, who experience true crises and can purchase goods worth enormous amounts in a very short time.

These phenomena must not be taken lightly. Doctors at Stanford University have studied the cases of 21 women suffering from the chronic disorder of "shopaholism." They prescribed an antidepressant called Cipramil. According to their conclusions, the drug "significantly improved the compulsive purchasing behavior of the women in the study."

Fashion victims

We have already mentioned their case in our indictment of the reprehensible practices of certain brands. It is true that brands can become such an object of desire that they lead certain more impressionable persons into more or less dramatic excesses. For others, brands, in their number and diversity, can offer consumers a kind of haven, the comfort of a world of illusion where they don't need to assert a personality of their own.

Conclusion

Clearly, certain categories of consumers are characterized by a certain susceptibility to the brand's actions: excessive credulity towards the advertising, uncontrolled purchasing, unconditional acceptance of the values and lifestyles proposed, and so on. Generally, the problems of these persons do not originate in their relations with brands. They have the same types of difficulty in their day-to-day lives with their environment, their family, their work, and their friends.

Obviously these people must be protected and dealt with carefully. Fortunately, they represent only a small percentage of the population. The great majority of consumers are capable of shopping rationally and responsibly. And that is the type of behavior we wish for and encourage, and to which we will now turn our attention.

The rational consumer

Before taking on the theme of the responsible consumer, we feel we should begin by asking a legitimate question: is it really possible to conceive of such a thing as a purely rational purchase? By rational, we mean the rigorous evaluation, with an eye towards objectivity, of the advantages and disadvantages of an act of purchase, followed by a decision that resembles a balanced judgment. Are consumers rational? The question may seem trivial. Yet it raises complex problems.

In his book on consumer choice,[6] J.-F. Bernard-Becharie proposes two enlightening examples. He describes a person who comes home unhappy about having spent his entire month's income in the space of one week. He nonetheless decides go out again and buy a desk lamp he doesn't really need and has to pay for on credit. A little later, he decides to take a vacation. He needs a little cash, so he sells his lamp to a flea-market merchant who buys it from him at half the price he paid for it. He ends up canceling his trip. He goes back to the flea market and buys the lamp back for a little more money.

The author then describes another person who hesitates between two models of car. He compares them in terms of acceleration, weight, speed, interior space. He defines two complex criteria of comparison using two variables: power and safety on the one hand, and interior comfort on the other. One of the models is better according to the first criterion, and the other according to the second criterion, so he hesitates between the two.

At first glance, the first person behaves in a quite irrational way, whereas the second is quite rational. But consumer theory throws another light on the cases. We saw in the preceding chapter how consumers can move from attitude to preference as a function of a prior frame of reference which conditions their perception of the different purchase stimuli. From this point of view, the first person is rational. Faced with a given situation, he can

---

6 J.-F. Bernard-Becharie, *Le choix de consommation*, Paris: Eyrolles, 1970.

decide quickly and make a choice that corresponds to his preferences of the moment. The supposed incoherence comes from the fact that he changes his preferences very often, but that doesn't change the coherence of each choice. The second person, on the other hand, doesn't really know what he wants. He attempts to reconcile criteria of choice that are heterogeneous, and as a result is incapable of deciding. He is the irrational person.

This example shows how difficult it is to analyze the notion of rationality. We will see first how consumers make a series of successive approximations, then we will describe the notion of stability of preferences, and finally that of progressivity.

The mechanism of successive approximations

Consumers are never either quite rational nor quite irrational, either from the point of view of consumer theory or that of common sense. Their purchasing behavior, observed over time, leaves the trace of an exploration of the available offering founded on criteria of satisfaction (if I'm not happy, I change). This schema is methodical, but tolerant. This implies that choices eliminated during an early stage can end up being chosen as the best compromise.

/ Consumers' purchasing behavior, observed over time, leaves the trace of an exploration of the available offering founded on criteria of satisfaction (if I'm not happy, I change). /

For example, the consumer sees an advertisement for a product and is persuaded. He or she buys the product and consumes it. In many cases, the consumption does not give satisfaction from all points of view and according to all criteria. The consumer is partially satisfied and partially disappointed. The next time, he or she buys a product of another brand. Again, the product is not entirely satisfactory, so the consumer goes back to the first brand, or else tries a third.

When consumer panels are studied, successive and irregular purchases of different brands are often observed. A person will buy Dannon yogurt with fruit, then Yoplait yogurt with fruit, then maybe Dannon again, then a store brand of yogurt, before going back to Dannon or Yoplait. Each time, consumers will act in a rational way, since they will decide as a function of their preferences; but these preferences themselves evolve as a result of their experience of the products. Often, a recurring purchasing behavior eventually stabilizes, but it can still evolve with the arrival of new products in the consumer's customary store, or with inventory problems or price variations. What results from these successive approximations, then, is behavior that is more or less unstable depending on variable dissatisfaction with the products, or of the variability of the offering of products in the category.

Time and stability of preference

When preferences for one brand or another are studied, it is generally done at a specific time. But these preferences also evolve over time, as a function of the experience of consumption. To measure the effectiveness of an advertising campaign, certain companies measure, for example, preferences before and after the campaign for a very broad sampling of consumers. They attribute the modifications of these preferences, according to a list of criteria, to the impact of the advertising. If the objective of an advertisement for Tasters Choice is to convince the consumer of the excellence of its coffee taste, then at the end of the advertising campaign, preferences for Tasters Choice in terms of taste should evolve positively. A study before and after the campaign should be able to confirm this.

However if this preference has not varied in a significant way, it doesn't necessarily mean that the advertisement was poorly done. It can mean that preferences in terms of instant coffee taste are too set or too stable, that the error was in the focus of the campaign itself. It might have been better to focus on ease of use or the fun aspects of the product. As can be seen, it's essential to understand the preferences acquired by the different brands in terms of different criteria, and the stability of these preferences, before determining the most effective advertising focus.

The progressivity of attitudes and preferences

We have tried to show that it's useless to try to change consumers' points of view if they are firmly fixed and are part of their pre-existing frame of reference. The mechanisms of selective perception and cognitive dissonance will come into play, and the advertising message will not be seen or will be modified.

Sometimes, though, the addition of a new element or of a new criterion can bring about progressive evolution of the pre-existing frame of reference. If a brand is perceived as expensive and of very high quality, there's no point in explaining to consumers that's it's not really that expensive. But the fact can be brought out that it offers additional services, that the after-sales service is free, or that the product is economical to use. This can eventually and progressively change the brand's overall perception.

We could cite the example of liquid detergents here. On the supermarket shelf, there are a great number of products whose price can vary by a factor of two, or almost. But they don't all necessarily have the same effectiveness. That can depend on the ingredients and the concentration of the liquid. If we can explain that a given product is more concentrated, more powerful, so that it takes less of it to wash a plate, then price becomes a more relative consideration. It may be that the most expensive product is also the most economical.

/ Sometimes the addition of a new element or of a new criterion can bring about progressive evolution of the pre-existing frame of reference. /

Successive approximations, stability of preferences, very progressive evolution of attitudes: as we can see, rationality is not absent from these three aspects of the complex mechanism that leads a consumer to a purchase, though it does comprise a great number of different parameters. So it is possible to be in the position of buying in a deliberate, considered manner, following the logic of preferences. Let us now see how that reasoning can be taken further, to finally arrive at a responsible act of purchase.

The responsible consumer

People are responsible to the extent that they can judge the consequences of their acts. Consumers can, as has been said, buy, sell, or abandon the same product within a very short time. Yet this does not mean that they don't know what they want. They prefer to buy and drive a car that doesn't pollute, provided that the service is as good as with other makes and that it doesn't cost significantly more. They may also boycott a brand because they don't like its advertising.

In making such choices, consumers show themselves to be aware of the reasons and the consequences of their purchases. They are intellectually responsible. However, in order to become socially responsible and appreciate the civic nature of the act of purchase, they have to become aware of the formidable power they have over brands, and recognize that they have the possibility of controlling enormous financial and human resources.

Any capacity for influence implies assuming responsibility and reflecting on the consequences of the exercise of that influence. This rule should hold for brand managers as well as for consumers. The latter, too often, are not aware of the extent of the real power they exercise when they go to the supermarket, or choose not to go there. They are no doubt more sensitive to the social problems of the world than of their ability to do something about those problems using their influence on brands. Once they have discovered this power and responsibility, the next small step is for the choice of a product to be based not only on immediate interests or comparison of benefits, but for it also to take all the brand's policies, and their consequences on our society, into account.

The act of purchase must be the result of motivations that go beyond impulse, habit, or the satisfaction of a considered personal need. It must be an action that has meaning, that supports the values expressed by the brand and its behavior in general.

Our two criteria of generation of social progress and respect for the dignity of the audience, used by managers of brands to judge the quality of their actions, find a new use here. They also serve as reference for consumers in examining the brand's identity and its behavior. It is undeniable that many recent actions by consumers demonstrate a growing sensitivity to the problems of our world, and that this evolution towards considering the act of purchase as an act of social responsibility already has its adherents. Awareness of the civic nature of the act of purchase is under construction.

The most recent case: in Chapter 4 we mentioned the Mecca-Cola brand, which promotes the cause of Palestinian children and supports other European NGOs. The arrival of the Mecca-Cola brand on the market in late 2002 and its immediate success within a certain specific market segment is the latest and clearest example of a mass-market brand that believes in the purchasing act going beyond the satisfaction of a physical need (in this case, quenching one's thirst). It has bet its very existence on the belief that a certain segment of the market is ready to buy a cola as a sign of adhesion to specific and clearly expressed social, and perhaps political, values.

> / The act of purchase must be the result of motivations that go beyond impulse, habit, or the satisfaction of a considered personal need. It must be an action that has meaning, that supports the values expressed by the brand and its behavior in general./

Conclusion

In the confrontation between the brand manager and the consumer, we have tried to determine the nature, the extent, and the limits of their respective powers. The increasing power of brands is undeniable, but that power also entails weighty responsibilities. It is also important that certain persons who are more susceptible because of their age, income level, or psychological fragility be protected from their persuasive power.

However, consumers remain in control of the game. To paraphrase the ironic passage from Brecht we use as an epigraph to this chapter, no brand manager can ever fire them! They can't be fooled for very long, and are often better informed about products than one might think. Their choices are generally rational and intellectually responsible, and should reflect more and more, in the years ahead, a new awareness of their social responsibilities.

We are now at an important turning point: the emergence of a consumer-citizen. We feel that everyone will benefit if that emergence takes place as transparently as possible, both to guarantee the balance of powers and to contain the risks of its being co-opted for the profit of special interests. That means that everyone must develop a consciousness of the idea that this banal, everyday act – the purchase of products or services – is taking on new meaning and power, and more and more openly becoming a civic act of social solidarity.

For consumers, this awareness is also the source of new responsibilities, symmetrical with those of the brand manager. They must inform themselves about the brands they buy, what they do, who runs them, what their values are. They must decode the brand's identity and verify its appropriateness to the two criteria we have mentioned. Further, the individual vote only becomes effective when it is added to a certain mass of identical choices. This means that consumers must share information and opinions, inform themselves, join together, and work to convince others. Finally, the exercise of the vote sanction is limited unless it guarantees, in parallel, the perspective of dialogue. We will develop these points in Chapter 9.

/ The act of purchasing products or services is taking on new meaning and power, and more and more openly becoming a civic act of social solidarity. /

We have said that brands' contribution to progress consists, through their qualitative excellence, in providing the physical, psychological, and moral comfort that puts consumers in a position to engender progress themselves. In other words, the brands "pass the baton," making consumers protagonists of social progress. In turn, consumers can exercise their citizenship, notably by letting the companies know that their expectations will by no means be limited to the satisfaction of immediate needs.

We may be permitted to dream of a virtuous – as opposed to vicious – circle within which the brands put consumers in a position to initiate progress, and where the latter in turn influence the brands, to make them commit themselves directly to causes of solidarity – or, at least, to improving the physical and moral quality of the lives of a great number of consumers.

9 Structured consumer action

There can be no daily democracy without daily citizenship.
(Ralph Nader)

Consumers are better informed about brands and about the purchases they make than is generally thought. Consumer isolation and passivity are not inevitable. Since the birth of the consumer movement in the 1960s, prosperous and powerful organizations have been working to inform consumers, assist them in choosing, and provide them with the means to compare the different product and service offerings available. These movements also do much more than that. They bring consumers together, giving them a chance to make their point of view heard and get organized. In certain cases, they can organize boycott campaigns to force companies to change their behavior.

The progressive awareness of consumers' rights has resulted in the implementation of laws and regulatory authorities, but also in the recognition of collective rights for consumer associations, which have given these groups weapons with which to defend themselves, take initiatives, and make their voices heard. In all the world's industrialized countries, the power of these groups is undeniable, and clearly generates progress by re-establishing the balance of power.

The Scandinavian countries, and in particular Sweden, are often held up as examples of the originality and effectiveness of their network of defense of consumers' interests. Nevertheless, for a certain number of historical and economic reasons, the United States is where the consumer advocacy movement has its modern roots; and it can be hoped that this country will play a crucial role in the coordination of future actions, on a global scale. That is why we will concentrate on the American example in this chapter.

Recent developments in relations between brands and organized consumers appear to be characterized by three traits. First, consumers have asserted their power and made themselves heard. Second, their demands have moved onto a vaster playing field – that of ethics, in particular. And the brands – and this is a new development – are listening to these demands and assuming their "global" responsibilities. Third, the danger of this power being confiscated for the benefit of specific interests has emerged, while consumers' primary expectations – product quality, for example – take a back seat. We feel that this imbalance could prove to be harmful.

We discuss these issues as we examine a radical and highly mediatized type of action: the boycott. While boycotts exist that are initiated by consumer associations for technical reasons to do with product quality, the recent trend is towards boycotts of an ethical nature. Using examples of this type of action, we will to try to characterize the issues behind these new structured consumer movements.

The emergence of consumer law

The concern for the respect of competition – and thus, for the protection of the consumer – is as old as commerce and law. Examples are to be found in Roman legislation. Nevertheless, it was in the United States, some 40 years ago, that the modern concept of consumer legislation emerged. Of course, other laws or initiatives in this area existed, at least embryonically, throughout the industrialized countries, but the skyrocketing of American capitalism led the United States to take action very early and very vigorously on the issue of "the hegemony of vendors."

The first association for the defense of the rights of the consumer, the Consumer Union, was founded in 1936. But it was in the early 1960s that the concept of defense of consumer rights began to take on considerable importance. This emergence is part of an old tradition in US political thought, viscerally attached to preventing any hegemony from threatening the economic or political equilibrium. The long struggle for the implementation of antitrust legislation in the United States extended all throughout the first half of the twentieth century. It is based on two fundamental laws – the Sherman Antitrust Act of 1890 and the Clayton Act of 1914 – and on various jurisprudence that has defined their interpretation. Basically, these laws control situations of monopoly, anti-competitive practices, price fixing, and cartel agreements. They are guaranteed by two federal authorities, the antitrust division of the Justice Department and the Federal Trade Commission. We tend to forget how much the existence of these control structures has marked the history of US capitalism, and remains a determining factor today. We could cite the breaking up of the Standard Oil monopoly, headed by Rockefeller, in 1911; the controversy around the price-fixing agreements between General Electric and Westinghouse in the 1960s; the Ford Motor Co. versus United States case in 1972, in which Ford was found guilty of hampering competition and forced to divest Autolite; or, recently, the suits against Microsoft for attempting to monopolize the software market.

/ The existence of control structures has marked the history of US capitalism, and remains a determining factor today. /

Starting in the 1950s, the question of individual rights became determinant in political life. The concept of "civil rights" was to mark several generations of Americans. The progressive reforms of the Warren Supreme Court (1953–69) completely reshaped civic life. Through the issues of equality before the law, the judicial system, and voting rights, US society worked to achieve an ideal of the citizen-individual that was to become its very foundation.

Around the same period, voices like that of economist John Kenneth Galbraith were calling the free-market economy into question, underlining the danger of excessive control over the consumer society by producers. In Galbraith's analysis, certain companies, with cheaper capital than others, take full advantage of industrial concentration and succeed in buying out their competitors or gaining control of all the technologies in their business sector. Their organization becomes rigid and a threat to the freedom of individual consumers. In this context also came the revelation of the techniques of mass communication and of their power, through social-psychology surveys.

While it remains even today an essential factor in US political life, control of the concentration of capital has shown its limits and is not sufficient to guarantee the rights of the consumer. It therefore becomes essential to create a counter-power, or rather to encourage its development. In 1962 President John F. Kennedy sent Congress, for the first time, a "Special Message to the Congress on Protecting the Consumer Interest." Starting in 1964, a Special Assistant on Consumer Affairs was appointed to the President's Executive Office.

John F. Kennedy's message underscored the fact that marketing can become detached and impersonal, and that consumers are subject to the influence of mass advertising that does not necessarily provide them with the means to judge whether, for example, a drug meets minimum requirements for safety, quality, or effectiveness, or how much a bank loan will really cost over the entire period of reimbursement. Based on simple – and doubtless somewhat extreme – cases, Kennedy defined what he considered to be a new Bill of Rights: the right to product safety, in terms of reliability and hazardousness; the right to be informed, to be protected against fraudulent communication – whether advertising, labeling, or in other forms; the right to choose, that is, to a sufficient variety of products; and finally, the right to be heard.

On this last point, Kennedy lamented the fact that consumers are "the only important group in the economy who are not effectively organized, whose views are often not heard." Without really saying so, the President was implying that it was high time the actions carried on by producers' lobbies were counterbalanced by action on behalf of consumers. The latter needed to be organized in a much more systematic way.

In 1962 a Consumer Advisory Council (CAC) was created in Washington. The Council very quickly determined a list of ten priority areas in which it was to intervene:

- standards for consumption (labeling, quantities, product performances, definition of quality standards)

- organization of consumption between consumers and the public authorities

- representation of consumers and consumer advocacy entities with the public authorities

- credit, and in particular mortgage loans and management of cases of over-indebtedness

- coordination of federal and local policy on the defense of consumers

- acceleration of economic growth and aid to growth beneficial to consumers

- the special case of consumption by groups of consumers with very low incomes

- the struggle against price fixing by producers

- access to decent housing for all citizens

- specific practices regarding health and medical care.

Having defined its policies, the CAC went on to take action in all the areas in this list, which 40 years later has lost none of its relevance and coherence. It might even be called the founding act of consumer advocacy, though the historical importance of the antitrust legislation must not be forgotten.

Today the Consumer Advisory Council no longer exists, but the Federal Trade Commission has been transformed. It is no longer an authoritarian, "top-down" public entity. A center for responding to consumers' needs was created. Two commissions have also taken over certain tasks identified by the CAC, and which we mentioned above: the Consumer Product Safety Commission and the Federal Communications Commission. The purpose of these entities is to protect the public interest and the consumer.

The implementation of these governmental structures is also accompanied by the recognition of collective rights for consumer organizations, which they may assert in a court of law. Such legal empowerment has made it possible for these associations to play a significant role, which compensates in part for the technical or economic weakness of isolated consumers against producers and mass retailers.

Consumer advocacy movements in the United States

Ralph Nader is considered to be at the origin of consumer advocacy in the United States – John K. Galbraith and John F. Kennedy preceded him by a few years.

Ralph Nader and Public Citizen

Born in 1934, a graduate of Harvard Law School, Nader worked for a Senate subcommittee. In this capacity, he produced a report on the disadvantages of certain types of instrument panels and steering columns during traffic accidents. The report apparently had little impact. As a result, Nader published *Unsafe at Any Speed* in 1965.

/ Ralph Nader is at the origin of consumer advocacy in the United States. /

The book did not get a lot of attention at first, even though it directly accused the General Motors Corvair of being a death trap. In fact, the controversy arose from the pressure the auto maker brought to bear on Ralph Nader. He subsequently succeeded in forcing the president of General Motors to apologize before a televised hearing of a Senate committee. Sales of the Corvair soon plummeted, and the car was withdrawn from the market.

In the meantime, Ralph Nader became a celebrity. From the General Motors affair, he developed the elements of a method: study a case in depth, launch an information campaign, call in the press, and demand reform. Nader also became interested in the need to protect local residents from the construction of oil pipelines, then in the dangers of the use of electrical equipment in hospitals.

Nader continues to organize. He enlists young students to help conduct in-depth surveys of companies or public authorities and publishes their results. He has published works on the negligence of the Federal Trade Commission, on dangerous chemicals found in food, and on the dangers of air pollution and its industrial causes. With member contributions, he founded the Public Interest Research Group, which hires young journalists and attorneys. He has encouraged his collaborators to run in union and political elections, but without great success.

In 1971 Ralph Nader founded an organization, Public Citizen, whose objective is to represent consumers' interests before Congress, the public authorities, and the courts. This group refuses to accept any subsidy or contribution from the government or from companies. It is financed exclusively by individual memberships. Since its creation Public Citizen has taken action, in particular, in the defense of consumers before the courts and in promoting clean, safe, renewable energy sources, fair trade, environmental protection, and the promotion of effective and reasonably priced drugs. In 1997 Nader brought out a study on the consequences of mergers in the pharmaceuticals sector on the availability of affordable medications.

/ One might wonder whether concern for immediate defense of consumers has not given way, in Nader's actions, to an activism with more general scope, aimed more at social reform than concrete improvement. /

In 2001 Public Citizen accused Ford of requiring Bridgestone to ship tires that were 10 percent lighter for its Ford Explorer vehicles. This reduced fuel consumption, but increased the risk of accidents caused by tread separation.

Ralph Nader has become a central figure in consumer advocacy. He was one of the first to call for the dismantling of Microsoft, or at least for the imposition of new rules of competition. His group was particularly active in Seattle during the demonstrations against the WTO. However, one might wonder whether concern for immediate defense of consumers has not given way, in his actions, to an activism with more general scope, aimed more at social reform than concrete improvement.

Consumer Action

Another consumer advocacy group is Consumer Action, founded in 1971 in San Francisco by Kay Pachtner. Its objectives are more limited, focusing on defense of consumers, accompaniment of their court actions against producers, education, and the dissemination of information on products and services. This organization, despite a modest budget and only 17 permanent employees, has a network of 5000 volunteer centers around the United States. It has telephone hotlines and an interactive web site to help consumers around the country.

Consumer Action has taken some very firm actions against certain companies or certain sectors. Among its publications are *Break the Banks: A Shopper's Guide to Banking Services*, and *Deceptive Packaging*. The group went after automakers with actions like its "Lemonstration" protest in 1975. It has also sued the Bank of America for fraudulent advertising; the bank lost and had to pay heavy damages. Consumer Action has also recently published an exhaustive guide to the costs of telephone use.

Consumer Action also cooperates with companies and public entities (American Express, Edison Electric Institute, Pacific Bell, US Department of the Treasury) to produce educational documents. It sees that consumers' point of view is taken into account, and provides them with relevant, honest information about products and services.

The Consumer Federation of America

Finally, the most institutional organization is probably the Consumer Federation of America, a structure that includes 285 local or specific consumer advocacy organizations and which goes back to the first Consumer Advisory Council created by John F. Kennedy. It has no individual members, but is funded by membership fees paid by the local associations.

This organization, founded in 1968, in fact plays the role of sounding board. It can take action at the political level, and defend points of view or projects prepared by one of its 285 member groups. It provides different types of training and communication for its members. It conducts studies on the behavior and needs of consumers, and publishes many memoranda and reports intended for its members or for the public authorities.

The Consumer Federation of America specializes in six major areas of consumer concern:

- financial services: in this area, it works for clarification of the service offerings of financial institutions

- utilities: water, electricity, gas, and telephone

- product safety

- transportation, and in particular automobiles, freeways, and rail and air transportation

- healthcare and drugs

- food safety and the struggle against all forms of bacterial contamination.

The federation recently brought out a study on the risk of over-indebtedness of credit card holders. It has also fought for reduction of telephone rates and installation fees for cable television systems. Finally, the Consumer Federation of America works with Congress to improve consumers' position as regards credit and price competition, product safety and the quality of user instructions, utility regulation, and all aspects of relations with government.

/ The three associations, Public Citizen, Consumer Action, and Consumer Federation of America, constitute an extraordinary arsenal for the evaluation of products and protection of the consumer. /

Despite their differences of structure, and sometimes of approach, these three associations, Public Citizen, Consumer Action, and Consumer Federation of America, constitute an extraordinary arsenal for the evaluation of products and protection of the consumer. They take vigorous action whenever a producer has shown a lack of concern for a consumer or has failed to provide the quality of products or services to which consumers have a right.

Consumer advocacy movements in Europe

In Europe, each country has a system of consumer advocacy that more or less corresponds to its political and public traditions.

The French system

The French system is based on a public entity and a union originating in the citizens' association movement. L'Institut national de la consommation was founded in 1967. It is managed by a board of directors with 23 members; 12 are appointed as consumer representatives and the other 11 represent industry associations. More than 40 percent of its budget consists of government subsidies.

This institute is a technical organization which assists the various consumer advocacy associations and conducts specialized studies. It has its own magazine, *60 millions de consommateurs*, and has a voice in the various debates on issues affecting consumers.

The Union fédérale des consommateurs (UFC) is a federation of associations created in 1951. Today it has 85,000 direct members and a magazine, *Que choisir?*, with a circulation of 335,000. The group's mission is to federate and represent other associations that are weaker on the national level – in particular ORGECO (created by members of the FO, CGC, and CFDT labor federations), family and women's associations, and other labor movements. These associations have a few government subsidies, but function essentially on membership fees and subscriptions to their publications.

Statements by the president of UFC-Que choisir, Marie-José Nicoli, characterize the organization well. Among its most visible actions have been its information campaigns against pollution of beaches (1973), against hormone-raised veal (1980), against fees charged by banks for checking (1986), in favor of phosphate-free detergents (1989), against high water rates (1998), and again against fees for paying by check (2000). In 2002, UFC-*Que choisir* published the answers to the questionnaires it had sent to the major candidates in the presidential election.

This association is like a French equivalent of Public Citizen in the United States. It is more concerned with major campaigns and stands on political issues than with neutral, systematic information and consumer-awareness efforts.

/ UFC-*Que choisir* is more concerned with major campaigns and stands on political issues than with neutral, systematic information and consumer-awareness efforts. /

It's interesting to look at the percentages regarding consumer issues and the most frequent areas of action: disputes having to do with housing account for 26 percent, problems with household goods 16 percent, insurance 9 percent, problems with cars or cycles 9 percent, and with banks 7 percent.

Italian movements

The Unione Nazionale Consumatori (UNC), founded in 1955, has a budget which is financed half by memberships and 20 percent by public subsidies. The remainder of the budget is made up by subscriptions to publications – the daily *Le scelte del consumatore* and its monthly supplement, aimed at members, the media, and public, cultural, and social organizations.

The German system

In Germany one organization, the AgV (Union of Consumer Associations), serves as umbrella for some 30 national, family, household, or religious associations, with a total of approximately 10 million members. This group publishes *Argumente zur Verbraucherpolitik*. This bulletin is issued frequently, but its distribution remains limited to political and governmental decision makers. For the member associations, its purpose is above all to serve as a means of representing their point of view in "high places" and getting a hearing when they propose changes in regulations or systems of protection.

A second entity, the Stiftung Warentest (Foundation for Product Testing), is an independent structure made up of equal numbers of representatives of consumers and producers. It has large public subsidies and regularly organizes comparative tests which it publishes in its magazine, *Test*.

Scandinavian organizations

The Scandinavian organizations are often direct extensions of the public authorities. There are, for example, the Finnish National Consumer Research Center, the Danish Institute for Informative Labeling, and the Swedish Consumer Agency (Konsumentverket). They sometimes work with associations of consumers, which operate in a highly structured and active cooperative network, whose development is encouraged by the authorities. In Sweden, consumer cooperatives number some 150 local groups with more than 2 million members. These synergies are further strengthened by the existence of two more innovative entities: the National Board for Consumer Complaints and the consumer ombudsmen.

Elected by the Swedish Parliament, ombudsmen are a kind of independent inspector with the right to investigate governmental entities, which they can exercise freely. Their mission essentially consists of defending citizens. There is an ombudsman for the Parliament, who protects citizens against unjust application of the law, and a press ombudsman, who protects against disinformation and libel. The one that interests us here is the consumer ombudsman. Ombudsmen can act in liaison with the Commercial Court, either at their own initiative or at the request of consumers. This gives them total autonomy and the possibility of intervening at any time, for example to halt a fraudulent advertisement or to negotiate with a producer, backed up by the threat of possible court action.

The power and scope of consumer movements

Several times, the consumer movements mentioned earlier have played a significant role. They have forced public authorities or companies to improve their practices. They have also helped consumers become better informed, more astute, and more vigilant. They play an essential role in making brands more comprehensible and encouraging both parties to play their respective roles responsibly. A distinction needs to be made between habitual actions and exceptional mobilizations.

Habitual actions

These actions have to do above all with educating consumers with the goal of developing more reasonable purchasing behaviors. Comparative product tests play an essential role in this area. We have seen how in Germany they were conducted by an entity that represents consumers and industry equally. In France, such tests are carried out either by a government body or by a consumer association.

By empowering purchasers to exercise their fundamental freedom of choice with objectivity, comparative tests have a crucial role to play in relations between brands and consumers. Unfortunately, they are sometimes open to criticism, in particular in France, and their failings sometimes reduce the scope of their effectiveness.

Some entities can be criticized for being overly aggressive towards companies. There is a tendency to describe the services provided by producers as necessarily dishonest activities. This is a natural tendency of criticism, one that can be seen at work in *No Logo*. One gets the impression that certain "testers" have made a priori judgments. Too often, the accounts give the impression that the company is making no effort to provide consumers with products of the highest possible quality. This is a silly assumption, if you think about it for a minute – as silly as the narrow view taken by certain companies or marketing agencies that insist on continuing to treat consumers as if they were imbeciles. It also shows that both sides have much to gain from a reconciliation.

/ By empowering purchasers to exercise their fundamental freedom of choice with objectivity, comparative tests have a crucial role to play in relations between brands and consumers. /

The product can be looked at as a tool of mediation between consumers and the brand. The brand has spent time designing, manufacturing, and promoting it; the consumer will spend time using it. This creates grounds for understanding. We see it as natural for product tests also to take place in a neutral space of mediation. The testing body should not be in the manufacturer's "camp," but neither should it be in that of the critic. That is why we feel that the German approach is more constructive.

Another, more technical, criticism has to do with sampling faults or errors of observation. We can use the characteristic example of champagne. The comparative tests conducted in France by consumer advocacy institutes using panels of consumers or oenologists reach absolutely incompatible or inexplicable results from one study to another. According to the experts, to obtain reliable results, you would have to test not one bottle chosen at random for each brand, but probably 20 or 100 that had undergone the same conditions of storage and transport. Going to a supermarket and buying a bottle of champagne that has just spent three weeks sitting next to a neon lamp, after two weeks in an overheated warehouse, is not the same as choosing a bottle that has been transported in winter and has never been taken out of the case. A test conducted under such conditions cannot produce solid statistics.

/ The product can be looked at as a tool of mediation between consumers and the brand. The brand has spent time designing, manufacturing, and promoting it; the consumer will spend time using it. /

Specialists in comparative tests will object that after all, they found the given bottle on the shelf of a supermarket, and consumers are likely to find similar bottles under identical conditions. And they are right. But if the study gives no information on the conditions of storage and the probability of adverse conditions that could affect the wine, its value as purchasing advice becomes more or less nil. A measurement has no scientific validity unless it can be reproduced under identical conditions, with very similar results being recorded each time.

It seems a shame that producers end up losing interest completely in these tests. The joint German system, here again, seems to us to be the most appropriate. The simple fact is that the company, after all, knows its product best and has the most technical skill for evaluating it. The brands, accustomed to conducting tests of all kinds – in particular for consumer products – have a considerable technical lead over consumer associations. It's high time that independent comparative tests had the same level of reliability. Here again, the solution could come from mediation.

Exceptional mobilizations

By mobilizing on exceptional issues, consumer movements depart from their mission of information and education and take on a role that seems more like that of a labor union. This is true in particular in the case of legal actions aimed at condemning certain commercial practices. A recent example was the successful suits against the overbilling practiced by mobile telephone operators in France.

While they are exceptional, and sometimes of limited scope (when they act on behalf of a small category of users, for example), such actions guarantee the visibility of the movement because of the media attention they draw. Beyond the day-to-day defense of the rights of consumers, these associations want to show their determination and safeguard their credibility. Like union actions, these media coups are more an end in themselves than a means of affecting public life.

Consumer movements can make their voices heard by the public authorities and give consumers' points of view when a bill affecting competition, advertising, financial products, or any other area where the citizen is in the role of consumer is being prepared. Such means, less visible than a lawsuit against a major group, are no less effective. There is no doubt that the finest victories of consumer movements have been quiet ones, where their point of view has been taken into account in a new regulatory text.

/ Beyond the day-to-day defense of the rights of consumers, these associations want to show their determination and safeguard their credibility. /

In addition to legal actions, the exceptional pressure brought to bear by associations of consumers on brands can also take the form of boycott calls. They are a dangerous exercise for both parties, to the extent that the power struggle leaves the judicial arena and projects itself into the stores themselves, at the moment of the act of purchase. Sales figures can affect the reputations of both parties, even though they are not always accurate reflections of the negative effect on a brand caused by actions over the middle and long term.

We will analyze the mechanisms of these spectacular actions in more detail. We have chosen to deal with them separately because, as we will see, they are not the exclusive province of consumer movements. Boycotts unite other participants, and the issues at stake combine demands of an ethical and political nature, and rarely involve consumer advocacy alone.

Boycotts and their effectiveness

The mechanism of the consumer boycott has taken on particular importance during the last 20 years, but governments, companies, and unions practiced them throughout the twentieth century in order to put pressure on a company or group of companies by paralyzing its economic activity. Boycotts between companies exist, in particular pitting producers against retailers. France's Leclerc supermarket chain has regularly been a target since the 1960s, and there was the violent "cigarette war" in Belgium in 1934, between the federation of tobacco retailers and consumer cooperatives.

The term originally had an ethical and unionist coloration. It comes from the name of Charles Boycott, an agent for an English landowner in Ireland at the end of the nineteenth century who incited the anger of the Irish Land League as a result of the inhuman conditions under which his agricultural workers lived.

We will look at some characteristic examples of consumer boycotts. They have several things in common: a structured group of determined activists, a large base of sympathizers, and a cause of a collective nature, concerning the public good, or sometimes the interests of a community.

The first boycotts

The first consumer boycotts we will look at took place in the 1970s and 1980s. They correspond to the birth and development of a new generation of activists, concerned with civil actions rather than politics, sensitive to international issues, and determined to challenge the expansion of the private multinationals.

The Nestlé boycott

One of the first and most famous boycotts began in the 1970s. Nestlé was accused of promoting the sale of its powdered milk in the poorest countries in place of mothers' milk. Reconstituted milk does not provide the anti-bodies present in breast milk, and can be dangerous when water quality is a problem. Therefore specialists recommend breast feeding.

According to the promoters of the boycott, Nestlé used women, some-times dressed as nurses or doctors, to convince young mothers of the virtues of its formula. The poor quality of the water caused diarrhea and very serious diseases in the babies. In addition, the poorest mothers tended to dilute the powder too much in order to make it go further, which resulted in cases of malnutrition that were discovered too late. According to the World Health Organization, these practices may have been directly or indirectly responsible for 1500 deaths a year.

The campaign against Nestlé quickly became very aggressive. In 1974, the journalist Mike Muller published a book entitled *The Baby Killer*,[1] which was

---

1 Mike Muller, *The Baby Killer*, War on Want, 1974.

translated into French and published in Switzerland. Nestlé, which had not reacted to the English-language publication, then brought suit against the author, focusing its communication on a defense of the quality of its products. An enormous controversy developed. The boycott began on July 4, 1977 in the United States. It was supported by the National Council of Churches. The organizer, INFACT (Infant Formula Action Coalition), succeeded in getting support from the staff of Senator Edward Kennedy. The issue was debated at the World Health Organization in Geneva. This entity defined a Marketing Code which Nestlé accepted. The campaign stopped in 1984.

But only temporarily. Since that date, regular accusations of violation of the Code have resulted in further, more or less successful, actions against Nestlé. In 1991 the Church of England decided to launch a new boycott, which lasted three years. Students at the University of Dublin took over in 1994. Finally, in October 2000, American organizers (Action for Corporate Accountability) resumed their actions against the brand, feeling that Nestlé had gradually reneged on its commitments made in 1984.

Admittedly Nestlé, through the 1990s, showed extreme inflexibility in managing a crisis that nevertheless went to the very heart of its brand identity. For a long time the company defended its positions, publicly trumpeting the soundness of its policy of free distribution of formula in maternity hospitals, countering the findings of international medical organizations with studies of its own, criticizing these same organizations and saying that it wanted to approach reform very prudently. The lawsuits brought by its lawyers and the revelation of a project to "neutralize critics" by the Ogilvy and Mather agency in 1989 did not help improve its image.

General Electric

The same organization, INFACT, orchestrated a boycott against General Electric, which it criticized for manufacturing components used in nuclear weapons. INFACT urged hospitals – in particular those run by religious organizations – to stop buying radiology systems and scanners from General Electric. According to INFACT, these actions resulted in a loss of US$40 million in equipment sales for General Electric. The company contests these figures, arguing that during the period in question, its sales increased from US$32 to 58 billion.

Shell and apartheid

In 1987, it was Shell's turn to undergo a boycott when the secretary of the British Anti-Apartheid Movement, Mike Terry, accused the company of not respecting the United Nations embargo on petroleum products. A spokesman for the company said that "Shell abhors the apartheid system, as we have stated many times, but Shell South Africa has South African employees and has been going 70 years. No one can believe that if you change its name, it will not carry on as a company."

At this point a plan of action called "Strategy Neptune" was put in place: Shell decided to sue all local governments or public officials who attempted to implement the boycott by refusing authorizations to operate to Shell service stations. Little by little, cities like Lewisham and Sheffield in England and Stavanger in Norway dropped their actions. The only city that maintained a very strong position, Hilversum in the Netherlands, was forced to end its boycott on order of the Crown. The Dutch Foreign Ministry said that "municipalities were banned from conducting foreign policy."

Boycotts against animal experimentation

In 1990 a boycott was launched by the British Anti-Vivisection Association against a series of companies – including L'Oréal, Elida Gibbs, Gillette, Colgate, Chesebrough-Pond's, Bristol-Myers, and Reckitt & Colman – whose hair-care products had been tested on animals.

Conclusions

A few basic traits are apparent in these first boycotts. A study by Monroe Friedman in the United States, covering 90 cases of boycotts, describes their major characteristics.[2] In 21 cases the boycott was organized by labor unions, in 19 cases by groups that defend racial minorities, in 10 cases by religious groups, and in only two cases by consumer movements. And of these 90 cases 27 were organized as a result of labor or personal problems, 26 over the treatment of certain racial minorities, and only 11 because of maltreatment of consumers.

Three things can be noted. First, during this initial phase, the boycott, which would seem to be the ultimate weapon of consumer advocacy movements, is used much more often for other purposes and for different problems. Then, as regards the famous examples, the companies that are most highly exposed are those that take the most inflexible attitude of defense against what they perceive as pressures of an essentially ideological nature. The stand-off between Nestlé and its opponents clearly shows the gulf that exists between the ethical issues championed by the opponents and the very concrete concerns of the company. Nestlé in the 1980s above all took the position of defending

---

2 Monroe Friedman, *Journal of Consumer Affairs*, vol. 19, no. 1.

the quality of its products and legally challenging the legitimacy of the boycott, using the issues of libel and free exercise of its activities. It had not yet become aware of the new responsibilities towards the totality of consumers its international image imposed on it. It felt – which is not completely false – that it was the target of an "oriented" movement and not of a more general concern uniting the public in solidarity. In any case, Nike reacted to the sweatshop scandal rapidly and with much more vigorous measures.

/ The companies that are most highly exposed are those that take the most inflexible attitude of defense against what they perceive as pressures of an essentially ideological nature. /

Finally, the financial effects of these boycotts have yet to be evaluated. The organizations active against Nestlé claim a 3 percent decrease in sales of Nescafé in 1993, and a significant increase in the company's advertising budgets in the 1990s. But it is probable that the effects will be felt above all in terms of image, over the long term.

Current boycotts

We will focus essentially on four boycott movements here: the one against Nike by the black community in the United States, that of Esso in the UK, and finally the one against Procter & Gamble and Danone.

Nike and Operation Push

The example of Nike is fairly characteristic of a new category of boycotts, and the reaction of the company must be compared with its attitude in the face of the sweatshop controversy. In 1990 Operation Push, originally founded by the Reverend Jesse Jackson and under the direction of the Reverend Tyrone Crider at the time, launched its boycott. According to the organization, 30 percent of Nike's shoe sales is to black consumers. In poor neighborhoods, Push said, these shoes are the equivalent "of the three-piece suit on Wall Street." Nike, therefore, should change its organization in the United States – by appointing a black to its board of directors, by using a bank belonging to blacks for part of its financial activities, by choosing a black advertising agency, and, in general, by recruiting more African-Americans at all levels of its organization.

Nike's directors didn't agree. According to their figures, they said, only 13.8 percent of the US sales are to African-Americans. Further, all production shops have been relocated to places where the ethnic problem can't be envisaged in the terms presented by Push. Finally, Nike did not intend to change its organization or its American mode of operation. The company also pointed out that 75 percent of the funds it spent on humanitarian causes was on behalf of minorities. Finally, Nike suggested that the fact that its major competitor advertised in the Push organization's magazine might have had something to do with the launch of the boycott.

The boycott began with a noisy demonstration outside Nike's general shareholders' meeting in Portland. Large demonstrations followed in front of certain stores, in particular Footlocker. And then – nothing. A few weeks later, Nike reported quarterly sales that were up 29 percent and an increase in orders of 39 percent. The operation was a failure for Push.

In the sweatshop affair, documented in *No Logo*, on the other hand, the company identified a problem of social justice early on, a source of concern among a significant proportion of its consumers. The controversy arose in the late 1990s. Nike rapidly took vigorous measures with its subcontractors and invested in wage improvements and social protection for Third World workers. At the time of the publication of *No Logo*, in 2001, Nike could claim that the majority of the examples cited by Naomi Klein corresponded to dysfunctions it had already taken steps to remedy.

In neither case, to our knowledge, did the company undertake legal action. Instead, its public response to Naomi Klein took place at the level of ideological debate, and reaffirms Nike's acceptance of constructive criticism. Clearly, significant progress has been made since the Nestlé case.

Esso and the Kyoto Accords

Environmental protection movements accused Esso of being behind the decision by President George Bush, Jr. to refuse to sign the Kyoto Accords on the problem of global warming. The company was suspected of having supported the American Petroleum Institute in dissuading China from ratifying the protocol, which supposedly could have hampered economic development in China. The Chinese decision was Bush's pretext for his refusal to sign.

On March 12, 2001, the National Association of Bulk Truckers (ANCAI) in Canada began to recommend a boycott of Esso in Quebec – in part because of the Kyoto Accords, but also because Esso wanted to increase the price of diesel fuel. During the summer the movement reached England. A certain number of associations – Greenpeace, Friends of the Earth, People and Planet – took over organization of the boycott. They were supported by celebrities: Anita Roddick, founder of the Body Shop, Bianca Jagger, Annie Lennox, Ralph Fiennes. Esso has 370 service stations in the UK; on December 1,

2001, demonstrators massed near the stations to discourage drivers from buying gas from Esso. Anita Roddick promised that two Body Shop delivery trucks would display huge posters saying "Boycott Esso."

According to a spokesperson for the company, these actions had a negative impact above all on the independent franchise owners using the Esso brand in the UK and on the brand's British employees. Attempts to extend the boycott to the European continent were made, but misfired. We still don't know today whether British consumers have changed their fuel purchasing behavior in a lasting way.

Procter & Gamble's black year

The misadventure of Procter & Gamble (P&G) we will now recount dates from late 2000. In fact it comprises a whole series of actions against the brand that year, by various interests. A first boycott, organized by the Gay and Lesbian Alliance Against Defamation, condemned P&G's advertising investments in the TV show of Laura Schlesinger, a journalist aligned with conservative interests and an outspoken opponent of homosexuality. The company withdrew all its ads from the broadcast – and immediately faced another boycott by conservative religious associations that support Schlesinger.

Then came the boycott organized by People for the Ethical Treatment of Animals (PETA), which denounced P&G's use of animal experiments in developing its products. The movement ended when the company announced it would halt all animal testing for 80 percent of its brands. But the year 2000 was not over. Two organizations, the Screen Actors Guild (SAG) and the American Federation of Television and Radio Artists (AFRA) organized a boycott against three P&G brands – Crest, Ivory and Tide – for the company's use of non-union actors in some of its advertising spots. The solidarity of the American entertainment industry came into play. Stars like Julia Roberts and Susan Sarandon lent their support to the movement. Demonstrations against P&G were organized in New York, Los Angeles, and Cincinnati, where the company has its headquarters. The movement lost steam after a few months, and the impact on sales diminished little by little.

A very important aspect of the mechanism of boycotts is apparent here: the notoriety, and even the "spectacular" dimension of the targeted brand. Here, unlike the cases of Nestlé and Nike, where the accusations are of a type that can result in a general outcry (if they prove to be accurate), the critiques remain specific and have little chance of rallying a majority of the population – with the exception of animal testing, which is a highly sensitive subject in the UK. This doesn't prevent groups of determined activists from vigorously attacking the brand, which takes on the value of a symbol in the promotion of a greater cause. For decades, P&G has had an extremely strong presence and visibility in the field of televised communication in the English-speaking world, particularly with its policy of advertising during daytime serials. This, in fact, is the historic origin of the expression "soap opera."

The case of Danone

The last boycott we will discuss is that of Danone, the leading French food and beverage group and the parent company of the US Dannon, in April 2001. The employees of the plants in Ris-Orangis and Calais launched a boycott against the shutdown of these two facilities, which produced LU cookies. The general plan called for 570 job cuts in France and a total of 1600 in Europe. Workers at both plants were to be offered "job reclassifications."

The employees' call was picked up by the CGT labor federation, the Communist Party, then ATTAC, the French Greens, and the Socialist Party. Certain rightist legislators got on the bandwagon. The oddest aspect is that this boycott, organized in protest of the closing of two LU cookie production sites, was never aimed at the baking division. It concentrated on Danone dairy products, no doubt because the brand is visible in the name of the group. This is a good example of how the name of a brand can take on psychological dimensions that go beyond the structural realities of an organization.

What was the impact on sales of dairy products in France? You would need to have access to the Nielsen ratings to know exactly. There is talk of a 20 percent drop in sales of the group's dairy products at the central market in Rungis, and a 10 percent drop in French sales during the month of April 2001. The company's management explains that it had immediately postponed most of its promotional operations and reduced its ad campaigns, explaining part of the decrease. However, Danone claims that overall results for the first semester of 2001 were very good, including for dairy products, but of course those are consolidated figures.

Conclusions

The Nike, Esso, Procter & Gamble, and Danone boycotts have a certain number of points in common:

- These boycotts all began for reasons other than the products themselves or protection of consumers.

- They have almost always been picked up by the media, in particular via personalities from show business and politics.

■ Their magnitude is proportional to the emotion they inspire. When they campaigned for very specific causes (in terms of the general interest), the organizers of these boycotts have not been very effective. On the other hand, when a large number of consumers – even non- participants – have felt concerned, they have had a significant impact on sales.

■ They have been taken seriously by the companies. In contrast to what they did in response to the "first-generation" boycotts, the companies did not concentrate their efforts in the legal arena. They have made a point of taking action and communicating their point of view, even if they have had trouble getting it across.

From a dubious anti-commercial practice, the boycott has taken on the status of a more or less collective movement for expressing social demands. The novelty is that the companies now take part in the process. They can vigorously contest the legitimacy of the motives, but they no longer challenge the principle. And that represents a turning point in the awareness of their collective responsibilities.

An assessment of boycotts and the true means of consumer advocacy

What stands out in this description of recent boycotts is that consumers some-how get left behind. The actions are almost never aimed at ensuring that they will be able to buy and consume better yogurt at a more reasonable price. In fact, consumers knowingly allow themselves to be "used" by political or social movements. The problem of the passive consumer-voter is visible here again. These movements often have extremely positive consequences in terms of social progress, especially since their relevance, quite democratically, is judged by the magnitude of the mobilization they succeed in awakening. In any event, the generalization of the phenomenon can no longer be ignored.

Marc Drillech, in a 1999 book on the question,[3] speaks in terms of a cultural transition from militancy to activism. Consumers are more and more conscious of their power, and they use it not for actions in defense of consumers, but for other goals. They attack Danone, who according to Drillech "was long perceived as one of the most virtuous companies, both as regards its labor policy, its communication, and the quality of its prod-ucts." But, he adds, "activists, whether politically Right or Left, have a tendency to attack their own camp rather than that of their opponents."

---

3 Marc Drillech, *Le boycott*, Paris: Presses du Management, 1999.

The limits of such actions – in particular in terms of relevance – call for two caveats. The first is the risk of co-option of this new power for the benefit of specific interests, for example political ideologies, or even direct competitors with few scruples. The second is more a regret: while the individual act of purchase or non-purchase is consumers' natural means of expressing their support or rejection of a brand's values, it would seem to be a good thing if boycotts could also serve as a means of expression for consumers as a group, and not only as "citizens of the world." That brands are agreeing to assume their global responsibilities certainly represents progress. But they are also accountable as regards their core business activity – the products or services they offer. And the responsibilities of consumers also include recognizing merit or lack thereof in the area they know best: consumption.

/ In fact, consumers knowingly allow themselves to be "used" by political or social movements. /

The limits of activism

Clearly, the associative-activist model is in the process of profoundly remodeling our Western societies. But all social movements can't be entrusted to scattered initiatives, led by small but determined groups supported by a passive base. It is in everyone's interest for reactive activism to move little by little towards institutionalization, generalization, and open cooperation with public and private stakeholders, as social progress spreads. Other, more radical activisms will arise, and perhaps constitute the seed bed for tomorrow's progress.

What we seem to be seeing today is the burgeoning of a worldwide civil society or planetary social movement. We should cite:

- the worldwide popular actions against free trade and the WTO
- the World Social Forum
- the International Forum on Globalization
- ATTAC (Association for the Taxation of Financial Transactions for the Aid of Citizens)
- Global Trade Watch
- United Students Against Sweatshops
- the Drop the Debt campaign

- Friends of the Earth

- the Confédération Paysanne agricultural group

- the Direct Action Network.

New actions from these ten national or international associations can be expected, aimed at new targets.

Where do companies stand in all this? They no longer have any choice, if they aren't already doing it, other than to conduct virtuous, sustainable policies. These associations, that observe corporate behavior on a daily basis, leave no choice open but to define operational practices and strict rules of ethics that are beyond criticism.

/ It is in everyone's interest for reactive activism to move little by little towards institutionalization, generalization, and open cooperation with public and private stakeholders. /

And the consumer? For us, they are where the problem lies. One gets the impression that so far, they have "missed the boat." The discussions now going on are above their heads. They are called upon to act and react to political calls to action. They comply, to a greater or lesser degree depending on the case, but they aspire to other things. So, boycotts have their uses, but also abuses and limitations.

Towards a responsible consumer

There are other channels, however. Consumers can, for example, join or support organizations of a new type, whose goal is to help consumers buy responsibly. Once they do, they cease being passive consumers of ideologies and become full-fledged players in the transactions they are involved in. The movement began in the United States where, for ten years, the guide *Shopping for a Better World* has been published.

In France the Observatoire de l'éthique, founded in 1993, has the goal of promoting individual, civil, and professional ethics. The organization judges companies and brands according to seven principal criteria:

- Strategy: Is it clearly defined? Does it take the human dimension into consideration, and is it based on real values?

- Employees: Is labor policy clearly defined, and is concrete action taken in favor of employment?

- The environment: Is there an environmental charter?

■ Sales: Can the company guarantee the traceability of its products that involve risks? What commitments have been made towards customers and suppliers?

■ Transparence: Are customers provided with clear and precise information on packaging and labeling?

■ Humanitarian issues: Does the company have requirements regarding the working conditions of the employees of its suppliers and subcontractors?

■ Sponsorship and corporate citizenship: What are the company's commitments in these areas?

It almost seems as if consumers, with boycott actions co-opted by political organizations or pressure groups, were creating a new system, more effective and closer to the grassroots, for imposing on producers and brand managers what they really want: better and more ethical products, produced under irreproachable conditions. And in the field, this time, companies seem to be listening more, prepared to play the game and improve their procedures and their behaviors.

Organizations like Public Citizen, ATTAC, and Push are interested in changing society as a whole. Of course their action is not without its usefulness, if only in serving as a goad, but it could well be that the most concrete actions will be brought about by the ethical-control organizations. Cooperation is the most constructive path.

As we have often said in the course of this book, seeing trade as an open war between brands and consumers may be one way of waging politics – while masking the identity of the real guilty parties – but that vision isn't likely to transform it in a meaningful way. As a system of exchange, trade is an essential, though not sufficient, component of social life. It is a truly human activity which must be defended by those who participate in it. This means keeping in mind what the purposes of the exchange are, and the respective roles of the vendor and the purchaser.

/ The most concrete actions will be brought about by the ethical-control organizations. Cooperation is the most constructive path. /

The individual is the guarantor of the process of selecting products, and, imperceptibly, is responsible for their improvement. Individuals have all the tools needed to apply pressure and force the correction of errors and excesses. They serve as the indispensable link between the brand's identity and their own identity.

IV

Conclusion

10 | Brands and globalization

> We all call barbarism that which does not fit our usages.
>
> (Montaigne)

What makes people want to attack McDonald's? The poor eating habits it promotes? The chain is no temple of gastronomy, of course, but the major fast-food brands stand out because of their criteria of hygiene and respect for the refrigerated food distribution chain, which are much better than what is to be found in traditional fast-food outlets. The hegemony of multinational capitalism? Of the 25,000 McDonald's restaurants in the world, 80 percent are managed as franchises by local operators from the regions where they do business. In France, McDonald's buys 80 percent of its supplies on the national market.

No, the reason is its symbolic value. What bothers people about McDonald's is not the policy of local management of an economic activity, but the "free-market globalization" it seems to connote. This brings us back to Naomi Klein's book. As must be clear by now, our purpose was not to refute her point by point. We share certain of Naomi Klein's analyses. We also acknowledge the excellent survey and documentation work she has done, which provides an excellent panorama of anti-brand activism today. What we did intend was to respond to an informal climate of latent hostility which has been felt in the wake of the book, and which is often based on a vague interpretation of her theses. We do feel, however, that the author partially encourages that ambiguity.

This is our feeling: Naomi Klein identifies brands and branding as the prime targets of activism – much more so than governments, for example. She shows how vulnerable and reactive to pressure the major brands are. And we agree with her. Her work also reactivates certain critiques of international capitalism that have existed for some time. And indeed, these issues are still in debate. But replacing the word "capitalism" with "branding" seems to us to be mere artifice. It is not enough to base an entirely new reflection on. The problems enumerated in *No Logo* are real, often accurately described, and sometimes tragic. But we don't go along with the idea that brands and branding are their causes. We have to look further.

/ Replacing the word "capitalism" with "branding" seems to us to be mere artifice. It is not enough to base an entirely new reflection on. /

For activists, brands provide a convenient entry into civic expression – even if real progress cannot come from confrontation alone. For an analyst, on the other hand, they are only a convenient scapegoat, a disguise for a historical phenomenon that is much more general. It is called globalization today, but its origin is indistinguishable – at least in the strict economic sense – with the beginnings of capitalism. That, finally, is the main objection we can raise against *No Logo*, and above all, against the movement it has inspired. Brands don't "make" globalization any more than soldiers "make" war. That is why, in this conclusion, we would like to look at the problem from a perspective that seems more logical to us, and look at the role of brands in a context that goes far beyond them.

Global brand, or "global" as a brand?

The power of a fashionable word is surprising. It is capable of mobilizing the masses, changing minds. "International," "multinational," and "transnational" have lost serious market-share points to "global," an emerging new brand, positioned on the sector of ideology. It is everywhere – on posters, in newspapers, on activists' leaflets and bulletins from corporate banks. It has its origin: the famous "global village"; its extensions: "globalization" and "anti-globalization"; it even has its derivative products, with the slogan "No global." The *Herald Tribune* now calls its celebrities column "The global class," and its advertising leaflet for subscriptions promotes "global news for the global class." Our old globe has never been talked about so much.

The demonstrations, with their sometimes dramatic consequences, of the partisans of "No global" at the world summits in Seattle, Davos, Genoa, Porto Alegre, and New York have refocused debate on the problems of poverty, inequalities, injustice, and the evolutionary model of our planet in general. These activists maintain that globalization is the root of all evil: the cultural Americanization of the world, the growing gulf between wealth and living standards in wealthy and poor countries, inequality and social injustice, the exploitation of labor in the developing countries, and so on. All these evil consequences are said to be the result of capitalism pushed to its limits, in confrontation with governmental institutions, national and international, which are incapable of providing effective forms of political or social control of the economy.

The partisans of economic laissez-faire argue the opposite position. These evils, they say, can be explained by insufficient globalization. It is precisely the last remaining protectionist obstacles, the last interventionism on the part of states, that prevent the free circulation of capital and prevent economic equilibrium from being reached.[1] To them, globalization is the root of all progress: growth, development, technological advances, the reduction of poverty and so on.[2]

On both sides we find simplistic visions, often partisan and purely arithmetical. If it is true that multinationals (but not brands) are the principal players of this movement, and that the new information and communication technologies are its accelerators, globalization can be seen as neither a plague nor a panacea. It is a process of general evolution our world has been undergoing since human beings began living in society. The recent acceleration of the phenomenon is caused by market forces and by technological progress, both factors for exchange. The dimensions of time and space have changed.

Globalization is a phenomenon of the same nature as the development of a brand: it is irreversible rather than polemical. We must work to improve its positive effects and attenuate its negative ones. In addition, its scope goes well beyond the economic domain. The Spanish Royal Academy recently incorporated the term into its dictionary under the following definition: "The tendency of markets and companies to extend and attain a worldwide dimension which goes beyond national boundaries." But isn't this the intrinsic movement of any trade activity, and of any collective human activity?

/ Globalization is a phenomenon of the same nature as the development of a brand: it is irreversible rather than polemical. We must work to improve its positive effects and attenuate its negative ones. /

Globalization is the progressive reduction of the importance of national borders. It is instantaneous worldwide access to information. It is a more intense and rapid flow of merchandise, services, and people. It is the planet

---

1 The recent example of Argentina (the crisis in 2001–2), ruined by the maintenance of an artificial parity between its currency with the American dollar, could be a sad illustration.
2 It should be noted that, for the first time, the number of persons living on less than US$1 per day was reduced by 200 million in 2000.

being considered as the natural field of action of each company and each individual. Already in the sixteenth century, with Montaigne, the idea arose that all humans are united in the same humanity, from the savages of the New World to the courtiers of powerful Europe. But the concern also arose that those men and women, alarmed by such a vast common space, might take refuge behind easy accusations. Each of us is the other's barbarian.

The phenomenon, then, is not new. It has seen innumerable developments: the invention of the compass, the first guides to navigation, the discovery of America by Christopher Columbus, the advances of the great explorers., the invention of the wheel, of printing, of electricity, wireless telegraphy, the internal combustion engine, the transistor, and the integrated circuit, to give only a few examples, have all contributed to it. The ingenuity of humans is constantly improving their living conditions; their imagination, their ambition, and their sense of effectiveness are the real driving forces. Everything that has contributed and continues to contribute to increasing exchanges of products, services, ideas, and customs, everything that extends our knowledge of the Earth and its peoples, is part of this movement.

In 1817 David Ricardo, with his theory of comparative advantages, clearly illustrated this mechanism of exchange, which encourages optimum use of the resources of a group of regions or countries to internationalize products.

Admittedly, technological progress in the communication and information sectors has encouraged the economic and financial development of activities controlled by multinationals with capitalist motivations. At this stage, there is also no doubt that the political, social, judicial, and environmental areas are lagging behind as regards the degree of integration that can be achieved by entrepreneurial structures with more simple, purely profit-driven motivations and more rapid decision-making systems. We feel that the recent process of awareness should result in an understanding of globalization as an evolution towards a better world and a better society, free of ideologies and at the service of human beings.

/ We feel that the recent process of awareness should result in an understanding of globalization as an evolution towards a better world and a better society. /

It will take time: time for changing attitudes, for institutions with the authority and the supranational means for confronting the major problems of the planet to be put in place. But we are optimistic about the ability of the human race to meet the challenges. Our survival depends on it.

Faced with these contradictory aspects, which fuel what are often ideological debates, we prefer to concentrate on the role of brands and branding in this process, and on the cultural aspects associated with globalization of the economy.

Brands and multinationals

Behind the presence of a brand, we often tend to imagine a powerful multinational company with innumerable ramifications. Kodak film and Dannon yogurt can be found in Morocco, South Africa, and Malaysia. For consumers, themselves "globalized," this ubiquity of course has its advantages. Brands are part of a social experience, and when traveling far from home – in Africa, for example – discovering brands, products, and packaging we have never seen before can transform an ordinary visit to a store into an adventure. But this enjoyment of the exotic often stops at the door of the pharmacy. Admittedly, it is very convenient to be able to buy the same products you use at home everywhere, and with the same confidence.

This global extension of brands, however, raises questions about the transformation of the worldwide economic system. For almost 50 years, with the appearance of the "Third World" trend, the multinationals have been accused of exploiting labor in the developing countries, and more generally of perpetuating an economy based on unacceptable differences in standards of living.

Globalization accused

The criticism of globalization is surely most vehement where economic development is concerned. Yet we should beware of stereotypes. Is this really the age of total laissez-faire? We have noted that the United States, often pointed to accusingly, in reality has very active entities for regulation of capital. In fact, free trade developed above all in the second half of the nineteenth century, resulting in considerable growth of the economy, and above all of European and American industry. The twentieth century, by contrast, tended to be a period of latent protectionism and weak economic development, above all between 1910 and 1939 and between 1975 and 1995.

From a macroeconomic perspective, the criticisms of globalization can be classified into two categories: either that it changes the terms of trade in favor of the wealthiest countries, reduces the value of the raw materials produced in developing countries, and keeps these countries in a situation of dependency and regression due to a lack of infrastructure and education; or, in the words of Jimmy Goldsmith, that it makes "the rich in the poor countries get richer, and the poor in the rich countries get poorer." In other words, it has no real and immediate effect on the well-being of the great majority of the poor people in these emerging countries.

It has to be recognized that the transformation of China into "the world's factory" has not had much of an effect, for the moment, on the peasants in rural areas. But in the long term, in 20 or 30 years, the standard of living of the Chinese can only improve. Economic mechanisms are always very slow to show their effects. We can predict that the future will hold a certain degree of prosperity. In any case, it would be an exaggeration to say that nothing is happening in China. A third of China's GDP today comes from private companies, generally created thanks to foreign capital, and producing products that are most often intended for export. If, in the long term, the situation can only improve, the living conditions of 200 million Chinese, generally located in the cities, are a far cry from what they were 10 or 20 years ago.

As the author Alessandro Baricco points out,[3] individuals should not be considered the ineluctable victims of the system. We can trust their capacity to adapt, to take stock of a situation, and to turn globalization to their advantage before it alienates them. Consequently, analyses of globalization in terms of internationalization of the class struggle (with capitalist countries pitted against worker countries) or the emergence of transnational classes (the nouveaux riches in the emerging countries) are not sufficient to describe the phenomenon.

/ Globalization operates at all scales and also percolates into the tiniest interstices of social structures. It's not true that the poorest people never benefit from it and that the richest are always spared its negative effects. /

Globalization operates at all scales and also percolates into the tiniest interstices of social structures. It's not true that the poorest people never benefit from it and that the richest are always spared its negative effects. Working conditions in the Third World are above what they were 10 or 20 years ago, and they continue to improve. As Jean-François Revel very accurately points out, " the growth of income in the poorest nations is, percentage-wise, the same over the long term as in the rest of the world's countries."[4] This is what David Dollar and Aart Kraay call "the Law of One to One."[5] Nevertheless, globalization of information has given inhabitants of the developed countries a much sharper awareness of the difficulties faced by citizens of the developing countries.

---

3   Alexandro Baricco, *Next*, Paris: Albin Michel, 2002.

4   Jean-François Revel, *L'obsession antiaméricaine, son fonctionnement, ses causes, ses conséquences*, Paris: Plon, 2002.

5   See, e.g., David Dollar and Aart Kraay, *Growth Is Good for the Poor,* Washington, D.C.: Development Research Group, World Bank, April 2001.

In this process of increasing awareness and the implementation of concrete solutions, the brand/consumer equation is a decisive accelerator and a real driving force for progress.

Brands and relocated labor

In the late 1990s, Nike came under heavy attack because of this issue. Sweatshops – relocated production facilities where work is most often subcontracted – were the scene of very real abuses. Aside from low wages, often aligned with the standards of the countries involved, there are the poor social benefits given workers, the repression of union organization, prison-like working conditions, and workers being forced to pay for goods and services (such as emigration fees, housing, and food) at sometimes grossly abusive rates.

This episode is well documented in *No Logo*. We won't go into the details. However, Nike's response to Naomi Klein deserves to be mentioned. The company does not deny the accuracy of the facts Klein reports, but points out that the most scandalous of these practices were corrected, in the months following the controversy, by a program of energetic action.

The example of Nike illustrates remarkably how a large movement of consumers can succeed, at the initiative of an avant-garde that is more aware of ethical issues, in forcing a company to face up to its responsibilities and improve working conditions for its workers around the world, in its own factories, but above all in its subcontractors' sweatshops. This extension of the debate to the independent subcontractors constitutes decisive progress. It is also the logical corollary of the brands' "power of ubiquity." If they want to disseminate their logo and their values at all levels of social life, it seems only natural that the phenomenon should also work upstream in the chain of production.

/ The example of Nike illustrates remarkably how a large movement of consumers can succeed, at the initiative of an avant-garde that is more aware of ethical issues, in forcing a company to face up to its responsibilities. /

Of course, the problems are far from being solved. A study of some ten Indonesian subcontractors of Nike, conducted in February 2001 by the Global Alliance for Workers and Communities (GAWC) – an organization Nike helped found in 1999 to increase control of its subcontracting shops – revealed cases of verbal, physical, and sexual harassment in certain factories. Other studies are under way in Vietnam, India, and China.

For its part, Gap promulgated a code of professional ethics in 1995, after coming in for criticism due to the deplorable working conditions in its factories in El Salvador. The GAWC is also surveying its operations in Asia. Chicco, the Italian brand of children's products, drew up a code of behavior in 1997, under pressure from the three major Italian labor unions. The promulgation followed a serious accident in a plant in China.

Undeniably, living conditions in the Third World are greatly inferior to what we know in the industrialized countries. Work is harder, jobs are more unstable, and safety conditions and social protection are often beneath the dignity of human beings. Despite what hard-core free-trade advocates say, the profit motivation alone is not enough to reduce these injustices and bring prosperity to everyone in the world as if by magic. But this is where consumers can, and must, make their voice heard. Who will listen? The brands. Today, in the countries of the Third World, they are the ones that are operating under the best possible conditions.

Of course, their humanism is not spontaneous. The pressure groups mentioned above, like Global Trade Watch and United Students Against Sweatshops, have played a considerable role, organizing press campaigns and boycotts to force these companies to be better citizens and adopt more humane attitudes. But what does it matter? To accuse the companies of cynicism would be to fail to understand the natural vocation of a brand, and to forget that each of us has to deal with our individual values and the objective constraints of what we do. What politician has never had to postpone an unpopular measure intended to achieve progress in order to have time to explain it, or, on the other hand, to alter his or her own judgment under pressure from constituents?

/ What is being asked of companies as economic systems is to be consistent with themselves: that is, reactive. The morality will come from the men and women who make them up and those with whom they do business. /

What is being asked of companies as economic systems is to be consistent with themselves: that is, reactive. The morality will come from the men and women who make them up and those with whom they do business, through the intermediary of national and supranational public legislation and private codes of conduct. Like political systems, brands combine values and special interests in a relationship of compromise. The important thing is that the blind logic of compromise always exists, and that it depends on our individual initiative to push it in the direction of progress. That requires that each of the partners in the exchange be in good faith, open to confrontation as well as to dialogue, and prepared to assume its responsibilities.

The paradox, which Naomi Klein points up very well, is that the better known and the more powerful a brand is, the more it is a target for action by these pressure groups, and the more it must adapt its behavior, everywhere in the world, to show that it is above reproach. This progress is not automatic, but, with responsible consumers and under the watchful eye of citizens' associations, it is inevitable. Brands, with their economic power, are on the leading edge of improvement of working conditions in the poor nations.

Brands and cultures

It is true that cultures are being homogenized around the world? The concern is all the greater because the issue is a highly emotional one.

The US empire

The idea of a US empire is gaining currency. One thing is certain: no nation has exercised such economic, technological, military, and cultural domination since the Roman Empire. John F. Kennedy himself said that since the time the first settlers landed in Virginia and began moving west, the United States had been embarked on conquest. This position of domination must be accompanied by responsibilities.

With Europe slow to emerge as a real power on the geostrategic playing field, the United States remains the only military power capable of intervening far from its own territory. Its influence extends to the political, economic, and cultural levels.

The major US brands are the privileged vehicles of US economic expansionism. An Interbrand document published in August 2003 lists the global brands according to their capacity to engender future profits.[6] Thirty-four of the first 50 (68 percent) and 62 of the first 100 of those brands are US-based. However, the sheer size of the US national market weights the statistics somewhat, and 41 percent of the brands in the classification are automobiles, beverages, food, furniture, clothing, and accessories – all expressions of specific local lifestyles or cultures. The proportion is higher in the case of non-US brands (68 percent). This shows a clear desire on the part of the markets for diversity in products that are symbols of culture.

The overrepresentation of US brands among the global brands, coupled with the progressive integration of economies, doesn't necessarily point to an Americanization of lifestyles, and above all, of attitudes. Diversity remains the rule.

---

6 *Business Week*, op. cit.

The apparent homogenization of cultures

/ The overrepresentation of US brands among the global brands doesn't necessarily point to an Americanization of lifestyles, and above all, of attitudes. Diversity remains the rule. /

Beyond an apparent homogenization, American-style, of certain visible aspects of daily life, attitudes and ways of thinking remain strongly linked to local cultures. If we construct a pyramid of three cultural levels – beginning with the most deep-seated and persistent and ending with the most visible and volatile – only a symbolic point, the most visible part of the pyramid, is affected by the products or services that show the greatest competitiveness on the worldwide level. In our opinion the foundation, the basic cultural tenets, is not affected. (See Figure 10.1.)

The visible part: global products

Shorts and T-shirts, the Western-style jacket and trousers, the refrigerator, the automobile, the airplane, and now the cellular phone are constantly transforming the visible aspects of our world. They are founded on technological progress, and in fact urban landscapes and their populations converge as far as their external appearance is concerned.

From the images the painter Joaquin Sorolla painted of life in the Spanish provinces between 1911 and 1919 for the Hispanic Society of America, to the traffic jams in Spanish cities at the start of the twenty-first century, is it possible to imagine we are talking about the same country? The twentieth century transformed the appearance of cities and their

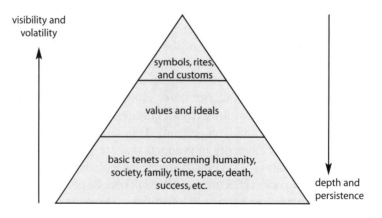

Figure 10.1 The cultural pyramid

inhabitants as never before. At one time, a traveler could recognize the region he or she was in just by looking at the way its inhabitants were dressed. In this competition on a planetary scale, the global products and brands that achieve success are not only American or European products – far from it.

American consumers are not deaf to the siren call of foreign products. A recent survey of 500,000 motorists conducted early in 2002 by Consumer Reports shows a clear preference for foreign cars. In the ten categories used, the best car was the BMW 530i; Toyota received four mentions; BMW and Honda, two each; Subaru and Volkswagen, only one.

In Japan, the younger generations have created their own culture, based on manga, robots, tribes, and virtual celebrities. Certain aspects of this Otaku phenomenon remain specifically domestic. The major publishers of video games continue to differentiate certain products according to whether they are aimed at the domestic or the export market. However, as the vogue for manga in the United States and in Europe shows, it is becoming more and more global. Borrowings from Japanese-style cyberculture and formal references to Asian popular film are becoming more and more numerous in the American entertainment cinema: blockbusters like *The Matrix*, or the Hollywood success of Hong Kong filmmakers (John Woo, for example) show this.[7]

The tiramisu, a typically Italian dessert, has been extremely popular in Japan for the last ten years or so. A Tokyo entrepreneur has even taken advantage of the trend to launch a clothing brand under that name.

But let's return to the brands. Branded products that have become global fall into three categories:

- Products that represent tangible progress and supplant all other offerings for reasons related to comfort, price, durability, reliability, and so on.

- Products that appeal to taste (food, cigarettes, fashion, and so on).

- Products that become global for reasons more directly related to the intangible values expressed by the brand. Absolut vodka is a striking example. What could be more difficult to differentiate for the average consumer than a vodka? Snob appeal, fashion, or simply superb communication that strikes just the right chord with certain social classes, impeccable distribution, retailing and advertising presence: all these can create global success for a product.

---

7 This is not a new phenomenon. In the 1930s, Hollywood welcomed European émigrés (Joseph von Sternberg, Erich von Stroheim, Fritz Lang, Ernst Lubitsch, and so on), whose Expressionist tendencies would revolutionize American film.

The visible elements have changed. Tastes in clothing, food, and decoration evolve. But what about attitudes? One can appreciate sushi and sashimi without losing one's American or European culinary bearing. A French connoisseur of fine wine, after all, is well equipped to savor a Rioja or a Chilean vintage, and so is a citizen of Japan – where formal wine tastings have undergone a considerable vogue. Wearing jeans, taking your family to McDonald's occasionally, driving a Jeep, or having a shot of bourbon after a meal doesn't mean that you're losing touch with your European or Asian values.

Global dissemination plays on the intrinsic merits of the product, the effectiveness of its methods of internationalization, and on the relevance and the potential universality of the offering. So there is no real hegemony, even if the size and dynamism of their domestic market makes certain US brands very competitive, increasing the resources at their disposal.

The reality: modes of thought

To Europeans and Asians, the overcommercialization of products under US brands might seem to have resulted in a mental Americanization of the world. Is the entire world tending to think like an American? The strong presence of the US social model in the media (films and TV series) sometimes produces visible side-effects. The presiding judges of French courts experience them each time a young defendant addresses them as "Your Honor." Among young people, intuitive notions about the law are emerging, derived directly from American culture, which don't necessarily have equivalents in French legal philosophy. A recent poll on racism conducted in French housing projects left analysts perplexed. On the one hand, a great majority of young people expressed strong moral condemnation of racist statements and behaviors; yet just as large a majority expressed sympathy for the idea of tolerance towards the expression of such ideas. From an "Americanized" perspective, in the light of the First Amendment of the US Constitution, what might seem a contradiction in European terms disappears.

/ Global dissemination plays on the intrinsic merits of the product, the effectiveness of its methods of internationalization, and on the relevance and the potential universality of the offering. /

Such effects remain surface phenomena, however. Cultures are made up of so many parameters, stemming from such a great variety of experience, that the idea that all societies are in danger of Americanization does not hold up. Tangible reality does not bear it out. In our opinion, even the idea of a homogenization of modes of thought is not valid. We like to compare the evolutions of different cultures to the slow movements of the tectonic plates. We would cite three eminent thinkers who corroborate our opinion.

In a study entitled *The Clash of Civilizations and the Remaking of World Order*,[8] Samuel Huntington argues that the essential causes of future conflicts will be neither ideological nor economic, but cultural: "The fault lines between civilizations are replacing the political and ideological boundaries of the Cold War as the flash points for crisis and bloodshed." His reasoning is based on the identification of eight distinct civilizations. The terrorist attacks of September 11, 2001 brought Huntington's thesis on cultural antagonisms back to the center of attention.

Francis Fukuyama, while he presents the thesis that the only system which will continue to extend its hold in the world will be that of Western liberal democracy,[9] makes a point of adding that this doesn't mean the disappearance of cultures, but simply that it is difficult to find another mode of civilization in which human beings could desire to live. Following the September 11 attacks, Fukuyama publicly repeated this point.

Finally, we would mention the work of Professor Ronald Inglehart at the University of Michigan and his World Values Survey (WVS).[10] His conclusions, founded on a rigorously scientific approach, draw a vision of the evolution of cultures in the world that takes in all the complexity of the evolution of values over time. Between Karl Marx and Daniel Bell, who argued that economic development brings about profound cultural changes, and Max Weber and Samuel Huntington, who describe durable cultural values which have an autonomous influence on society, the results of the WVS underscore the effective coexistence of profound cultural changes in distinct cultural traditions. Economic development, through the feeling of greater security it engenders, results in the progressive abandonment of rigid norms in favor of the values of tolerance, trust, and solidarity. But religious and political heritages leave imprints that persist beyond modernization. Inglehart's theses seem to confirm the existence of a cultural dynamic in constant evolution, through generations who live in different contexts, where factors such as the level of security have a much more determining influence than the advertising of the megabrands.

Cultural homogenization, then, does not seem to us to be a real danger. Cultural differences are not about to disappear anytime soon. The quote from Montaigne that serves as epigraph to this chapter unfortunately still has currency, and we can only hope that it will one day no longer ring true.

---

8 Samuel P. Huntington, *The Clash of Civilizations and the Remaking of World Order*, New York: Simon and Schuster, 1996.

9 Francis Fukuyama, *The End of History and the Last Man*, New York: Free Press, 1992.

10 See, e.g., Ronald Inglehart, *Modernization and Postmodernization: Cultural, Economic, and Political Change in 43 Societies*, New Haven, CN: Princeton University Press, 1997.

But here again, we feel that brands play a very positive role, which we will now attempt to describe.

/ Cultural homogenization does not seem to us to be a real danger. Cultural differences are not about to disappear anytime soon. /

Brands as promoters of multiculturalism

Underlying all the criticisms of Americanization of the world is the premise that cultural diversity and multiculturalism are positive factors, while uniformization is necessarily a threat. This attitude follows the same reasoning as that behind the protection of endangered animal and plant species: the disappearance of part of a culture represents an impoverishment of the human heritage. This is a simplistic and rigid vision of complex evolutionary phenomena. There is a fundamental difference between the extinction of a culture and its blending with other cultures.

The emigration of poor populations to the wealthier countries is a daily source of debate, but from the beginnings of the Industrial Revolution to the First World War, the United States built its economic prosperity on the massive influx of immigrant populations. Europe has seen innumerable migratory movements, and Latin America has been a melting pot of European nationalities. The most strongly established national identities nearly always show a vast plurality of cultural input. The difference is that with the objectivity the passage of time brings, the phenomenon of integration is more visible, whereas in the short term, behaviors appear more diversified.

Cultures and identities are not partitioned, hermetic, rigid, and immune from fluctuation. A language is the expression of a culture. We love our language and we speak and write it, but we also recognize that it is a dynamic system, in constant evolution, enriched over the centuries by innumerable borrowings from other languages. But this does not prevent it from remaining an expression of our identity.

The danger, to our way of thinking, is not the disappearance of cultural specificities. In her book devoted to the myths of nationhood in Europe, researcher Anne-Marie Thiesse stresses how vital they seem to be, today more than ever, thanks to the new tool for dissemination that is the Internet: "Are national identities threatened by globalization? In any case, for the moment they have found new vitality thanks to this planetary medium that is itself a symbol of the changes in progress."[11]

The issue is rather, as Montaigne says, that of ending the mutual accusations of barbarity. We feel that multiculturalism, within a single society,

---

11 A.-M. Thiesse, *La création des identités nationales,* Univers historique, Paris: Seuil, 1999.

is the inevitable pattern towards which we are moving. This phenomenon can be extremely dangerous if it is not accompanied by an attitude of respect, curiosity, and acceptance of differences. What is important is for the different cultures to coexist dynamically and constructively. The great cultural centers that have influenced the history of civilization have always valued and practiced these attitudes. No culture can represent absolute values, and each individual has the capacity to broaden his or her horizons.

In their way and at their level, brands participate in this promotion of tolerant multiculturalism. We have already seen that brands are very often the reflection of the cultural environment in which they developed. Their identity is founded on the geographical, historic, gastronomic, technological, or esthetic traditions of their native region. Their offering of products, diversified according to these criteria, encourages multiculturalism. It allows consumers to discover and appreciate an infinity of cultural wealth that was unknown or inaccessible. That can only mean progress for civilization.

/ Multiculturalism, within a single society, is the inevitable pattern towards which we are moving. /

Brands also facilitate the understanding of cultural differences by providing the possibility of trying out new products and services. This benign experimentation associates consumers in a culture that is not their original one. It lets them become familiar with and understand these new values, and become accustomed to differences. It encourages tolerance. Japanese who drive Mercedes, Chinese who drink cognac, Americans in Chanel ensembles, or Italians carrying Hermès handbags are participating in this cultural exchange, accepting and understanding diversity.

Brands are important players in the process of globalization. As such, they contribute to global cultural change. Never before have individuals had the possibility of "thinking out of the box" of traditional patterns of belonging to a group. The advent of the postmodern individual, via immediate access to global information and the brands' multicultural offerings, enables us to choose to break with traditional social behaviors and stroll through the "hypermarket of lifestyles," to use Gilles Lipovetsky's expression.[12] What is more, by learning to appreciate elements of diverse cultures, people become forces for the evolution of their cultures of origin.

Brands are not only the expression of local cultural values. They also, as in the field of sports, for example, promote universal values without strongly localized cultural attachments. Sports, products of a leisure civilization (most of them were invented by idle British aristocrats who wanted to test their mettle against one another) and spread by colonization, have become in a

---

12 Gilles Lipovetsky, *L'ère du vide*, op. cit.

half-century one of the most effective forces for globalization, but also for social emancipation. And that is where we find the most globalized brands: Nike, Adidas, Reebok, Lacoste, Puma, Fila, and so on.

The global brands, issued from multiple and varied cultures, present in our downtown areas, promote the very principle of the concomitance of choices in a competitive context. Their very existence affirms the values of liberalism and democratic choice. Of course, the respective strengths of brands on the markets imply no judgment of the cultures they represent. It is not legitimate to set up a scale of values between cultures. This doesn't imply blind tolerance, but to condemn certain aspects of a culture in the name of one's own values does not mean rejecting it as a whole.

/ Never before have individuals had the possibility of "thinking out of the box" of traditional patterns of belonging to a group. /

There are cultures without global brands, but that are not in danger of extinction because of it. All it means is that at a given point in time no brand project exists that would be economically viable or that has found an entrepreneur prepared to commit to it. The non-commercialization of the cultural values of the Touareg people implies nothing as regards the permanence of their culture or the possibility, in the future, of a brand's being based on these values. The Paris–Dakar rally and its logo, in any case, owe a lot to them. That organization has often been criticized for interfering in a culture that is different from its own. But it may have contributed, in its way, to making its characteristics known.

In conclusion, it is important to remember that brands are a rampart against the specter of a single economic and cultural model, one that is a reflection of the United States or of the West, warned against by the "No global" movement. We see brands as promoting multiculturalism, encouraging curiosity about and tolerant understanding of other worlds, but also as driving forces for cultural evolution and blending which, far from engendering homogenization, work to enrich the living heritage of humanity.

To conclude

We end this concluding chapter devoted to the role of brands and branding in the current context of globalization with an awareness of the difficulties, but affirming our optimism. What we have tried to show, throughout this book, is that brands, in the end, are only a reflection of ourselves. They will be factors of progress only to the extent that we ourselves want them to be, whether as brand managers or as consumers.

Brands carry meaning. Like the words in our language, they tell our own story, and we need them in order to affirm our humanity. And like words, they can be made to say anything and its opposite. But it depends on each of us, whether we are managers or laborers, brand managers or consumers, to speak out against such abuses and make our voices heard through these tools of exchange and communication.

In our respective careers, we have always insisted on viewing trade as an essential and worthy human activity. This is the point of view we have tried to substantiate in these pages. Of course voices have been raised, and continue to be raised, in condemnation of the abuses of the economic and political system that has become dominant in the world. We do not want to give short shrift to these objections. We are prepared to listen to them and debate them, all too aware that too many intolerable problems still exist. We also hope that it will have been understood how much importance we place on mobilizations of consumers and users in the exercise of fairer trade, and how much we believe in the civic importance of the individual act of purchase as an act of support for the ethical and esthetic values expressed by brand identities.

/ Brands carry meaning. Like the words in our language, they tell our own story, and we need them in order to affirm our humanity. /

Independently of our respective, sometimes diverging opinions, we have made a point of ruling out any profession of faith in an ideology. Above all, beyond certain clarifications we deemed necessary, we have tried to inform, to describe objectively, and to bring up the most urgent issues. But if our "response" to this informal wave of resentment against brands were to be summed up in a few words, we would say the following:

What we want to avoid above all is for the forest to be hidden by the trees, and for essential debates to end once a convenient scapegoat has been designated.

"Imagination and fiction make up more than three quarters of our real life," philosopher Simone Weil wrote.[13] To our mind, this is a good definition of the endless fascination of the universe of brands. Yet we must be careful to hold on to that last quarter, and not forget that, behind any brand phenomenon – the best along with the worst – are very real men and women. The true nature of our woes and of our victories resides with them, and they are the ones who must take up the formidable challenges of the century that has just begun.

---

13 Simone Weil, *Gravity and Grace,* New York: Putnam and Sons, 1952.

Postscript

We would like to add a more personal note. At the end of a book largely devoted to the concept of value, it seems only natural for us to state our own.

Our period is often referred to as "postmodern." What was defined for so long as our historical modernity – through the thirst for truth, universalism, the demand for meaning – now seems to be slipping away. "Postmodernism," as philosophers, sociologists, architects, and artists use it, has come to be the accepted term for this liberation from meaning and from history, expressed in certain sometimes contradictory phenomena, attitudes, and trends: the absence of stable doctrine, moral and cultural relativism, individualism, hedonism, pluralism, the emergence of urban tribes, pragmatism, freedom of choice, of speech, of opinion, and of information, mass culture, the culture of the day-to-day, of consumption, the empowerment of civil society, the techno-culture and the mass media, esthetic profusion, ephemeral and emotional relationships.

Are these the unavoidable symptoms of our time? Perhaps. But there is nonetheless the impression of a certain decline, visible in our failure to be demanding where effort, constancy, and rigorousness are concerned. Is it because we no longer want to, or because we have forgotten how? Motivation seems to have replaced will as the operative concept.

We can't help seeing a parallel, at this point in time, between the characteristics of postmodern behavior and the symptoms of acedia. We should not be put off by the unfamiliarity of this term. We are very familiar with this "delicate monster"! It is often characterized by a revulsion for spiritual things, but more generally by an inability to see meaning in our lives, to focus on a goal.

Acedia was originally the eighth deadly sin.[1] The word comes from the Greek akedia; it originated in the monastic world. Evagrius Ponticus (345–399), a monk of the Egyptian desert, analyzed this "obscure affliction" in detail in his *Praktikos*. Despondency, general discouragement, a refusal of effort, bitterness, negligence, discontent with the present, indifference, an aversion to action, an avoidance of confrontation, a lack of interest in the self and in others – the symptoms are multiple. People afflicted with acedia are bored, always in search of the latest novelty to cheer them up, wandering aimlessly physically and intellectually. The victim can also succumb to hyperactivity or an exaggerated concern for physical health.

This eighth deadly sin disappeared from the list during the Renaissance, probably because of the complexity and contradictory nature of its manifestations. Also, perhaps, it had become incomprehensible to Humanist thought at a time when modern science was being invented and humanity was being reinvented in the context of its expanding world. But in our time? The description of these symptoms somehow seems oddly familiar.

It may well be that many of the most common ills of today are new incarnations of this spiritual and moral dilution that a monk called Evagrius was coming to grips with in the Egyptian desert in the fourth century. A postmodern, acedic world: the term is almost pleonastic.

Our own conviction is that no period of history, regardless of the progress that has preceded it and the sacrifices made to bring it about, can ever escape responsibility for its own meaning, can never be fully realized unless it finds, and accomplishes, the destiny that justifies it with respect to past and future generations.

"And where do brands come in?" one might ask. Well, if a possible antidote to acedia lies in a renewed curiosity about the self and the world, in a courageous search for meaning in our own lives, we feel that they have a role to play. If, as we have argued in Chapter 8, consumers can influence brands' action in a decisive way, then there is hope that in time, the values expressed by brands will reflect their aspirations, their dreams, and their will.

If that time comes, it will be one in which the esthetic and the ethic of brand identities will contribute to giving human life more meaning, where the beautiful will engender the good, where positive content will influence form in promoting values that are, quite simply, human.

---

1 Fr. J.-C. Nault, "Le mal obscur: l'acédie selon Évagre le Pontique," *GESTS review*, Abbaye de Saint-Wandrille, France, 2002.

Index

3M, 20

A&P, 28
Aaker, D., 98
Abercrombie & Fitch, 64
Accenture, 30–1
Action for Corporate Accountability, 253
activism
    anti-globalization, 70, 244, 266–7, 280
    anti-tobacco, 59, 212
    consumer, 1, 164, 239–66
    feminist, 43
    graffiti, 41
    protest movement, 2, 52, 72, 205, 245
Adidas, 26, 160, 164
advertising
    costs, 17–20, 23, 74, 81, 91
    false, 63–4
    recognition, 53–5
    subvertisement, 41
    pornography in, 48–51, 62, 88
AIDS, 45, 52, 55, 62, 65, 211
Air France, 62
Altadis, 59
American Eagle Outfitters, 64
American Federation of Television and
    Radio Artists (AFRA), 257
americanization, 266, 274–8
American Petroleum Institute, 256
Angelini, G., 46
anorexia, 45–6
anti-narcotics organization, 47
Apple computers, 30, 33
Armani, 27, 82, 101–2, 135, 150
Arthur Andersen, 30–1, 164

Artz, E., 19, 151
ATTAC, 258, 260, 262
Aubade, 100
Audi, 69, 100, 170, 191
Avenir Publicité, 49
Avon, 62
Axa, 62

Bally, 35, 66, 100, 103, 113, 115–16, 185,
    196
Banania, 89–91
Banco Sabadell, 95
banking, 25, 30, 95, 245
Baricco, A., 270
Barthes, R., 41, 65
Barton, B., 97
BBC, 231
Beccaria, J. M. R., 45
behaviorism, 205–20
Bell, D., 277
Benetton, 48, 52–5, 59–60, 87, 119, 144,
    202
Benetton, L., 53, 59
Berluti, 65
Berluti, O., 65
Bernard-Becharie, J.-F., 233
Bernstein, D., 98
BMW, 136, 210, 275
Body Shop, 45–6, 119, 257
Boisvert, Y., 203
boycotts, 41, 54, 203, 240, 251–60
    animal experimentation, 254
    Danone, 258
    Esso, 256–8
    General Electric, 253